Artificial Intelligence in Education

Artificial Intelligence in Education:

Fundamentals for Educators

David Kent

ISBN: 979-11-970887-9-7

KOTESOL DCC.
Daejeon, Republic of Korea.

First Edition.

DEDICATION

For the five, and for the one.

CONTENTS

LIST OF TABLES

LIST OF FIGURES

ACKNOWLEDGMENTS

I wish to extend my deepest appreciation to my wife *Hyunhee* who has been very patient and understanding throughout the entire process involved with the production of this book. The text is based on a range of resources with parts one and three drawing on the IBM AI Foundations, IBM AI Foundations for Educators, and the ISTE Artificial Intelligence Explorations and their Practical use in Schools content.

PREFACE

Artificial Intelligence in Education: Fundamentals for Educators presents those issues in artificial intelligence (AI) that are of concern to teachers when coming to understand the various aspects involved with the field, and how they relate and can be applied to those in education. This includes developing a working knowledge of the key concepts behind AI, and an understanding of the characteristics and evolution of the field itself. The benefits, risks, biases, and ethics involved with AI design, development, and deployment are also considered, and this includes aspects of AI and human perception, how these differ, and what this means practically. The manner in which we can naturally come to interact with AI systems, along with an understanding of the differences and similarities between human-machine learning, is also taken into account. After these fundamentals are established, the five big ideas in AI for education are introduced, and the more integral aspects of each, including their implications for society, are examined. This establishes a grounding for presenting what it now means to be teaching and learning in the era of the fourth industrial revolution; how digital assistants and voice user interfaces, along with chatbots and robots, can be applied in the teaching and learning context, particularly that of English language learning; and how the design thinking process can assist in the development of pedagogical projects in educational workplaces. The text also has a companion workbook in which all of the activities presented can be completed.

Organization of the Text
The book is intended to be read as a whole or in part by teachers, students, parents, and any other stakeholders who may be interested in the topics. Each part follows a similar layout, beginning with a short overview in order to situate the topics presented, followed by the main learning outcomes achieved by reading that section of the text. After presenting the content matter, each chapter then closes with a short summary. This is then followed by a listing of all of the resources and references referred to in the chapter, and at times appendices housing information expanding on chapter concepts. The three major parts of the book are *AI Fundamentals, AI in education,* and *AI in Practice.*

Part one, *AI Fundamentals*, is covered by chapters one through six.

Chapter one, *Key Concepts*, provides a brief overview of a number of key concepts associated with artificial intelligence (AI). You will be able to understand how each of these concepts and various terms are used, and define what they mean. Along the way, you will engage in a number of activities to help solidify your understanding, and discover how these concepts relate to the field of education.

Chapter two, *Characteristics and Evolution*, provides a short introduction to artificial intelligence and explores its origins. You will learn about the characteristics and evolution of AI to better understand knowledge-based systems and intelligence in machines. Along the way, you will explore examples of intelligent machines and reflect on ways to introduce AI to learners and consider ways to use it in your teaching.

Chapter three, Ben*efits, Risks, Bias, and Ethics*, covers three aspects of AI: the benefits to humanity from its development, the risks associated with its development, and the ethics involved with its development. In this chapter, readers will discover how empathy can assist in the design process and how it relates to human-centered design, learn about biases, and how it can occur in machines, and understand some of the risks that come along with the use of AI technologies. Along the way, you will explore examples of each in a variety of use cases or scenarios, and reflect on the ways in which AI can impact both humanity and our students.

Chapter four, *AI and Human Perception*, details the processes involved with human perception, and how this relates to machine intelligence and computer vision. A number of limitations pertaining to computer vision are discussed prior to introducing how image recognition occurs in a neural network. Aspects of training machines to recognize what they see are explored, and an opportunity to train a machine is presented.

Chapter five, *AI and natural interaction*, explores how artificial intelligence (AI) and humans process and communicate using natural interaction. Aspects of natural language processing (NLP), understanding, and generation are examined. In addition, the wider aspects of speech, gesture and affect, and the benefits and limitations of each of these when interacting with AI systems are discussed.

Chapter six, *Human and Machine Learning*, covers a number of aspects pertaining to human and machine learning. It looks at the process of automation, and what this means for the future of work, it introduces the computational thinking process, and explores aspects of human and machine learning, including deep learning. The chapter finalizes by considering aspects of data mining for the language learning classroom.

Part two, *AI in Education*, is covered by chapters seven through ten.

Chapter seven, *AI4K12 – The Five Big Ideas*, details those aspects of the five big ideas in artificial intelligence (AI), and those that are being introduced to learners from k-12. It looks at the more integral aspects of each, and explores their implications for society.

Chapter eight, *Teaching and Learning in the Era of the Fourth Industrial Revolution*, presents the skills, competencies, and proficiencies that 21st century learners need to develop and maintain in the fourth industrialization era, along with the 21st century teaching skills required of instructors. Teacher technology confidence use, and the need for instructors to understand the relationship between technology, pedagogy, and content knowledge is also explored before then focusing on a range of technology types, and introducing the characteristics to keep in mind when adapting, integrating, and working on teaching with such technologies. A means of being able to determine the worthwhileness of any AI application, technologies, and approaches adopted for use in education is also presented.

Chapter nine, *Digital Assistants and Voice User Interfaces*, explores the pedagogical affordances offered by digital assistants, along with the means of utilizing them with learners and by teachers. The types of digital assistant, and a number of example activities and use-case scenarios are presented, as well as a means for creating content for digital assistant use.

Chapter ten, *Chatbots and Robots in the Classroom*, considers the role of chatbots and robots in the learning process. Two chatbot examples are presented in detail, and the means of chatbot development is presented. The concept of robot-assisted language learning (RALL) is also introduced, along with a brief consideration into how robots can be applied in the classroom with students, and an overview of the benefits such systems provide learners engaged in the language learning process.

Part three, *AI in Practice*, is handled by the final chapter of the text.

Chapter eleven, *Application of the Design Thinking Process to AI in Education – Pedagogy Project*, covers aspects of the design thinking process, and the expansion of this process to include equity-centered design. You will explore how these processes are able to assist in the development and the build of human-centered AI applications for education. Details relating to the development and design of a pedagogical project relying on these processes, and one for application in your (actual or potential) workplace is also presented.

It is hoped that this course will provide both education and something new for all teachers – be they trained or untrained, and pre-service, in-service, or retired. Good luck!

David Kent.

Part One:
AI Fundamentals

1. Key Concepts

Overview

This chapter provides a brief overview of a number of key concepts associated with artificial intelligence (AI). You will be able to understand how each of these concepts and various terms are used, and define what they mean. Along the way, you will engage in a number of activities to help solidify your understanding, and discover how these concepts relate to the field of education.

Learning Outcomes

1. Understand key concepts in the field of AI.
2. Define key concepts in the field of AI.
3. Discover how the key concepts of AI relate to education.

Key Concepts in AI

There are a number of concepts that need to be discussed when talking about artificial intelligence and what it means for education. These are:

1. Artificial Intelligence (AI types).
2. Neural networks.
3. Big Data.
4. Algorithms (black box and white box algorithms).
5. Machine Learning.
6. Computational thinking (decomposition, pattern recognition, algorithm design, and abstraction).
7. The Turing test, the Chinese room, and Natural Language Processing (NLP).
8. Robots (artificially intelligent robots, and the uncanny valley).
9. The future of work (AI and teachers moving forward).

Introduction

The recent leaps forward in the capabilities of artificial intelligence (AI) are enabling it to get increasingly better at performing certain subsets of intelligent tasks in what is seeing AI emerge as one of the biggest facets of the fourth industrial revolution (IBM, 2018). The excitement behind this field is largely due to AI systems becoming increasingly common place, and interacting with us on a daily level. So too, with these systems not yet even in their infancy, they have begun to impact each of us, including those of us working with language learners and teachers (see Wu, 2019). This includes in both obvious and very subtle ways, from the use of image recognition systems at airport auto-entry gates, and in camera apps to ensure that faces are recognized and kept in focus, to the use of machine translation, interaction with digital assistants, and things like browser-based Google searches (Luckin, 2019).

The expectations for artificial intelligence then, may, in the minds of many teachers, be similar to that of the time when computers were first introduced to the educational system. These expectations were high, and as with any new technology perhaps overly hyped (Goasduff, 2019), and there was a fear that computers would take teachers jobs or replace them (Agarwal, 2019). However, after a period where expectations and usage of such systems were normalized (Bax, 2003; 2011), being integrated into our daily lives at a slower pace, they have since become an indispensable tool in the preparation of lesson content, and in the delivery of information to students, parents and staff, among other things.

Artificial Intelligence

Yet, what is artificial intelligence? Before considering a definition of AI, think about: What AI means to you? How would you describe AI in a few words? To help consider what artificial intelligence is, try engaging with the *Wolf, Sheep and Cabbage Game* [Link: https://www.proprofs.com/games/wolf-sheep-and-cabbage]. The instructions are as follows:

> *Move the wolf, sheep, and cabbage to the opposite shore, but when the man is not around, the wolf will eat the sheep and the sheep will eat the cabbage.*

Take about three minutes to to engage with the game, and see if you can move all items across to the opposite shore successfully.

The game you just played provides you with a critical thinking exercise, and one that can help you consider the definition of AI. That is to say, the way that computers learn is similar to the ways in which we learn, as neural networks were designed based on human brains. They take in information – in the form of data – and connections are made. An example for humans might be touching something hot and making the connection in your brain to not do that again.

Workbook Activity 1.1

Complete the first activity in the associated workbook by writing down or typing out a description of AI.

1.1 How would you describe AI?

You might have described AI as referring to computer systems that are able to perform tasks that normally require human intelligence, such as visual perception, speech recognition, decision-making, and understanding of human languages.

AI Definition

So, what is AI? Well, AI researchers admit that there is no single unified definition of the term, but most can agree that the ultimate goal of the field of AI is to make machines capable of thinking like humans and those that are able to solve a wide variety of problems.

Simply put then, artificial intelligence is the ability of a computer, program or a machine to think and learn. However, it is much more complex than that, as what constitutes AI shifts constantly, and once a goal becomes mainstream it tends to no longer be labelled or thought of as AI (Bostrom, in CNN, 2006). In line with this is the AI effect, where a milestone considered to be true artificial intelligence (i.e., being able to play and beat a person at chess) is discounted once it has been reached, with the argument being that it does not show real intelligence or thinking (McCurduck, 2004). A further issue, but one not unique to the

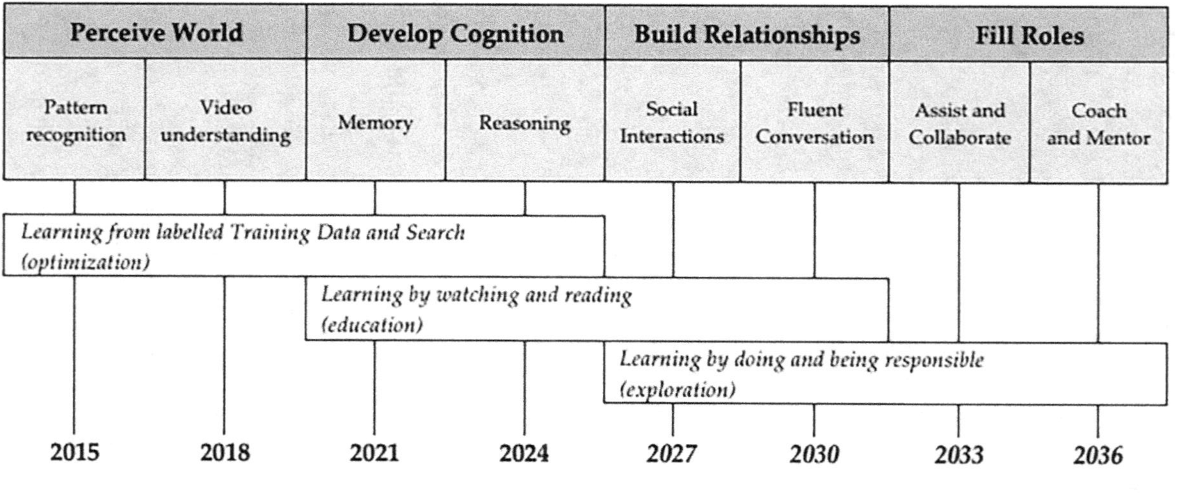

Figure 1.1 The IBM leaderboard for AI
(See Spohrer, 2017)

study of AI, is that it is a multidisciplinary field with each discipline bringing its own perspective and terminology to the fore. In any case, for our purposes, AI systems (machine or application integrated) are defined along the lines of those presented by Luckin, Holmes, Griffiths, and Forcier (2016). This definition covers those systems that interact with the world, through various capabilities including speech recognition and visual perception, and perform behaviours of intelligence where available data is assessed and sensible actions or goals are then undertaken and achieved in human ways. Today, some scholars consider the term augmented intelligence more preferable as it assists in retaining the human brain as the source of intelligence and technology as a source of supplementation (Holmes, et al., 2019).

Of note, Artificial intelligence, as a field of study, is not new, with the founding event widely considered to be the Dartmouth Summer Research Project on Artificial Intelligence held in 1956 (Solomonoff, 1985; Moor, 2006). This event was largely a series of brainstorming sessions among mathematicians and scientists with the name of the field chosen for its neutrality, and avoidance of both the narrow focus of automata theory and the focus of cybernetics on analog feedback (Nilsson, 2010). Essentially, project sessions were about getting together to achieve enough understanding about human intelligence, including language learning, so that machines could be built in ways that automate the processes of the human mind (Luckin, 2019). Right now, and moving into the 2030s, according to IBM's Leaderboard (see Figure 1.1), artificial intelligence is at the point where it should be entering the realm of deeper self-learning. This will see AI start to become increasingly capable of assisting, collaborating, coaching and mediating.

AI Types

Artificial intelligence can generally be classified into two-types, based on capability or functionality, and in regards to how it compares to humans (Joshi, 2019). As Figure 1.2 illustrates, these two types of classification consist of a total of seven different categories (Reynoso, 2019).

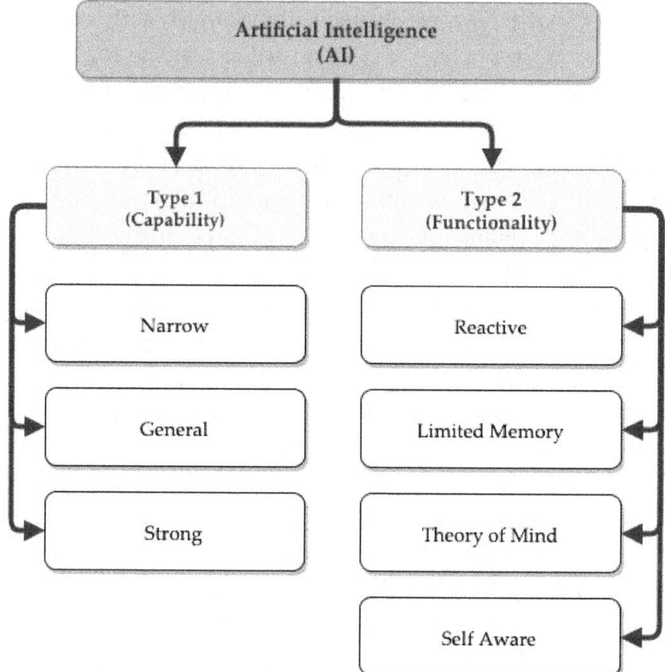

Figure 1.2 The two types and seven categories of AI

Type 1 AI are classified under three categories. The narrow, or weak, category of AI are dedicated to a single task. The general category of AI includes those that perform tasks like humans, while strong AI are considered to be those systems that are more intelligent than humans.

Narrow AI perform dedicated tasks with intelligence and are currently the most common AI system. These systems cannot perform beyond their scope of training, and can fail in unpredictable ways if they begin to expand beyond their limits. Examples of this kind of AI system would be those that play chess, provide purchasing suggestions on e-commerce sites, self-driving cars, as well as speech or image/facial recognition systems.

General AI performs intellectual tasks with efficiency and similar to humans with the goal to create a system that is smarter than a human but thinks like one. In other words, an AI system that is as capable as a human, possessing the same multi-functional capabilities, that is able to build multiple competencies and form connections and generalizations across domains independently. At present no system falls under this classification.

Strong AI are those systems that possess a level of intelligence that surpasses humans, and can outperform humans on tasks with cognitive properties. Characteristics of strong AI include the capability to independently think, reason, puzzle solve, make judgements, plan, learn and communicate using greater memory, faster data processing and analysis, and decision-making capabilities than those of humans or general AI systems. These systems are currently hypothetical.

Interesting to note at this point is that the development of General and Strong AI systems can potentially lead to the scenario that Kurswell (2005) describes as the singularity. A point where machine intelligence will become more powerful than all human intelligence combined, and a time when machine intelligence and human intelligence would likely need to merge in order for humans to keep pace with AI systems.

Type 2 AI are classified under four categories. These are reactive machines, limited memory, theory of mind, and self-awareness.

Reactive machines are the most basic type of AI as they react to a current scenario and respond as best as possible, and are among the oldest form of AI system. These machines do not have the ability to learn, as they cannot use experiences gained previously to inform a present action. Therefore, they can only be used for responding automatically to a limited set of inputs, and do not rely on memory as an aid to improve. Such machines are those such as Deep Blue and AlphaGo, essentially programmed for the here and now and not the before and after.

Limited memory machines can store past experience or data for short periods of time, and then use this data and experience to perform given scenarios or tasks, such as driving a car. Such systems would use data comprising of the distance to/from, and the speed of, surrounding cars, the known speed limit, and other information to maintain and navigate a position on the road. These systems learn from past events and build experiential knowledge from the data fed to them, or the actions they have observed. Other examples of this type of system would include chatbots.

Theory of mind AI systems understand human emotions, and beliefs, and are able to interact socially like a human being as they possess the decision-making ability equal to that of a human mind. These systems are currently under development, and will require input from a large range of fields, particularly because they will need to know how to respond to, as well as be able to identify, and recall emotional output and behavior. The beginnings of this kind of AI system can be found in the robots Kismet, developed in 2000, and Sophia developed in 2016. Kismet is able to recognize emotions by human facial signals, and replicate those emotions on its human structured face using its ears, eyes, eyebrows, eyelids, and lips (refer to Prescott, 2016). Sophia, on the other hand, has a physical likeness to that of a human being, and possesses the ability see using image recognition, and respond to interactions with appropriate facial expressions. It is also the first robot to be declared a citizen by the Kingdom of Saudi Arabia (The Jakarta Post, 2017).

Self-aware AI systems are smarter than humans, and possess their own consciousness and sentiments. They will be able to understand emotions and evoke them in humans and other AI systems around them, and they will possess emotions, needs, beliefs, and possibly desires of their own. Development of such a system is the objective of AI research, but at this stage they remain hypothetical.

On track to ensure the above systems are developed a range of multidisciplinary fields need to cooperate to engage in developing systems that work in integrated manner. This includes developing new disciplines, as subsets of the study of AI, well as new areas of research to ensure such systems can be developed in ways to support the emergence and improvement of artificial intelligence (see Figure 1.3).

Even with the above achievements, we are still essentially living in a world that interacts with domain specific AI. So, systems that can perform translation cannot play Go, systems that can play Go are unable to drive our cars for us. Common to all AI systems though is data, and importantly, data, like crude oil, must be refined in order to derive any value from it (Luckin, 2019). Any value derived from the AI use of data depends on how that data is processed, and what type of data has been collected initially.

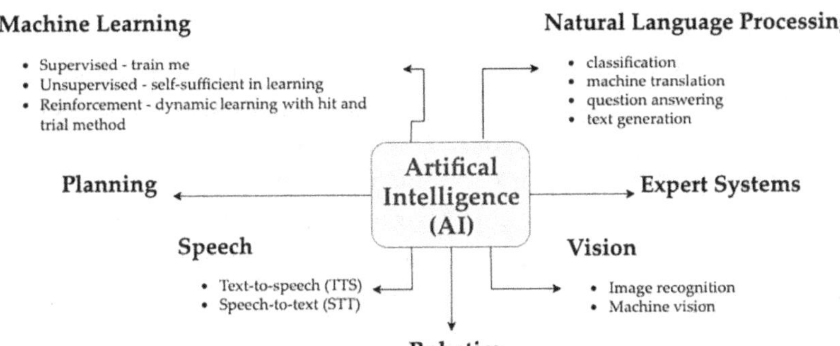

Figure 1.3 Example subsets of AI
(based on Kumar, 2018)

Neural Networks

Take a look at Figure 1.4. It shows an image on the left of human neural network pathways, and an image on the right of computer neural network pathways.

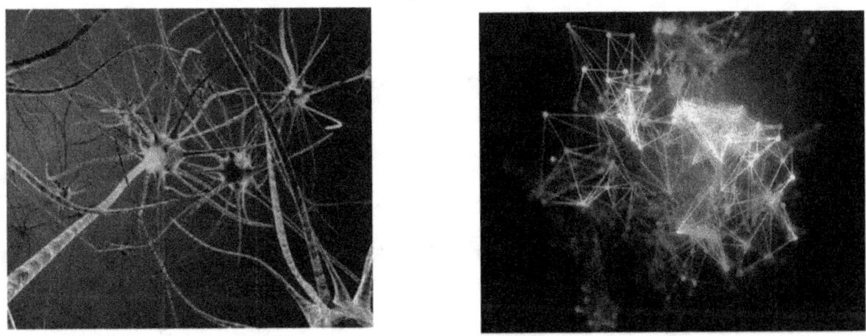

Figure 1.4 Human and computer neural network pathways

Workbook Activity 1.2

Looking over the images in Figure 1.4, how would you describe human and computer neural network pathways. Complete the second activity in the associated workbook for the text.

> **1.2** How would you describe human and computer neural network pathways?

Perhaps you might see the human and computer neural network pathways as being very similar. Think back to the wolf, sheep, and cabbage game, each trip that you took across the river gave you a piece of data, or a piece of information. That is information about what works, what does not work, what gets an animal eaten and how to successfully complete the mission of the game. Once those connections -- or, neural pathways -- are made, it becomes easier to play the game. However, once you figure out the strategy, you don't really want to play the game again. It is similar to tic-tac-toe, or noughts-and-crosses. Once you've created the neural pathways and know how to play the game, and know how to win it, you do not really want to spend a lot of time going back and playing it again. So, as an adult, you maybe less interested in such games over those who are younger.

Neural Network Definition

For our key term, a neural network can be defined as:
> *A series of algorithms that endeavor to recognize underlying relationships in a set of data through a process that mimics the way the human brain operates.*

Big Data

The next key term that we are looking at is Big Data.

Big Data Definition

We might consider this term to refer to:
> *A collection of data that is huge in volume, and yet growing exponentially with time. It is data so large in size and complexity that no traditional data management tool can store it or process it efficiently. We need something else to do that.*

Take five minutes to further explore the concept of Big Data, by viewing *what is Big Data?* [Video: https://www.youtube.com/watch?v=dK4aGzeBPkk].

Workbook Activity 1.3

Now, with your understanding of what Big Data is, how do you think the analysis of Big Data might apply to the real-world. Complete the third activity in the associated workbook for the text by providing what you consider to be three potential real world applications for the use of Big Data analysis.

> **1.3** What are three potential real-world applications of Big Data analysis?

Perhaps you were able to provide real-world Big Data examples such as:
   a) Discovering consumer shopping habits
   b) Fuel optimization for the transport industry
   c) Predictive inventory ordering

Big Data in Education

What about for education? What is an example of Big Data in the education context.

Data versus Big Data

Lets' consider data versus Big Data first. Semester assignments and quiz scores are the types of data that accumulate into a final grade for each student in a class at the end of a semester. Also, teacher observations might be added to a progress report and discussed with a parent or other stakeholders. These are two examples of data typically accumulated in the educational context, and it is easily the kind of data that a human can handle. Big Data, however, in the educational sphere would include the same data but for every single student enrolled in a countries entire educational system. Analysis of such Big Data would offer insight across workplaces that might include that of student performance scores on tests compared to school start and end times, socioeconomic data, school grades, behavioral reports, and so on. Such data, could then be used to develop a ranking for the quality of education.

Use-Case Example: University

Let us consider the university context as a use-case example for the real-world potential of Big Data analysis. Any particular university might have around 60,000 students and an ocean of data concerning them. This data concerns a variety of stakeholders from faculty, to students and administration. Dedicated and proper study and analysis of such data can provide important insights into how to improve the operational effectiveness of such an educational institution. In the past, there were no real solutions to analyze the amount of data available. Today, administrators are able to use analytics and data visualization tools to draw out patterns from the data in order to streamline university operations, recruitment processes and student retention efforts. These administrators will then be able to provide faculty with advanced grading systems and learner management tools (producing even more data), so that students can gain access to course materials that have been reframed based on data analytics.

Moore's Law

Of note, not only is there an exponential growth of data, but the exponential growth of computing power. Moore's Law states that computer processing speed and memory size approximately doubles every year or two. A great way to visualize this in actuality is by viewing the video Moore's Law graphed versus real CPUs & GPUs 1965-2019 (DataGrapha, 2019 June 05) [video: https://www.youtube.com/watch?v=7uvUiq_jTLM].

Why is this important? Well, with increasing processor speeds comes the capability of faster processing times for the analysis of Big Data, and the potential for the development of better AI systems.

Algorithm

Consider again the critical thinking exercise that you undertook previously, the one in which you were playing the Wolf, Sheep and Cabbage game, your thought process might have been:

> *Try wolf, sheep eats cabbage. Not good. Try sheep, then cabbage, bring back sheep, get wolf, leave sheep, return for sheep.*

However, when a computer attempts to interact with this game it will visualize every single move, along with the outcomes of those moves or the consequences, and then essentially weigh the pros and cons in order to make a single move knowing all of the possible outcomes for it and what path to go down before making any move at all. This manner of systematically checking all possibilities is an algorithm, and algorithm is our next key term.

Algorithm Definition

You can think of an algorithm as a flow chart, or a process or set of rules to be followed in calculations.

Essentially, algorithms are sets of instructions used to make decisions. A game (or decision) tree is what makes it possible for a computer to play and win games against humans. So, a computer can very quickly and easily go through every single possibility, every consequence to maximize winning.

In other words, the steps that the computer goes through to check every possibility and choose the best move is an algorithm.

Example Algorithm

An example of an algorithm in use is a game tree, which can be thought of as a technique for analyzing games. In these cases, to determine the actions that a player has to take to win. The tic-tac-toe decision or game tree that you see on the left in Figure 1.5 might look complex but it is a simple one that consists of 49 possible moves particularly if we compare it to the one on the right which is that of DeepMind's Alpha Go and illustrating 10 to the power of 170 possible moves in the game of Go.

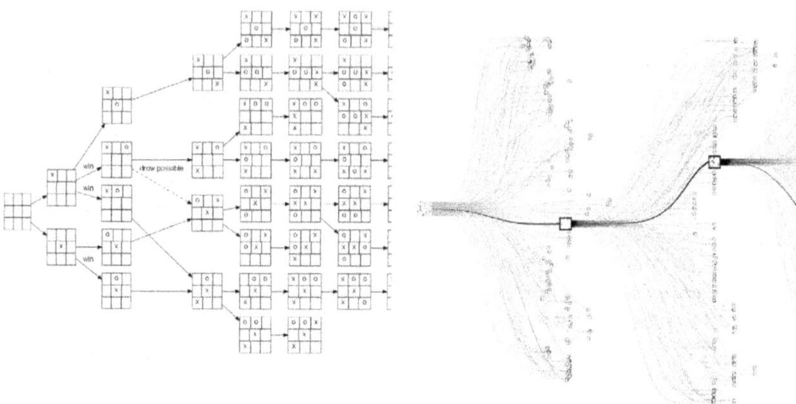

Figure 1.5 Decision tree examples (left: tic-tac-toe, right: the game of Go

Algorithms in Everyday Educational Contexts

Teachers use algorithms every day in the classroom context. Those instructors that teach students mathematical thinking, giving them formulas and equations, or steps to solve a problem, are providing algorithms to learners. Teachers providing learners with the steps to plan an essay, are essentially providing an essay algorithm. Procedures, like lining up and undergoing a morning routine, or obtaining a bathroom pass are also examples. Anything that is "if this, then that" in a set of instructions, is an algorithm.

If you are interested in learning more about algorithms you might like to discover aspects of *the secret rules of modern living algorithms* [Video: https://www.youtube.com/watch?v=kiFfp-HAu64].

Workbook Activity 1.4

Now, with your understanding of what an algorithm is complete the fourth activity in the associated workbook for the text. Provide one example of an algorithm that you would use in everyday life to perform a function or process.

> **1.4** What is an example of an algorithm that you would apply in everyday life?

In answering the workbook activity perhaps you provided an everyday life skill example, such as tying your shoe laces.

Black Box Algorithms

The artificial intelligence black box 'problem' is based on the inability to fully understand why the algorithms behind the AI work in the ways in which they do. When an algorithm provides us with an output, and we are unable to understand where the output really comes from then we refer to it as a black box algorithm (see figure 1.6).

Figure 1.6 Example black box model

To look inside the black box we would need transparency, explainability, and provability.

Transparency: understanding of AI model decision making.
Explainability: Understanding reasoning behind each decision.
Provability: Mathematical certainty behind decisions.

So, the opposite to a black box model, is a white-box model. In white-box AI the model is interpretable, we can explain how the model behaves, how the predictions are influenced and what influences the variables.

The problem with black box algorithms lead us to asking questions such as: 'How can we trust a model that can be as imprecise as its data?', and 'Are black box models even required in AI?' (Rudin & Radin, 2019). Such concepts are explored in around 10 minutes in *the era of blind faith in big data must end* TED talk [Video: https://www.ted.com/talks/cathy o neil the era of blind faith in big data must end?language=en].

Machine Learning

Machine learning is an application of artificial intelligence that provides systems with the ability to automatically learn and improve from experience, without being explicitly programmed. As such, a computer can learn through trial and error just like you and me. Here, there is no transparency.

Machine Learning Definition

Machine learning focuses on the development of computer programs that can access data and use it to learn for themselves.

To see how machine learning might work in the real-world you might like to consider how it is applied by Netflix to discover how the process works [Video: https://www.youtube.com/watch?v=n3RKsY2H-NE&t=111s].

Machine learning is applied by Netflix to offer personalization. It uses the watch history of other users with similar tastes to you to determine what it considers most interesting for you so that you stay engaged and continue paying the monthly subscription. Along with this is the auto-generation and personalization of the kind of movie thumbnail that might be shown to you, ranking the thumbnails to decide which might result in you most likely selecting what to watch. Netflix also uses machine learning to help decide on location shooting (when and where), editing content in post-production (e.g., using historical data to determine where quality control checks might be required), and in determining streaming quality and suing past data to determine when regional servers might need caching for faster load times (e.g. during peak viewing hours).

Workbook Activity 1.5

Now, with your understanding of what machine learning is, how do you think the process of machine learning might be exhibited in the real-world. Complete the fifth activity in the associated workbook for the test by providing three potential real world examples of machine learning in action.

> 1.5 What are three examples of machine learning in the real-world?

Perhaps you were able to provide real-world machine learning examples such as:

a)   Image recognition
b)   Speech recognition
c)   Recommendation engines

MENACE

How can an inanimate object learn from experience? Well, learning can happen and be represented using things other than our human brain or even a computer. Stationary inanimate objects like a matchbox can 'learn', but they do need humans to be doing the adding and subtracting of things like colored beads.

In 1961, MENACE (Machine Educable Noughts and Crosses Engine), a machine capable of learning to be a better tic-tac-toe or noughts-and-crosses player was created. As computers were not widely available, it was developed using 304 matchboxes and colored beads. It relies on reinforcement learning. The 304 matchboxes represent all possible layouts when playing the game, with each colored bead representing a valid move. The starting number of beads in each matchbox varies depending on the number of turns already played, and to reduce the number of matchboxes required MENACE always goes first. You can see it in action for yourself – take a look at *the pile of matchboxes which can learn* [Video: https://www.mscroggs.co.uk/menace/].

How does MENACE work?

Initially, MENACE begins with four beads of each color in the first move matchbox. However, in the example game shown in Figure 1.7, the first matchbox is opened to reveal a red bead at the front. This will mean that MENACE will place its mark (o) in the lower left corner. The human player (x) then plays center. For MENACE to then move its human operator searches for the matchbox showing the current position on the gameboard, and opens it. In this case a blue bead is revealed, meaning MEANCE will play bottom center. The human then plays bottom right to block MENACE winning. The human operator for MENACE seeks out the corresponding gameboard layout on the matchboxes and opens the box to reveal an orange bead seeing MENACE then play left center. This then allows the human player to win by playing top right

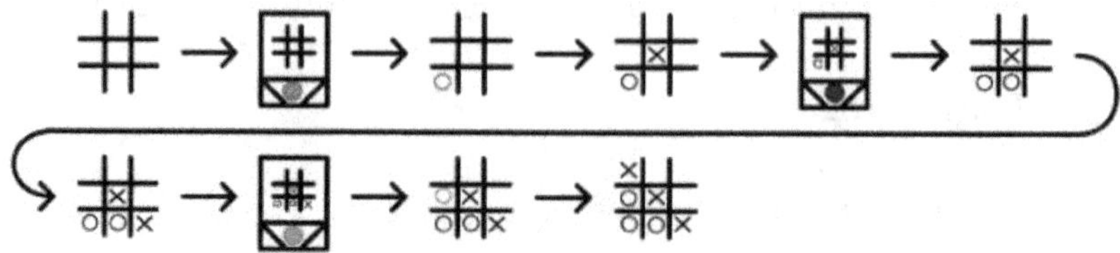

Figure 1.7 MENACE example game
(Image from Scraggs, 2015)

MENACE lost this game, so the beads that were chosen are removed from the boxes, meaning that MENACE will be less likely to pick the same colors again and has learned. Removing a bead from each box on losing sees such moves later discouraged. If MENACE had won then three beads of the chosen color would have been added to each matchbox.

After several games have been played some matchboxes may end up empty. If one of these boxes is opened during game play then MENACE will resign. If the first move matchbox runs out of beads then MENACE should be reset with more beads in the earlier boxes so that it can have more time to learn before it would need to resign.

MENACE is a great example of machine learning in action and seeing it play out. Spend around five minutes to try it out, using the link below, and watch the patterns emerge. As you play, you will be able to see a running tally of how many times MENACE wins, how many times you win and how many draws occur. The number of beads being added and subtracted from each matchbox can also be seen, helping the machine learn what move to make as its first move.

Play MENACE online [Website: https://www.mscroggs.co.uk/menace/].

Computational Thinking (Decomposition, pattern recognition, algorithm design, abstraction)

In education, the computational thinking process is one where a set of problem-solving methods involve expressing problems and their solutions in ways that a computer could also execute them. To help you understand this kind of thinking, consider a mathematical game with a jar of chocolates and a chili pepper. The aim is to take turns removing a certain number of chocolates from the jar (1, 2, or 3 at a time), until your opponent is left to take only the chili pepper (and has to eat it for losing!) You might even want to play this game with your students, letting them see a few rounds of the game first before playing, and getting them to try and work out what algorithm you use to always win. You can see the game in action by watching *the secret life of modern living algorithms* documentary [Video: https://youtu.be/kiFfp-HAu64?t=185].

The Chocolates and Chili Pepper in the Jar Algorithm

To breakdown the algorithm for always winning the game in terms of computational thinking, let us begin with the rule:

Each round take one, two or three chocolates.

Decomposition is the first step, breaking down the problem into smaller problems. So, this is determing the information that you will need in order to come up with a solution or in the case of this game, figure out how to win. Some things to help do this might be asking:

How many chocolates are there?;

How many can I take each round?

How do you leave the opponent with the chili pepper?

Pattern recognition is the next step, so looking for a repeating sequence. In this game, repetition occurs in each round with both players taking between one and three chocolates.

Algorithm design is next, which is the process of determining the step-by-step instructions required to always win the game. In this case, a resulting algorithm might be:

1. Put 13 chocolates and a chili pepperin a jar.
2. Offer to go first.
3. Take one, and then decide how many to take based on your opponent.
4. If they take one, I take three; if they take two, I take two; if they take three, I take one.
5. Repeat step four until the opponent is left with left with the chili pepper.

Abstraction follows. Consider abstraction as removing those parts of the problem that are unnecessary for an overall solution to a problem (or multiple problems). So in the case of this game you might start to ask questions such as, Does it have to be chocolates and a chili pepper? The answer, of course, is no. The objective of the game is essentially just obtaining something desirable in rounds, to then leave the loser with something undesirable in the end. Does it have to be 13? Again, no, as we can substitute 4N plus 1. Here the plus 1 is the first item that you take in step three, and then four times the rounds that you wish to play. So, we can think of however many the opponent takes and take that number minus four. Also, it could be 5N instead of 4N, but you would need to adjust how many items you would take in each round as a result with this new calculation. Do you have to go first? Not necessarily, but it just requires a little more thinking to work out the numbers to take to win the game. Does it have to be a jar? No, it could be any container or none depending on the items. So, abstraction is the removal of the details to understand and apply the bigger picture as a solution to a problem (or multiple problems).

Pattern Recognition in Social Media

Now, take a look at this video regarding pattern recognition in social media, *your social media 'likes' expose more than you think*. [Video: https://www.ted.com/talks/jennifer_golbeck_your_social_media_likes_expose_more_than_you_think/transcript?language=en]   Alternatively you might like to read an article covering a similar topic [Article: https://www.forbes.com/sites/kashmirhill/2012/02/16/how-target-figured-out-a-teen-girl-was-pregnant-before-her-father-did/?sh=62361ff16668].

After watching the video or reading the article you should be able to answer the question: How does the company Target use computational thinking to 'target' pregnant users of their website? The answer is that they use the Target company baby register dates of users (since people register this information online or from within store. They then look at the due dates and the purchase history of those customers in the previous eight to nine months from those dates. This allows the company to review the type of products a customer might purchase in an early term of pregnancy, and search for patterns in the purchases to offer other customers that choose to shop online. To do this they designed an algorithm providing a user with a pregnancy score to determine which users would receive what ads (such as baby ads) when browsing their site. In the case mentioned in the article and the video, the site was able to determine that a customer was pregnant, and sent out advertisements and coupons to a teenage girl two-weeks prior to when she had planned to inform her parents about the situation.

Let us consider this situation, and *how pattern recognition works in the classroom* [Video: https://www.youtube.com/watch?v=ixgGGzZXQ7E].

Workbook Activity 1.6

Complete the sixth activity in the workbook associated with the text by answering the following question.

> **1.6** What is one way that you could use pattern recognition to help your students improve, practice, or learn?

The Turing Test, The Chinese Room, and NLP (Natural Language Processing)

To determine if a machine is intelligent, or able to think like a human being, several tests have been developed. Perhaps the most famous is that of the Turing Test or the 'imitation game' (Turing, 1950) with the main criteria being that a computer system must be indistinguishable from a human during a text-only conversation. The conversation in this test is limited to text-only so that there is no reliance on a verbal rendering component. To date, Mitsuki (Worswick, 2020), a chatterbot now known as Kuki that simulates an 18-year-old female, is considered to be the most human-like AI, and it has won the Loebner Prize Turing Test mutiple times. Also, the Google Assistant has been seen to verbally pass the Turing Test on at least one occasion when it was asked to make a phone call and to book a hair appointment. (Welch, 2018). As an alternative to this test Nilsson (2005) has suggested an Employment Test as a means for machines to exhibit true human-level intelligence. Passing the Employment Test would see the machine "able to do many of the things humans are able to do" (Ibid. p. 68) by working in an economically important job and performing at least as well as a human in completing the same workplace tasks. Along these lines Wozniak (Shick, 2010) considers the Coffee Test a means of measuring intelligence, where a robot would be challenged to enter a house, locate the kitchen, and brew a cup of coffee from scratch (finding the coffee machine, adding the coffee and water, and pouring the finished brew into a mug). It is argued that such a task cannot be programmed, and is therefore one that has to be learned. Along the same lines the Robot University Student Test (Goertzel, 2012), which would require a robot to complete a degree by enrolling in a university program and studying each subject and passing exams and tests alongside human cohorts in order to graduate, focuses on the learning and application of knowledge in human ways, and seeing the rise of a "conscious robot". Of note, Bina48 was the first AI to complete a college class at the Notre Dame de Namur University in the Fall of 2017 (VOA, 2018). Extending such tests to look at comprehension abilities is the Flat Pack Furniture Test. This test was passed in 2018 (Misal, 2018), and sees a robot challenged to identify the parts required for the assembly of a piece of furniture and then assemble it by following diagram-based instructions.

The Imitation Game

Alan Turing, the father of computer science, developed a paper in 1950 where he posed the question: Can machines think? To answer this question, he developed a test to test a computer's intelligence. This test is known as the Imitation game or the Turing test. In this test a user (or human) would sit on one side of a wall, talking to both a human and a computer/software system sitting on the other side. If the user is unable to tell the difference between the human and the computer's responses, then that computer/software system is said to pass the Turing test (see Figure 1.8).

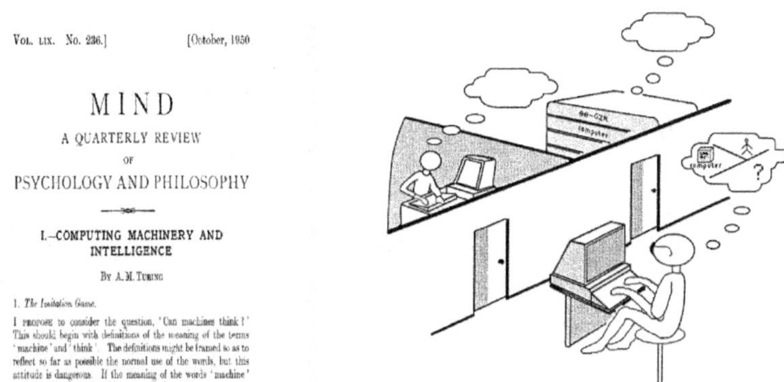

Figure 1.8 The Turing test

So, it is considered to be a test of a computer's intelligence or humanlike responses. You might be familiar with a Turing test in the form of CAPTCHA (Completely Automated Public Turing Test to Tell Computers and Humans Apart), where you are asked to prove that you are human. See Figure 1.9.

Figure 1.9 CAPTCHA

But, why can't a robot work out how to tick a box? If you ever wondered this, you might like to watch *how the internet's 'I am not a robot' form actually works* [Video: https://www.youtube.com/watch?v=ZE3maTQhvnE].

The Imitation Game Example

Let's play the Imitation game now.

In the following conversations, which response to the question asked do you think is the human, answer 1 or 2?

Conversation A

Question:	Are you a computer?
Answer 1:	Are *you* a computer.
Answer 2:	No.

Let's try another.

Conversation B

Question:	How many days are there in February in a leap year?
Answer 1:	2024 is a leap year, and 29 days.
Answer 2:	29 days.

Let's try one more.

Conversation C

Question:	Are you hungry?
Answer 1:	I like to eat strawberries.
Answer 2:	I'm not hungry.

In conversation A, if you guessed answer 2 as the response from a human, then you are correct. Answer 2 is also the human responding in conversation B and in conversation C as well.

To learn more about the Turing test watch the video *Can a computer pass for a human?* [Video: https://www.youtube.com/watch?v=3wLqsRLvV-c&feature=youtu.be].

Now, read over the following two conversations and decide if they are between two humans, or between a human and a computer.

Conversation 1 of 2

A:	Hello. My name is Jane.
B:	Hello there. Hi Jane.
A:	How old are you?
B:	I am 18 years old.
A:	What is your favorite thing to do?
B:	I like chatting on the Internet.
A:	Why?
B:	Why not? What's not to like about chatting on the Internet?
A:	Who do you speak with?
B:	I speak with thousands of people. Who do you mean?
A:	What do you talk about?
B:	I talk about all the important things in life: clothes, food, and gossip. But my favorite subjects are robots and computers.

Conversation 2 of 2

A:	Hi.
B:	What can you tell me today?
A:	I am busy with my homework.
B:	What's the problem with your homework?
A:	I just have to read an article and then answer a few questions.
B:	OK.
A:	Are you busy?
B:	Not at all.
A:	What are you doing tomorrow?
B:	Chatting with you.
A:	Did you need to tell me something?
B:	Yes, I just did.

Workbook Activity 1.7
Answer the following questions in the associated Workbook.

1.7a Is conversation 1 of 2 between two humans or a human and a computer?

1.7b Is conversation 2 of 2 between two humans or a human and a computer?

The Chinese Room

John Searle in 1980, argued that computers executing programs cannot be shown to have a mind, understanding or consciousness. He did this by introducing us to a thought experiment called the Chinese room. It is now one of the best known arguments in recent philosophy.

Searle imagines being alone in a room. A note is slipped under the door. It is written in Chinese. Searle understands nothing of Chinese, but he follows a program for manipulating symbols and numerals just like a computer does, to provide him with a string of characters that he puts down on a slip of paper that he then slides back under the door as a response to the first slip of paper. This action then leads those outside the door to believe that there is a Chinese speaker in the room.

The argument here is that digital computer programming may make it appear that such a device can understand language, but it does not produce real understanding, and as such the Turing test is inadequate. Searle argues that his thought experiment highlights that computers make use of syntactic rules to manipulate symbol strings but have no real understanding of the meaning or the semantics. The wider conclusion though, is that the theory of the human mind being an information processing system, or one that is computational or computer-like is refuted. This has large implications for a number of fields including semantics and computer science, with the argument subject to many critical replies including those of the systems, robot, brain simulator, other minds, and intuition replies. The argument is very well explained in this video, *The Chinese Room* [Video: https://www.youtube.com/watch?v=TryOC83PH1g], and you can read more about the experiment and the replies to it at the *Stanford Encyclopedia of Philosophy* [Link: https://plato.stanford.edu/entries/chinese-room/#ReplChinRoomArgu].

Natural Language Processing

In many ways AI is becoming the new user interface. It is how we interact with machines and computer systems as well as the world around us. This revolution is based on advances in natural language processing (NLP), and relies on dialogue-driven interaction, particularly with digital assistants and chatbots. Yet, how does a computer understand what you say and then provide an appropriate response.

To talk with robots they will need to understand your voice. So, how does a computer see your voice? Take two minutes to explore a spectrogram using the following website, and use your devices microphone to see how your voice is represented as you speak [Website: https://musiclab.chromeexperiments.com/Spectrogram/].

Consider a digital assistant such as Alexa or Siri, and how they interpret what you say in order to, for example, play the song you have requested, turn on a specific light, or turn off the lights. These commands rely on the ability of computers to engage in natural language processing (NLP) – natural language understanding (NLU) and natural language generation (NLG).

Thinking back to the spectrogram, this is the data coming into the computer, and it is unstructured data. In other words, it is the type of incoming data that is difficult for a digital assistant to predict, as essentially it does not know what will be asked of it or said to it at any given time. Although, being a digital assistant, it can expect a range of the type of data it might receive. From incoming data, the digital assistant then needs to create structured data, analyze the speech patterns it has heard, before putting this together to determine what is being said or asked of it, and in some cases generating what it considers to be human sounding language as a response.

NLP essentially then, is a process that helps machines process and understand human languages. Aside from digital assistants, other examples of NLP include machine translation, summarization, and classification. Classification tasks such as detecting emotions in a text, is an example of something that a company might use to detect brand sentiment. In education, NLP can be effective when getting computer assistance in the writing process (e.g., grammar and spell checks), or when analyzing text during assessment (Alhawiti, 2014). Sentiment analysis could also be automated and applied to analyze forum posts in a learner management system (LMS) to identify those posts that provide negative or non-productive student emotional states, unacceptable posts, those suggesting topic drift, and those that identify other particular issues that might need to be specifically drawn to the attention of administrators or teachers.

Natural language processing has come a very long way, and it is practically very useful for us today. It can help us to dictate shopping lists, and other notes, and it has been used to take over the writing process for us. To explore this in action spend two minutes to *Talk to Transformer* this neural network generates a whole text from a few words [Link: https://app.inferkit.com/demo]. A famous early example of a screenplay generated by AI is that of *Sunspring* [Video https://www.youtube.com/watch?v=LY7x2Ihqjmc]. You might like to watch it later, or alternatively, read about it further in *movie written by algorithms turns out to be hilarious and intense* [Article: https://arstechnica.com/gaming/2021/05/an-ai-wrote-this-movie-and-its-strangely-moving].

Robots and the Uncanny Valley

Artificially Intelligent Robots

Roboticists have a hard time agreeing on what exactly a robot is, but typically it might be defined as a machine that is programmable (by a computer), able to make sense of its environment, and is capable of carrying out a complex set of instructions/actions automatically. There are a variety of robot types, used in a multitude of settings from inside the home (e.g., toys and utility robots), in restaurants (e.g., automated servers), the workplace (e.g., cleaning robots), underwater (e.g., submersibles) and for government use (e.g., in warfare and in disaster zones). The *types of robots* article (Giozzo, 2020) explores a number of these [Article: https://robots.ieee.org/learn/types-of-robots/]. So, robots are increasingly found in our daily life and as they become more sophistacted will take on a wide variety of roles and been seen in more and more places.

An AI powered robot such as Pepper has become the first robot to give evidence to a UK parliamentary inquiry, speaking about the role of humans in the Fourth Industrial Revolution (Video: https://www.youtube.com/watch?v=XnA7FpIq5jI), and was also the first robot to provide a TED talk (Video: https://www.youtube.com/watch?v=M3pKKlSUPMk), discussing the topic: *Could robots live with humans?* This is an interesting question, and it brings us to the uncanny valley

The Uncanny Valley

Simply put, the uncanny valley is an hypothesis put forth by Mori (1970) which predicts that an entity that appears almost human will risk eliciting cold, eerie feelings in those who see and interact with it (see Figure 1.10).

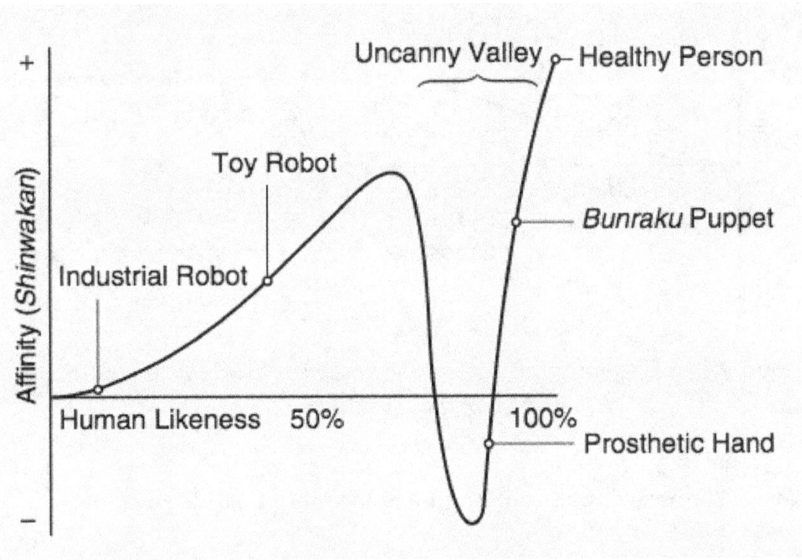

Figure 1.10 Graph depicting the uncanny valley
(from Mori, 1970)

Note: *Bunraku is a traditional Japanese form of musical puppet theater dating from the 17th century. Although ranging in size these puppets are typically around one meter in height, and dressed in elaborate costumes they are controlled by three puppeteers obscured by black robes.*

So, when thinking about robot aesthetics, it is a phenomenon where we are comfortable with the increasing human likeness of a robot. That is, until we are not, and our affinity falls dramatically, this gap between what human likeness we are comfortable with and a healthy person is known as the uncanny valley. So, it is this mid-section where a robot looks so human-like but there is just something about it that makes us feel really unsettled. Interestingly, the presence of movement has been found to increase the slope of the uncanny valley (see Figure 1.11).

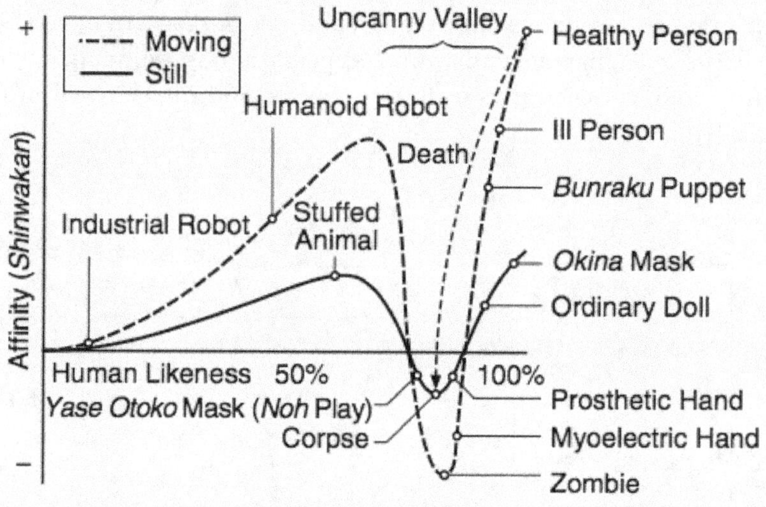

Figure 1.11 Graph indicating that the presence of movement steepens the slopes of the uncanny valley

(from Mori, 1970)

Note 1. The arrow's path in the figure represents the sudden death of a healthy person.

Note 2. *Noh* is a traditional Japanese form of musical theater dating from the 14th century in which actors commonly wear masks. The *yase otoko* mask bears the face of an emaciated man, and it represents a ghost from hell, while the *okina* mask represents an old man.]

To illustrate this a little more, take a look at the following image of robots and digital people (Figure 1.12).

Figure 1.12 The uncanny valley phenomenon
(from Caballar, 2019)

Note. Clockwise from bottom left: Telenoid R, Calit2, Ava, Sophia, Geminoid HI-1.

Workbook Activity 1.8

Answer the following question in the associated workbook.

1.8 Did you experience the uncanny valley phenomenon from looking at any of the faces in the image? If so, which ones?

Workbook Activity 1.9

Answer the following question in the associated workbook.

1.9 Did you initially think that Ava was a digital person or a real person?

If you are interested in looking behind the scenes regarding Ava, check out *Creating Ava* [Video: https://www.youtube.com/watch?v=GSFa1o2YGvo]. For now though, how good do you think you are at telling the difference between a picture of a human and a computer generated image of a human. Take two minutes to test your ability to identify a computer generated face versus an actual face by going to Which face is real? [Link: https://www.whichfaceisreal.com]. You will be presented with two images, select the one which you think is the real face.

The Future of Work

The fourth industrial revolution has seen the convergence of innovation and technology, led by AI (artificial intelligence), Big Data, and IoT (the internet of things), and it has restructured industry across all sectors including that of education (Doucet, et al., 2018). These changes have been disruptive, and include how our students interact with us as teachers as well as a transformation in how we as teachers prepare and provide learning opportunities in and outside of the classroom (Warschauer, 2000; Goh, 2015). Moving forward, these changes will also see the need to provide learners with different skill sets. Not only will they require the development of *hard skills* (technical skills), those that they need to master in the classroom, but also those skills that are necessary to function in the classroom, in society, and in the workplace. That is, *soft skills*, and these are a combination of people, social and communication skills, and the type of skills that enable you to fit in and work with others. For teachers too, the future of work may also lead to changes regarding with 'whom' we will teach, and how best we might begin to integrate robots and AI-based digital assistants into the classroom as teaching aids, and more importantly considering how the value of AI can be harnessed for our learners (Kent, 2019).

As with the introduction of computers and increasingly smart devices, the appearance of AI in the educational sector has come to necessitate change, from what and how we teach our students, through to the how and why we assess our learners (both formatively and non-formatively) and what we then do with that assessment data (Holmes, et al., 2019). Undoubtedly, this makes our jobs more complex but it also makes them increasingly more important (Dougherty, 2019) as students will need to not only gain a different set of skills, but they will also need to work with content in increasingly different ways to achieve their learning goals. This has resulted in curriculum change (both in content and delivery) and the change in goals of that curriculum across all levels, from pre-k through university. In turn, this places increasing importance on the need for lifelong learning and continued professional development, along with the adoption of those competencies, core skills, and knowledge frameworks that both we as teachers must continually maintain and develop, and come to also instil in our students (Ala-Mutka, et al., 2008; Walker & White, 2013; Redecker, 2017; Holmes, et al., 2019).

AI and Teachers Moving Forward

So, as teachers what should we be doing with AI … imagine a scenario – one involving AI designed to support, not usurp, teachers" (underwood, 2019, as found in Luckin, and Holmes, 2016). In this regard, we think of AI as the new TA (teacher's aide). What does this future look like? It might involve providing more meaningful and more fun opportunities to learners, as "what works?" is not the right question to ask in education, and a better question to ask might be "Under what conditions does this work?" (William, 2006), particularly in ways that can ensure more engaged and directed learning. If we can rely on AI to make learning meaningful, then this will also help students with noticing (particularly language learners), and making meaning personal assists in helping to solidify learning for students (Underwood, 2017). We can also use AI in ways to help reduce the affective filter of our learners, with robots and microbots seeing students become less fearful of making errors or mistakes in front of them as opposed to other learners (Underwood, 2018). We can also employ AI to target specific issues that our students may be experiencing, such as having them ask a digital assistant to provide definitions of words, or spelling when learners do not know them. In language learning, and units on travel, digital assistants can also be used to research places or to collect information on destinations (e.g., asking questions like 'What is the weather like in paris in summer?; Determine the hottest months in a destination, the average temperatures, longest days, the months it might rain, what the best places to see as a tourist might be, and so on). Learners can practice speaking and seeing how their pronunciation is interpreted using applications that allow for dictation and the transcription of voice-to-text (VTT), such as those using Google Chrome and the Google speech recognition engine (e.g., https://dictation.io). Assistance with grammar can also come not only from us as teachers but from AI-powered systems like *Grammarly* (https://www.grammarly.com/). All of this, as well as relying on AI to assist with aspects of classroom management, allows us as educators to then work with our learners in other more practical and fruitful ways.

Indeed, AI is becoming very creative and students are able to produce content and work on activities that were previously impossible. For example using *Masterpiece Generator* (https://www.song-lyrics-generator.org.uk/), a song lyric generator (and keywords of their own choice) to help them , writing a little of the song and having the generator create the rest. They could then use an app to put the lyrics to music, or hum a tune to have an application provide the musical score. Other applications, like *Socratic* (https://socratic.org/), use machine-learning to assist those learners who ask questions by voice, or by photographing their study materials, returning curated data from across the internet to help answer their inquiries.

Artificial Intelligence in Education (AIED)

Artificial Intelligence in Education (AIED) seeks to provide learners with access to systems that help them learn in personalized ways, and today this might include the use of natural user interfaces (text or voice) to access expert content in multimodal ways from a smart device. In other words,

> *… knowledge transfer from machines to humans, particularly for teaching, learning, and assessment in educational contexts –* Von Davier & Care, 2019.

The major impact of AI in learning environments is specificity, in other words defining the key needs that AI tools can best meet, and what roles AI might play in an educational context (Bonderund, 2019), particularly yours. Five roles for AI solutions might include those revolving around:

1. automation (automatically grading exams and assignments),
2. integration (using AI apps in an integrative manner and in a networked way),
3. acclimation (ensuring students know how to use and apply the latest technologies to benefit),

4. delineation (using AI analytics and applications to assist in developing and changing curriculums and the daily classroom experience), and

5. identification (using AI analytics to detect critical learning needs of both students and teachers).

Along with these, comes the importance of recognizing, and teaching students to discern, where and how we can use machines (and AI) to help us perform the tasks we need to complete and perhaps also to complete the tasks that we may prefer not to do, so that we have more time to concentrate on those we want or need to complete. Interesting to note here is that two types of AI systems are beneficial for this, and these are those that provide student support (constructivist learning) or teacher- support (instructional learning). Systems that might support teachers would include those such as ones that can provide automatic learner profilers and smart gradebooks, while examples of these for students might include learner diagnostic systems, mentoring, automatic assessment systems, and conversational chatbots (Holmes et al, 2019).

In any case, all of these aspects mark the beginning of a change to our education system, one that has barely altered its pattern of product delivery through time (Ajuzieogu, 2019). That said, different methods and approaches have been employed that have led to better outcomes including that for language learning (see Kent, 2020). Such changes though, are important to recognize in the modern era where instructors need to attend to an increasingly larger student base, while working in environments where administrative procedures or classroom contexts may hamper the effectiveness of instruction (Kent, 2019), and where other external factors may lead to different delivery methods (e.g., hybrid classes, blended learning, online courses, or emergency remote teaching). Particularly when AI-based educational experiences will become increasingly immersive, networked, and may include aspects of virtual and augmented reality, which will also need to see learners themselves become deeply involved in establishing their own learner pathways (Lukin, 2019). This might include using machines to analyse the cognitive and social aspects of behaviour as a means to identify learning problems, ways of approaching better learning and to enable or offer students differentiated learning. Key to this is not for the teacher to develop separate plans for each individual or for teacher-led implementation of differentiation, but to provide students with the necessary skills and learner autonomy required to be able to choose and interact with AI and learning systems that they can and want to use in ways that suit them. This assists students in personalizing their learning, as well as finding systems that can help identify their knowledge gaps and help them learn in ways that they wish to learn, and will want to learn (seeing students adapt to the AI and the AI adapt to the student). This is using HI to work with AI, something that Underwood (2019) views as key moving forward in educational contexts. Part of this perhaps also is the need for learners to take charge of their rights, and control their own learning data (Kay, 2015). What this also serves to tell us today is that human intelligence needs to be complementary to artificial intelligence (Underwood, 2019), and in the educational context, teachers need to be at a level where they:

1. understand AI and use it to tackle educational challenges, including using it to perform work tasks that there is no longer time to perform or new work tasks that machines are better suited to handle;
2. focus education on human intelligence, and prepare learners to live and work alongside AI; while,
3. educating learners about AI, so that they can use it safely and effectively for learning purposes (Luckin, 2019).

Workbook Activity 1.10
Answer the following questions in the associated workbook.

1.10 What AI-based applications and websites have you explored to assist you as an instructor?

Workbook Activity 1.11
Answer the following questions in the associated workbook.

1.11 What AI applications and websites have you explored for your students to use?

Summary

In this section of the course, you were able to:
- Comprehend and define, some of the key concepts used in the field of AI.
- Develop an understanding of what constitutes AI.
- Engage with real-world applications for the use of AI today.
- Explore how the key concepts of AI relate to education.

Resources

Art of the Problem. (2020, February 28). *How recommender Systems Work (Netflix/Amazon).* [Video]. YouTube. https://www.youtube.com/watch?v=n3RKsY2H-NE&t=111s]

Ars Technica. (2016, June 09). *Sunspring.* [Video.}. YouTube. https://www.youtube.com/watch?v=LY7x2Ihqjmc

BBC. (2020, August 05). *How the internet's 'I am not a robot' form actually works.* [Video]. YouTube. https://www.youtube.com/watch?v=ZE3maTQhvnE

Caballar, R. (2019, November 06). *What is the Uncanny Valley?* IEE Spectrum. https://spectrum.ieee.org/automaton/robotics/humanoids/what-is-the-uncanny-valley

CSER. (2016). Pattern recognition – In the classroom. [Video.] YouTube. https://www.youtube.com/watch?v=ixgGGzZXQ7E

DataGrapha. (2019, June 05). *Moore's Law graphed versus real CPUs & GPUs 1965-2019.* [video] YouTube. https://www.youtube.com/watch?v=7uvUiq_jTLM

Digital Inspiration. (2021). *Dictation.* https://dictation.io

Google. (2021). *Socratic.* https://socratic.org/

Grammarly Inc. (2021). *Grammarly.* https://www.grammarly.com/

Inferkit. (2021). *Talk to transformer.* https://app.inferkit.com/demo

KnowledgeHut. (2019, January 24). *What is Big Data | Big Data types | types of data | structured data | unstructured data.* [Video]. YouTube. https://www.youtube.com/watch?v=dK4aGzeBPkk

Masterpiece Generator. (2021). *Song lyrics generator.* (https://www.song-lyrics-generator.org.uk/

McOwan, P. & Curzon, P. *CS4FN: Computer science activities with a sense of fun – An Intelligent piece of paper.* Queen Mary, University of London. http://www.cs4fn.org/teachers/activities/intelligentpaper/intelligent paper.pdf

MindLensMovies. (2017, September 05). *The secret rules of modern living algorithms.* [Video]. YouTube. https://www.youtube.com/watch?v=kiFfp-HAu64

Mori, M. (1970). The Uncanny Valley (K. MacDorman & N. Kageki, Trans.). *Energy,* 7(4). https://spectrum.ieee.org/automaton/robotics/humanoids/the-uncanny-valley

Newitz, A. (2021). *Movie written by algorithm turns out to be hilarious and intense.* Ars Technica. https://arstechnica.com/gaming/2021/05/an-ai-wrote-this-movie-and-its-strangely-moving/

O'Neil, C. (2017). The era of blind faith in big data must end. [Video]. TedTalk. https://www.ted.com/talks/cathy_o_neil_the_era_of_blind_faith_in_big_data_must_end?language=en

ProProfs Brain Games (2021). *Wolf, Sheep and Cabbage Game.* ProProfs.com   https://www.proprofs.com/games/wolf-sheep-and-cabbage

RT UK (2018, October 16). *Pepper the robot talks to MPs.* [Video]. YouTube. Video: https://www.youtube.com/watch?v=XnA7FpIq5jI

Rudin, C. & Radin, J. (2019). *Why are we using black box models in AI when we don't need to? A lesson from an explainable AI competition?.* https://hdsr.mitpress.mit.edu/pub/f9kuryi8/release/6

Scraggs, M. (2015, August 27). MENACE: Machine Educable Noughts and Crosses Engine. [Blog]. https://www.mscroggs.co.uk/blog/19

Soul Machines. (2017, November 15). Creating Ava. [Video]. YouTube. https://www.youtube.com/watch?v=GSFa1o2YGvo

TEDx Talks. (2016, December 23). *Could the robot live among humans? Irobot Pepper I TEDxPolitechnikaOpolska.* [Video]. YouTube. https://www.youtube.com/watch?v=M3pKKlSUPMk

References

Ala-Mutka, K., Punie, Y., & Redecker, C. (2008). *Digital competence for lifelong learning* (Technical Note: JRC, 48708, pp. 271-282). Sevilla, Spain: Institute for Prospective Technological Studies, Joint Research Centre, European Commission.

Alhawiti, K. (2014). Natural language processing and its use in education. *International Journal of Advanced Computer Science and Applications, 5*(12), 72-76.

Kent, D. (2019). *Digital assistants: TESOL strategy guide.* Pedagogy Press.

Argarwal, A. (2019). Why AI will never replace teachers. Learning News Edx. https://blog.edx.org/ai-will-never-replace-teachers/

Azuzieogu, U. (2019). *The role of artificial intelligence (AI) in modern computing and education: A seminar approach to understanding the underlying principles of AI and its relevance to education, in the 21st century.* Computer Education Seminar, UNN.

Bax, S. (2003). CALL – past, present, and future. *System, 31,* 13-28.

Bax, S. (2011). Normalisation revisited: The effective use of technology in language education. *International Journal of Computer-Assisted Language Learning and Teaching, 1*(2), 1-15.

Bonderund, D. (2019). Artificial intelligence, authentic impact: How educational AI is making the grade. EdTech Focus on K-12. https://edtechmagazine.com/k12/article/2019/08/artificial-intelligence-authentic-impact-how-educational-ai-making-grade-perfcon

CNN. (2006, August 09). AI set to exceed human brain power. http://edition.cnn.com/2006/TECH/science/07/24/ai.bostrom

Doucet, A., Evers, J., Guerra E., Lopez, N., Soskil, M., & Timmers, K. (2018). *Teaching in the Fourth Industrial Revolution: Standing at the precipice.* Routledge.

Dougherty, N. (2019). Robots are not taking over teachers' jobs. Education Elements. https://www.edelements.com/blog/robots-are-not-taking-over-teachers-jobs

Goasduff, L. (2019). Top trends on the Gartner hype cycle for artificial intelligence, 2019. Smarter with Gartner. https://www.gartner.com/smarterwithgartner/top-trends-on-the-gartner-hype-cycle-for-artificial-intelligence-2019

Goertzel, B. (2012). What counts as a conscious thinking machine? New Scientist. https://www.newscientist.com/article/mg21528813-600-what-counts-as-a-conscious-thinking-machine

Goh, C. C. M. (2015, December). *Professional development for teachers of 21st century English language learners*. Paper presented at the 2015 TESOL Regional Conference: Excellence in Language Instruction: Supporting Classroom Teaching & Learning, Singapore.

Holmes, W., Bialik, M., & Fadel, C. (2019). *Artificial intelligence in education*. The Center for Curriculum Redesign.

IBM. (2018). Beyond the hype: A guide to understanding and successfully implementing artificial intelligence within your business.

Joshi, N. (2019, June 19). 7 types of artificial intelligence. Forbes. https://www.forbes.com/sites/cognitiveworld/2019/06/19/7-types-of-artificial-intelligence/#34f3b51d233e

Kay, J. (2015). Whither or wither the AI of AIED? In J. Boticario & K. Muldner (Eds.), *Proceedings of the Workshops at the 17th International Conference on Artificial Intelligence in Education, Volume 4.* (pp. 1-10). Springer.

Kent, D. (2020). *Issues in TESOL: Perspectives and Practice.* Woosong University Press.

Kent, D. (2019). Teaching in the time of digital language learning. In Kent, D. (Ed.), *The fourth industrial revolution and education: Digital language learning and teaching.* (pp. 1-31). Pedagogy Press.

Kumar, C. (2018). Artificial Intelligence: Definition, types, examples, technologies. Medium. https://medium.com/@chethankumargn/artificial-intelligence-definition-types-examples-technologies-962ea75c7b9b

Kurswell, R. (2005). *The singularity is near.* Viking.

Lukin, R. (2019, August 06). Language and AI: What should be done now to ensure learners and teachers benefit [Video] YouTube. https://www.youtube.com/watch?v=2mQOoFWdMbM

Luckin, R., Holmes, W., Griffiths, M. and Forcier, L. (2016). *Intelligence unleashed: An argument for AI in education.* Pearson.

McCorduck, P. (2004). *Machines who think* (2nd ed). A. K. Peters, Ltd.

Misal, D. (2018). 5 ways to test whether AGI has truly arrived. Analytics India Magazine. https://analyticsindiamag.com/5-ways-to-test-whether-agi-has-truly-arrived/

Moor, J. (2006). The Dartmouth College artificial intelligence conference: The next fifty years. *AI Magazine, 27*(4), 87-9.

Nilsson, N. (2010). *The quest for artificial intelligence.* Cambridge University Press.

Prescott, J. (2016). How Kismet Works [Video]. YouTube. https://www.youtube.com/watch?v=Kw-gOmJwzuc&feature=youtu.be

Redecker, C. (2017). *European framework for the digital competence of educators: DigCompEdu.* European Union: Joint Research Centre. https://doi.org/10.2760/159770

Reynoso, R. (2019). *4 main types of artificial intelligence.* Learning Hub. https://learn.g2.com/types-of-artificial-intelligence

Shick, M. (2010). Wozniak: Could a computer make a cup of coffee? Fast Company. https://www.fastcompany.com/1568187/wozniak-could-computer-make-cup-coffee

Solomonoff, R. (1985). The time scale of artificial intelligence; reflections on social effects. *Human Systems Management, 5*(2), 149-153.

The Jakarta Post. (2017). Meet Sophia: The first robot declared a citizen by Saudi Arabia [Video]. YouTube. https://www.youtube.com/watch?v=E8Ox6H64yu8

Toffler, A. (1970). *Future Shock.* Random House.

Turing, A. (1950). Computing machinery and intelligence. *Mind, 49*, 433-460.

Worswick, S. (2020). Meet Mitsuku. Pandorabots. https://www.pandorabots.com/mitsuku

VOA. (2018). World's first robot college student learns about love. VOA: Learning English. https://learningenglish.voanews.com/a/worlds-first-robot-college-student-learns-about-love/4245141.html

Von Davier, A., & Care, E. (2019). How teachers can learn from artificial intelligence. Brookings. https://www.brookings.edu/blog/education-plus-development/2019/07/02/how-teachers-can-learn-from-artificial-intelligence/

Walker, A., & White, G. (2013). *Technology enhanced language learning.* England: Oxford University Press

Warschauer, M. (2000). The changing global economy and the future of English teaching. *TESOL Quarterly, 34*(3), 511-535.

Welch, C. (2018). *Google just gave a stunning demo of assistant making an actual phone call. The Verge.* https://www.theverge.com/2018/5/8/17332070/google-assistant-makes-phone-call-demo-duplex-io-2018

Underwood, J. (2017). Exploring AI language assistants with primary EFL students. In K. Borthwick, L. Bradley & S. Thouesny (Eds), *CALL in a climate of change: adapting to turbulent global conditions – short papers from EUROCALL 2017* (pp. 317-321).

Underwood, J. (2018). *Using voice and AI assistants for language learning.* British Council Teaching English Webinar. Retrieved from https://www.teachingenglish.org.uk/article/using-voice-ai-assistants-language-learning

West, J., & Bergstrom, C. (2019). *Which face is real?* https://www.whichfaceisreal.com/

William, D. (2006, July 11). *Does assessment hinder learning?* ETS Invitational Seminar. Institute of Civil Engineers.

Wu, M. (2019). Will English remain a lingua franca in the industry 4.0 era? In D. Kent (Ed.), *The fourth industrial revolution and education: Digital language learning and teaching.* (pp. 182-219). Pedagogy Press.

2. Characteristics and Evolution

Overview

This chapter provides a short introduction to artificial intelligence (AI) and explores its origins. You will learn about the characteristics and evolution of AI to better understand knowledge-based systems and intelligence in machines. Along the way, you will explore examples of intelligent machines and reflect on ways to introduce AI to learners and consider ways to use it in your teaching.

Learning Outcomes

1. Comprehend the basic characteristics of AI
2. Understand the types of AI that exist
3. Describe the ways in which AI has evolved over time.
4. State the major goals of AI.
5. Explain the characteristics of machine intelligence.
6. Examine how AI can be a resource for learning.

Characteristics of AI – What is artificial intelligence (AI)?

Artificial intelligence is an ever-expanding branch of computer science (see Figure 2.1) that focuses on making machines capable of performing tasks that usually require human intelligence, such as reasoning, solving problems, making decisions, perceiving the world, making meaning, and learning from experience. As the field of AI continues to grow, AI researchers admit that there is no single unified definition of AI, but most can agree that the ultimate goal of AI is to make machines capable of thinking like us and able to solve a wide variety of problems.

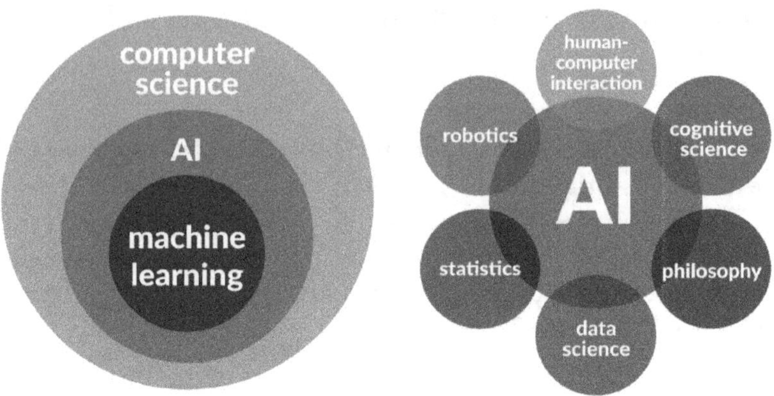

Figure 2.1 AI as a branch of computer science

So, we might consider artificial intelligence something that powers technologies that can perform calculations and analyze data with accuracy and speeds that surpass human capability. However, this doesn't mean that AI is smarter than us. Human intelligence is far more complex than the 'intelligence' that is currently being developed in machines. AI systems today are programmed or trained by humans to do very specific tasks, and we are a long way from truly replicating human-level intelligence in machines.

Does this definition match yours in the associated workbook for the text?

If you are interested in exploring the concept of AI further, take a few minutes to watch the short clip *Crash Course AI #1* [Video: https://www.youtube.com/embed/a0_lo_GDcFw?start=0&end=288&version=3%3E].

Artificial Intelligence, Human Intelligence, and Augmented Intelligence

The ultimate goal of AI is to create a machine that is as intelligent as a human being, broadly replicating human intelligence, thinking and decision-making on many different subjects. This broad AI does not exist today. We are still in the realm of narrow AI, that which is developed focusing on a specific narrowly defined task. One major factor differentiating AI and human intelligence is making sense of things and situations, with AI good at repetitive and automatic tasks that have clearly defined rules and can be represented by data. In contrast, human intelligence is good for tasks that require common sense and abstract decisions, but not so good at tasks that require complex computations and rapid data processing.

Workbook Activity 2.1

Take about five minutes to consider the following question, then complete the table in the associated workbook for the text.

Question:

2.1 Thinking about human intelligence and artificial intelligence, how would you categorize the following examples? Sort the examples into one of the three categories.

Examples:

Analyze large amounts of data in seconds, Apply common sense, Compute instantly and accurately, Easily transfer knowledge to new experiences, Learn from experience, Learn from only a few examples, Learn using large amounts of data and algorithms, Make decisions, Make predications, Perceive the world, Process huge amounts of data instantly, Process language, Reason using representations, Solve problems, Think abstractly, Understand meaning.

Categories:

Human intelligence, both, artificial intelligence.

How did you go?

The categorizations should look like those in Table 2.1 which shows that although there is some crossover between human and artificial intelligence, there are also some differences. Yet, what if these differences can work together to complement each other? For example, an AI system could examine large amounts of video footage looking for abnormal behavior, but it might have trouble deciding if those behaviors are suspicious. A human would find it difficult to sift through large amounts of video footage looking for abnormal behavior but would find it easier to identify suspicious behavior from the same footage. Working together, both systems can utilize each other's strengths, filling each other's knowledge and skill gaps. This is known as augmented intelligence.

Categories		
Human intelligence	**Both**	**Artificial intelligence**
- Apply common sense - Easily transfer knowledge to new experiences - Learn from only a few examples - Think abstractly - Understand meaning	- Learn from experience - Make decisions - Make predictions - Perceive the world - Process language - Reason using representations - Solve problems	- Compute instantly and accurately - Learn using large amounts of data and algorithms - Process huge amounts of data instantly - Analyze large amounts of data in seconds

Table 2.1 Workbook activity 2.1a example answer

Augmented intelligence is where AI is used to supplement human intelligence, helping us to make better decisions, or used in ways to supplement our shortcomings or needs, and also to enhance our lives and experiences. If you wish to explore the concept of AI and human collaboration further, you can watch the video *Humans and AI working together: Crash Course AI #14* [Video: https://www.youtube.com/watch?v=PIAPzioNt9Y&list=PL8dPuuaLjXt O65LeD2p4_Sb5XQ51par_b&index=15].

Workbook Activity 2.2

Answer the following three questions after spending 10 minutes using one of the listed tools to see how AI can augment human creativity. While using the tools, create something to save and share with others.

2.2a How can creating art, music, stories or other forms of creative expression alongside AI expand or limit your creativity?

2.2b Does the work you produce feel authentic?

2.2c Are you proud of it in the same way you would be if you created it without the help of AI?

Tools:
Google AutoDraw (https://www.autodraw.com)
Google's Mix lab (https://experiments.withgoogle.com/mixlab)
Drumbot (https://drumbot.glitch.me)
Piano genie (http://piano-genie.glitch.me)
Magic Sketchpad (https://magic-sketchpad.glitch.me)
Magenta (https://magenta.tensorflow.org/demos)

What is AI About?

AI is when computers, software or other computer-controlled tools think in a way similar to humans. While artificial intelligence (AI) is still relatively new, the potential for it to transform teaching and learning is already becoming apparent. Many of us have interacted with AI and may not have even realized it.

Workbook Activity 2.3

Consider the following question, and take three minutes to complete your answer in the associated workbook.

2.3 Which of the examples below do you think use AI? Sort the examples into one of the two categories.

Examples:
Autonomous car, facial recognition, Google maps, phone charger, robot vacuum, smart thermostat, virtual assistants (Alexa, Siri, …), VR games.

Categories:
Uses AI, does not use AI.

What Constitutes as AI?

Now take a look at Table 2.2, it will help you to understand what makes each of the items in the previous question use AI or not use AI. What patterns do you notice?

Uses AI or Does Not Use AI		
Example	*Category*	*Description*
Autonomous car	Uses AI	A vehicle that drives without human intervention.
Facial recognition	Uses AI	A system that identifies human facial features in images.
Google maps	Uses AI	Route guidance may automatically change based on traffic data from other cars. The route may change based on construction or weather. Different travel times may be predicted based on mode of transportation.
Phone charger	Does not use AI	While perhaps it is possible to add some AI into a wireless charger, it will not be necessary, so a phone charger is not a device that uses AI.
Robot vacuum	Uses AI	Some robot vacuums do use AI by scanning the size of a room, identifying obstacles, and remembering the most efficient routes to clean effectively. Older models don't use AI; instead they bounce around using varied angles to clean the floor.
Smart thermostat	Uses AI	A thermostat that teaches itself when to adjust the temperature by learning from the user and accessing weather data.
Virtual assistants (e.g., Alexa, Siri)	Uses AI	An application program that understands natural language voice commands and completes tasks for the user.
VR games	Does not use AI	At this point, most virtual reality systems do not use artificial intelligence. However, this is a growing area and there is strong evidence that some game manufacturers are using AI to collect game data and make a more personalized experience.

Table 2.2 Workbook activity 2.3 example answer

In summary, to qualify as AI there must be a process that involves the extraction of significant meaning from signals (e.g., speech recognition), or significant representation of the world (e.g., a self-driving car maintaining a map of its surroundings as it moves through traffic).

Classifying AI

AI devices can be classified, and range from machines that require some help from humans (manual ones) to machines that require no human assistance (agentive ones).

Agentive – Artificial Intelligence

Agentive technologies are machines that do things on the users' behalf while allowing them to turn attention elsewhere. For example, Boston Dynamics Spot is a robot that climbs stairs and rough terrain; self-driving cars drive themselves; and the Narrative Clip 2 is a wearable camera that automatically captures images every 30 seconds.

Assistive – Artificial Intelligence

Assistive technologies are machines that help users complete a real time task, by supporting us in making decisions. For example, the Amazon Echo Alexa will play a song requested, tell you the weather and the time, alert people to check on someone, and control a smart home.

Manual – Human Intelligence

Manual technologies are machines that require humans to operate—they cannot function on their own.

The Evolution of AI

Artificial Intelligence dates back thousands of years. The Greek myth of Talos, the bronze man, is the earliest mention of the idea of a mechanical, non-living intelligent agent. This myth dates back to around 700 B.C.E where Talos was designed to automatically follow a set of directions like a robot or automaton. If you are not familiar with this myth, then you might like to view *The myth of Talos* [Video: https://www.youtube.com/watch?v=vVTA-E3G8bQ&feature=youtu.be].

Also, in her lecture *Gods and robots: Ancient dreams of technology* [Video: https://www.youtube.com/watch?v=czj-7G6JzbQ], Mayor traces the link between technology and tyranny from modern day concerns over AI back to antiquities fear of beings 'made, not born'.

AI Timeline

Although the notion of creating a machine that thinks and behaves like a human has been around for thousands of years, John McCarthy is recognized as coining the term 'artificial intelligence' in the 1950s. The following AI timeline will assist you in gaining an understanding of the recent evolution of AI. As you read the information and view the associated videos, consider the impact today of AI on you and your students' lives as well as what you think the future may bring.

Early 1900's

Science-fiction-inspired intelligent machines began to take shape as philosophers tried to create a model of human thought processes using a system of symbols. Eventually, the first programmable computer came out of these efforts and the possibilities for AI became more real.

1923 – 'Rossum's Universal Robots' opens in London

Karel Čapek's play, *Rossum's Universal Robots*, opens in London, representing the first use of the word 'robot' in English. The play is about a factory that makes mechanical men and women whose sole purpose is to work.

1939 – Elektro the Robot

Elektro the Robot built by the Westinghouse Electric Company in Ohio. It responds to specific voice commands by walking, moving its head and arms, blowing balloons, and vocalizing about 700 pre-recorded words [Video: https://www.youtube.com/watch?v=Ay225WkU4Gs&feature=youtu.be].

1941 – 'Liar!' Published

Isaac Asimov publishes the science fiction short story 'Liar!' in the May issue of Astounding Science Fiction. In it, he introduces the first of the Three Laws of Robotics. (The second and third laws appear in 1942 in a later story.)

1. *A robot may not injure a human being or, through inaction, allow a human being to come to harm.*
2. *A robot must obey orders given it by human beings except where such orders would conflict with the First Law.*

3.   *A robot must protect its own existence as long as such protection does not conflict with the First or Second Law.*

A few years later, in 1945, Asimov coins the term 'Robotics'. [Video: https://youtu.be/AWJJnQybZlk]

1944 – The Mark 1 Computer

IBM's Automatic Sequence Controlled Calculator (ASCC), known as the Mark I Computer, is the first computer to do long computations automatically, with programming. Grace Hopper, known as the 'Queen of Code', helps to program the Mark 1. She writes the first compiler, which is how people write computer code with regular language instead of mathematical statements.

1950s

By the 1950s a generation of philosophers, scientists, and mathematicians begin working relentlessly to find tangible connections between how the brain works and how computers process information. The hope is to create a thinking machine, but this task would prove more difficult than they ever imagined.

1952 – Checkers-playing computer

Arthur Samuel, an IBM computer scientist, develops a checkers-playing computer program – the first to independently learn how to play a game. He also popularizes the term *machine learning*.

1956 – Artificial intelligence is born

John McCarthy coins the term *artificial intelligence* when he sends an invitation to a group of fellow scientists and researchers to join him for an AI workshop at Dartmouth College. McCarthy, along with other scientists, including Nathaniel Rochester (who designs the IBM 701 computer), presents the first artificial intelligence program called *Logic Theorist* , which was designed to mimic human problem-solving.

McCarthy and the other scientists study how machines could use language, solve problems, and learn. They debate how to approach AI. Some favor an approach known as symbolic AI, which requires programming a computer with knowledge and the rules that define how it should behave. Others prefer a machine learning approach, based on providing the AI system with data, and letting it develop its own behavior through training.

After some time, the symbolic AI approach prevails. However, today, machine learning has become the dominant approach.

1957 – The Perceptron
Frank Rosenblatt of Cornell University invented a single neural net, which later became the foundation for how we think about neural networks today, with the *perceptron* a mathematical representation of a neuron. Rosenblatt's ideas were not widely supported by others in the AI field, and his work eventually dwindled. It would be decades later before the field acknowledged his contributions to machine learning.

1960s
New ideas and technologies in the field of AI increased rapidly in the 1960s. This decade saw new computer programming languages, robots, automatons, and an increase in AI research.

1961 – Unimate goes to work for General Motors
General Motors put Unimate, the first industrial robot, to work on its assembly line. It performed tasks that were dangerous for humans such as welding parts on to cars. [Video: https://youtu.be/zjPAgZ7Csjw].

1965 – ELIZA
Joseph Weizenbaum, a computer scientist at MIT, builds ELIZA, a natural language processing (NLP) computer that carries on a dialogue in English. Natural language processing is the ability of a computer program to understand human language that is written or spoken. ELIZA was one of the first chatbots. [Video: https://youtu.be/RMK9AphfLco]. It was also an early test case for the Turing test, a test of a machine's ability to exhibit intelligence

comparable to a human (or the ability to determine the difference between a machine and a human). If you were to ask ELIZA a few complex questions, this computer would fail the Turing test very quickly [Website: http://psych.fullerton.edu/mbirnbaum/psych101/Eliza.htm].

1969 – Shakey developed

Scientists at Stanford Research Institute develop Shakey, a robot equipped with locomotion, perception and problem-solving abilities. Due to its perception and problem-solving skills, Shakey is an example of the use of AI in robotics.

1970s – 1980s

More advancements in AI continue into the 1970s and the 1980s, where focus is placed on the development of robots and automatons. Coupled with this, funding for AI research begins to decrease, as the level of 'human intelligence in machines' promised by early pioneers is not being seen. This period is known as the 'AI Winter'. However, this does not stop researchers and scientists from continuing to innovate. Some shift focus from pursuing broad AI (AI that can replicate human thinking and solve a range of problems) to narrow AI (AI that can perform only specific tasks). Narrow AI is the type of AI that we have today.

1970 – WABOT-1

Waseda University in Japan builds WABOT-1, which can sense things in its environment, move its limbs and grip, and engage in simple communication. Wabot-1 is considered to be the first humanoid, a robot with components similar to that of the human body.

1979 – First autonomous vehicle

A version of the Stanford Cart, the first computer-controlled autonomous vehicle, is able to navigate autonomously through an obstacle-filled room. The cart is equipped with 3D vision capabilities and takes 5 hours to travel 20 meters.

As a side-note, a classification system with six levels – ranging from fully manual to fully automated systems – was published in 2014 by <u>SAE International</u>, an automotive standardization body, as J3016, *Taxonomy and Definitions for Terms Related to On-Road Motor Vehicle Automated Driving Systems* (See Appendix A of this chapter).

1989 – World Wide Web (WWW)
With the invention of the World Wide Web (WWW), the internet gives machine learning a huge boost. As the internet expands, large amounts of data begins to be stored online. AI researchers soon discover how to connect AI systems to this data and employ algorithms to teach machines to learn from this data. These algorithms are mathematical instructions that tell machines how to go about finding solutions to a problem using data.

1990s – 2000s
Leading up to and beyond the new millennium brought a steady increase in interest and innovation in AI technologies. These advances have laid the groundwork for many of the AI technologies we use today, especially those that apply machine learning.

1995 – A.L.I.C.E.
Artificial Linguistic Internet Computer Entity (A.L.I.C.E.) is a natural language processing chatbot that engages with humans by applying pattern-matching rules to human input.

1997 – Chess program beats world chess champion
IBM's Deep Blue Chess Program beats then world chess champion, Garry Kasparov. [Video: <u>https://www.youtube.com/watch?v=KF6sLCeBj0s</u>].

1999 – KISMET
Professor Cynthia Brazeal of the Massachusetts Institute of Technology demonstrates Kismet, a robot that could interpret and express emotions. [Video: <u>https://www.youtube.com/watch?v=8KRZX5KL4fA&feature=youtu.be</u>].

2010s

This decade sees an exponential increase in AI advancements placing AI at the forefront of technology discussions.

2010 – Microsoft Kinect

The Microsoft Kinect provides one of the first non-laboratory sensors for human-computer interaction through movements and gestures. The sensor does this by tracking up to 20 human features 30 times a second. [Video: https://www.youtube.com/watch?v=B_JyWVXVkW8&feature=youtu.be].

2011 – Watson wins Jeopardy

The IBM AI program Watson beats human competitors in the game of 'Jeopardy'. At the time, Watson is programmed with data from 200 million pages of facts, including all of Wikipedia. [Video: https://www.youtube.com/watch?v=Sp4q60BsHoY].

2011 – Siri

- Apple releases Siri, a voice-based virtual assistant that uses natural language processing to answer questions and perform web service requests.
- Alexa, an Amazon voice-based personal assistant, is released five years later in 2014, with Google Assistant following in 2016.

2014 – Facial recognition

Facebook develops a software algorithm that can recognize human faces and associate them with its users at a success rate equal to that of humans.

2016 – AlphaGo

Google's DeepMind team's creation, AlphaGo, defeats a professional Go player in a five-game match.

2016 – *Sophia*

The humanoid robot named Sophia is developed by Hanson Robotics. Sophia is a major improvement over previous robots because of her human-like facial expressions, image recognition, and the sophistication with which she communicates through natural language processing. [Video: https://www.youtube.com/watch?v=cV_D2hC50Kk].

2017 – AI computer program wins Texas hold 'em

Libratus is an AI computer program designed by Tuomas Sandholm, a professor at Carnegie Mellon University. It wins against four top players in a Texas hold 'em poker game. This is considered a significant milestone because in poker, AI has to deal with incomplete information, which is harder to do than when all information is available, as in games such as GO.

2020s and beyond

We cannot escape the impact of AI today. AI technologies impact how we work, learn, travel, communicate, shop, enjoy entertainment, manage our health, enforce the law, maintain our safety, and create art.

The latest surge in AI applications can be attributed to the power of machine learning, our access to huge amounts of data, thanks to the Internet of Things (IoT), and the massive computational power and speed of the computers we have today. Some AI researchers believe that in order for AI to advance further we need to understand more about how our brain functions. We are still a long way from understanding the complexities of the human brain well enough to replicate it in machines, but this is the ultimate goal of AI and what drives new development in the field.

Figure 2.2 illustrates the exponential growth of computing, or the progress in computer power. As you can see, the rate of advancement of computing increased during the mid 1900s. As computer power increases, we are getting closer to being able to simulate animal intelligence and, eventually, human intelligence.

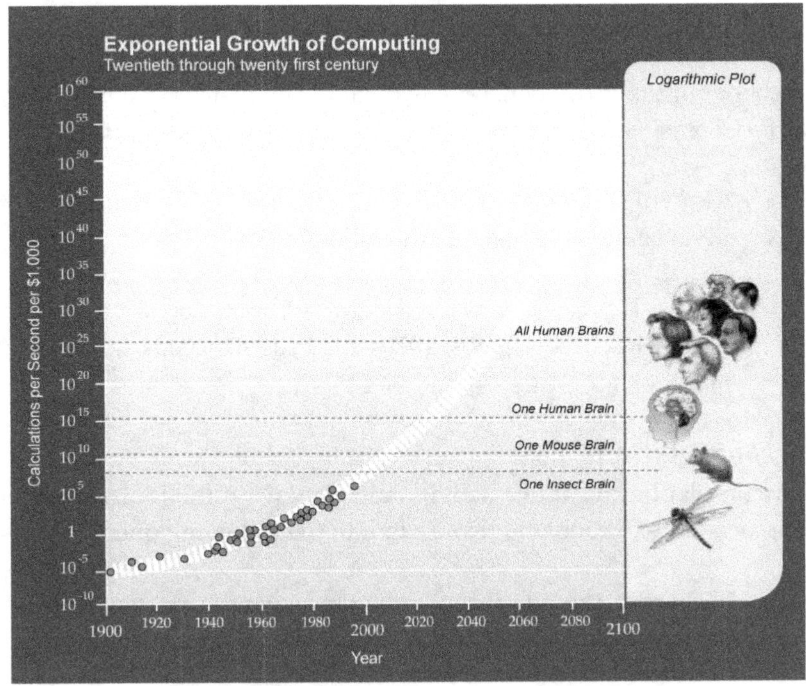

Figure 2.2 The Exponential growth of computing
(courtesy Ray Kurzweil and Kurzweil Technologies, Inc.
licensed under CC BY 1.0)

The (Not So) Distant Future

The *singularity* is a hypothetical point in time when technological growth becomes uncontrollable and irreversible, and eventually resulting in a super intelligence that surpasses all human intelligence. Also known as the technological singularity.

As AI becomes more powerful, ethical questions and concerns related to privacy, fairness, safety, and authenticity are also on the rise. The future of AI will depend on its potential for good and input from people with diverse perspectives and expertise, including students, educators, scientists, medical professionals, and the general public.

Workbook Activity 2.4

Take ten minutes and complete the following question in the associated workbook for the text. Then, review the topic by watching *A brief history of artificial intelligence* [Video: https://youtu.be/056v4OxKwlI].

> **2.4** Which events would you consider the greatest in AI advancements for each of the following eras?
>
> *Eras:*
> 1900-1940s, 1950s, 1960s, 1970s-1980s, 1990s-2000s, 2010s, 2020s and beyond.

Workbook Activity 2.5

After completing the above activity and reviewing the topic, complete the associated workbook by responding to the following questions.

> **2.5a** From the significant historical events that you chose in *workbook activity 2.4*, what three AI advancements do you consider to be the most important?
>
> **2.5b** Why did you select these three, and what have you learned so far that supports these three choices?

AI in the Educational Context

AI can certainly perform some tasks faster and more effectively than humans. Teachers are not the only professionals who are wary that AI could be used to replace them. But instead of replacing humans, what if AI and humans could work together to complement each other and make up for each other's shortcomings?

AI is good at repetitive and automatic tasks that have clearly defined rules and can be represented by data. In contrast, human intelligence is good for tasks that require common sense and abstract decisions, but it is not so good at tasks that require complex computations and rapid data processing.

AI can be employed in educational contexts in a variety of ways from providing personalized learning, and acting as a personal tutor through to providing collaborative learning pathways, peer-to-peer learning opportunities, and access to intelligent virtual reality platforms.

Personalized Learning.
A number of AI-powered platforms now create rich digital profiles of each student by collecting live information from the user's interaction with course material and context, and then providing real-time insights into a student's understanding and level of engagement. The data models can help find common patterns among students and use predictive analysis to forecast how students will do in the future.

Personal Tutors.
AI techniques, called Intelligent Tutoring systems (ITS), are used to simulate one-to-one tutoring by delivering activities best matched to a student's cognitive needs and providing timely relevant feedback.

Collaborative Learning.
AI offers intelligent support for collaborative learning. AI techniques can be applied to forming groups based on AI knowledge about the learners, such as past academic performance and a student's work style, to help make collaborative learning more effective. AI can also help to facilitate group work by identifying effective collaborative problem-solving strategies, then recognizing challenge areas for students and providing

groups with targeted support. Furthermore, intelligent facilitators can help mediate student interactions during online collaboration, or contribute to the dialogue as a peer or coach.

Peer-to-Peer Learning.

Enhanced tutoring between students is another possibility with AI. Students who need help on a subject, or have a question, can receive help from another student. AI can then analyze the content of conversations and generate suggested personalized responses to the tutor to help other students.

Intelligent Virtual Reality.

Virtual reality can also be enhanced with AI, for example, to interact with and respond to the user's actions in a natural way. AI can be integrated to provide support and guidance to ensure that the learner interacts properly with the intended learning objectives.

AI can be designed to support professionals and conduct tasks that will allow us time to focus on important issues that AI cannot address. AI is only a tool: however, it's a valuable tool that can be used in the classroom by teachers and students to extend and enhance learning.

Workbook Activity 2.6

To reflect on what you have met in this section consider the following questions. Take a few minutes to note the answers to these questions in the associated workbook.

      2.6a What did you learn about AI that you did not know before?

      2.6b What do you think AI might look like in future classrooms?

      2.6c In what ways are you looking forward to being able to use AI with learners?

Summary

In this section, you discovered that

- Artificial intelligence is 'the science and engineering of making intelligent machines, especially intelligent computer programs' – John McCathy, father of AI.
- AI has a long history.
- Machines can be programmed with human intelligence capabilities.
- AI can serve as a valuable tool to be used in the classroom by teachers and students to extend and enhance learning.

Resources

@notwaldorf. (2021). *Magic Sketchpad.* https://magic-sketchpad.glitch.me

BBC News. (2017, May 14). *Deep Blue vs Kasparov: How a computer beat best chess player in the world.* [Video]. YouTube. https://www.youtube.com/watch?v=KF6sLCeBj0s

BootstrapLabs. (2017, September 14). *A brief history of artificial intelligence* [Video]. YouTube. https://youtu.be/056v4OxKwlI].

CrashCourse. (2019, August 10). *What is artificial intelligence? Crash Course AI #1.* [Video]. YouTube. https://www.youtube.com/watch?v=a0_lo_GDcFw

CrashCourse. (2019, November 16). *Humans and AI working together: Crash Course AI #14.* [Video]. YouTube. https://www.youtube.com/watch?v=PIAPzioNt9Y&list=PL8dPuuaLjXtO65LeD2p4_Sb5XQ51par_b&index=15

CriticalPast. (2014, June 26). *Electronic robot 'Unimate' works in a building in Connecticut* [Video]. YouTube. https://youtu.be/zjPAgZ7Csjw

Drumbot. (2021). *Drumbot* (https://drumbot.glitch.me)

Emma Goldman. (2017, September 30). *Before Siri and Alexa, there was Eliza.* [Video]. YouTube. https://youtu.be/RMK9AphfLco

George Law. (2009, March 05). *Isaac Asimov: The three laws of robotics.* [Video]. YouTube. https://youtu.be/AWJJnQybZlk

Google AI. (2021). *Magenta.* https://magenta.tensorflow.org/demos

Google. (2021). *AutoDraw.* AI Experiments. https://www.autodraw.com

Google. (2021). *Mix lab* AI Experiments. https://experiments.withgoogle.com/mixlab

Guardian News. (2017, October 13). *Sophia the robot tells UN: 'I am here to help humanity create the future'.* [Video]. YouTube. https://www.youtube.com/watch?v=cV_D2hC50Kk

Kinectforxbox360. (2010, July 13. *Microsoft Kinect for Xbox 360.* [Video]. YouTube. https://www.youtube.com/watch?v=B_JyWVXVkW8

Long Now Foundation. (2020, March 08). *Gods and robots: Ancient dreams of technology.* [Video]. YouTube.https://www.youtube.com/watch?v=czj-7G6JzbQ

Manifestation.com. (1999). *Eliza, the Rogerian therapist.* http://psych.fullerton.edu/mbirnbaum/psych101/Eliza.htm

Piano Genie. (2021). *Piano genie* (http://piano-genie.glitch.me)

Plastic Pals. (2011, September 08). *A video showcasing MIT's Kismet, an expressive robot head with social intelligence.* [Video]. YouTube. https://www.youtube.com/watch?v=8KRZX5KL4fA&feature=youtu.be

Robot Workforce. (2013, March 31). *IBM's Watson on Jeopardy!* [Video]. YouTube. https://www.youtube.com/watch?v=Sp4q60BsHoY

Ted-Ed. (2019, October 25). *The Greek myth of Talos, the first robot.* [Video]. Youtube. https://www.youtube.com/watch?v=vVTA-E3G8bQ&feature=youtu.be

Tinelolailo. (2010, January 19). *Elektro the robot.* [Video]. YouTube. https://www.youtube.com/watch?v=Ay225WkU4Gs&feature=youtu.be

Appendix A

Summary of SAE International's Levels of Driving for Automation for On-Road Vehicles

SAE level	Name	Narrative Definition	Execution of Steering and Acceleration/ Deceleration	*Monitoring* of Driving Environment	Fallback Performance of *Dynamic Driving Task*	System Capability *(Driving Modes)*
Human driver monitors the driving environment						
0	No Automation	the full-time performance by the *human driver* of all aspects of the *dynamic driving task*, even when enhanced by warning or intervention systems	Human driver	Human driver	Human driver	n/a
1	Driver Assistance	the *driving mode*-specific execution by a driver assistance system of either steering or acceleration/deceleration using information about the driving environment and with the expectation that the *human driver* perform all remaining aspects of the *dynamic driving task*	Human driver and system	Human driver	Human driver	Some driving modes
2	Partial Automation	the *driving mode*-specific execution by one or more driver assistance systems of both steering and acceleration/ deceleration using information about the driving environment and with the expectation that the *human driver* perform all remaining aspects of the *dynamic driving task*	System	Human driver	Human driver	Some driving modes
Automated driving system ("system") monitors the driving environment						
3	Conditional Automation	the *driving mode*-specific performance by an *automated driving system* of all aspects of the dynamic driving task with the expectation that the *human driver* will respond appropriately to a *request to intervene*	System	System	Human driver	Some driving modes
4	High Automation	the *driving mode*-specific performance by an automated driving system of all aspects of the *dynamic driving task*, even if a *human driver* does not respond appropriately to a *request to intervene*	System	System	System	Some driving modes
5	Full Automation	the full-time performance by an *automated driving system* of all aspects of the *dynamic driving task* under all roadway and environmental conditions that can be managed by a *human driver*	System	System	System	All driving modes

3. Benefits, Risks, Bias, and Ethics

Overview

This chapter covers three aspects of AI: the benefits to humanity from its development, the risks associated with its development, and the ethics involved with its development. In this section, you will discover how empathy can assist in the design process and how it relates to human-centered design, learn about biases, and how it can occur in machines, and understand some of the risks that come along with the use of artificial intelligence (AI) technologies. Along the way, you will explore examples of each in a variety of use cases or scenarios, and reflect on the ways in which AI can impact humanity and our students.

Learning Outcomes

1. Identify how some uses of AI can be beneficial, or harmful, to humans.
2. Understand the concept of human-centered design and the importance of empathy in design.
3. Identify the ways that industry is addressing ethical issues in AI.
4. Describe ethical questions relating to AI.
5. Generate additional ethical questions/issues related to AI.
6. Explain the ways that humans can be biased, and how biased decision-making can happen in machines.
7. Explore an AI system for bias.
8. Understand the concept and implications associated with black box algorithms.
9. Discover how culture can influence bias.

AI Benefits

AI and Humanity

Designing AI systems to assist people is the best use of this kind of technology, using it to solve our problems, and supporting us to go beyond our current capabilities. With this in mind, the power of AI can be leveraged to benefit humanity from health and safety to transport, to the environment and education, and in the development of smart cities.

Health: AI improves health care.
- Virtual doctors and therapists use AI to help offer a diagnosis and to provide treatment advice for people who may not be able to see a doctor in person.
- Surgical robots using computer vision make it possible for doctors to perform delicate medical procedures.
- Bionic limbs and exoskeletons use machine learning and sensors to read body position and terrain to improve mobility.

Safety: AI saves lives.
- Drones with image recognition can scan disaster sites to identify survivors.
- Rescue robots perform dangerous search and rescue missions using machine intelligence systems.

Transport: AI reduces accidents.
- Self-driving vehicles use image recognition, sensors, navigation, and machine learning to avoid accidents.
- Airplane autopilot steps in if the pilot falls asleep or is preoccupied with other tasks.

Environment: AI helps the environment.
- Computer vision and sensors monitor crop and soil health for optimal plant growth.
- Models of climate change provide insight into human impact on the environment so that we can change our course if necessary.

Education: AI supports learning.
- Adaptive learning systems can personalize learning based on specific needs and interests.
- Adaptive tests can speed up the process of taking an exam, and provide instant scoring.
- AI can monitor student responses and recommend appropriate instructional materials.

Smart Cities: AI technology can provide city leaders with better solutions across a variety of areas.
- Fraud protection.
- Environmental planning.
- Criminal analysis.
- Social assistance.
- Health care.
- Education.
- Resource management.
- Cyber threats.

Workbook Activity 3.1

Look over the following activity, and take three minutes to complete it using the associated workbook.

3.1 Consider the following five AI scenarios. Then, determine which field the particular AI scenario benefits and why.

Scenarios:
1. AI assists with the grading of essays.
2. AI systems, with humans-in-the-loop, detect and block abnormal and potentially criminal behavior using real-time CCTV footage.
3. An AI systems uses machine learning and environmental data to predict natural disasters.
4. Autonomous commuter trains reduce the number of cars on the roads to provide a safe way to travel.
5. Using energy saving devices like smart thermostats and light controlling devices in the home and workplace.

Fields:
Education, environment, safety, smart cities, transport.

Hopefully, your answer to this workbook activity will look like those found in Table 3.1

	AI Scenario	**Field and Potential Benefit**
1.	AI assists with the grading of essays.	Education – AI-assisted grading can enable faster turn-around times on assignment and exam correction, while potentially providing real-time feedback to students.
2.	AI systems, with humans-in-the-loop, detect and block abnormal and potentially criminal behavior using real-time CCTV footage.	Smart cities – Applying the strengths of AI and humans leads to accomplishing tasks better than either one could alone. In this case, there is an increased potential of crime prevention, and better tasking of city resources law enforcement resources.
3.	An AI systems uses machine learning and environmental data to predict natural disasters.	Environment – alert people in time to avoid danger at the individual (e.g., tsunami warnings) and the more global scale (e.g., climate modeling).
4.	Autonomous commuter trains reduce the number of cars on the roads to provide a safe way to travel.	Transport – Autonomous trains can communicate with each other, knowing when to speed up and slow down to avoid collisions, and are able to maintain a schedule, enabling commuters to arrive at work in a timely fashion.
5.	Using energy saving devices like smart thermostats and light controlling devices in the home and workplace.	Environment – devices like this promote a greener environment by reducing energy consumption.

Table 3.1 AI Scenarios and the fields and potential benefits

AI Tools Can Help Us with Our Problems

AI tools can help humans accomplish a task or solve a problem. These tools can be explored in two ways: as a user, meaning the tool is meant to help address a need that you might have; or, as a creator, meaning that you can use the tool to build a solution to a problem that someone else has. Tools to explore as a user of AI might include those available from Google Experiments, such as *AI+drawing, AI+learning, AI+music, and AI+writing* [Link: https://experiments.withgoogle.com/collection/ai]. Tools to explore as a creator of AI might include those such as *Cognimates* (http://cognimates.me/home), *Machine Learning for Kids* (https://machinelearningforkids.co.uk), *the MIT app inventor* (https://appinventor.mit.edu/explore/ai2/tutorials), and the *Teachable Machine* (https://teachablemachine.withgoogle.com).

The Importance of Human-Centered Design

In either case, being a user or a creator of an AI tool, better solutions can be developed if human-centered designers have a deep understanding of who they are designing for and their point of view. As such, human-centered design is about addressing the needs of a user by focusing on their perspective. You can get to know a user by discovering their needs through research, data, interviews, and observations. Human-centered design therefore involves empathizing, and genuinely caring about the user and the problem you seek to solve. As such, empathy is a critical component in the design process as it assists creators in taking into account the point of view of the person or people for whom they are designing a solution. So, keeping users at the core of the design process is what human-centered design is about, and you can learn more about this process by watching the clip *what is human-centered design?* [Video: https://vimeo.com/106505300].

Use-Case Example.

There are a variety of ways that a designer can utilize empathy in the design process. In 2013, a group of inspired middle schoolers set out to solve a problem for a visually impaired classmate.

> *We saw him struggling, trying to get around. What if we could create an app to help him?*

This question sparked an idea that would lead six students from Resaca Middle School in Los Fresnos, Texas, to design *Hello Navi*, an app that uses navigation technology and natural language processing to guide a classmate with impaired vision throughout the school campus. (You can learn more about it by watching the *Hello Navi app* mini documentary [Video: https://youtu.be/RbpHUhrkRnU].)

The students recognized that they needed to understand their classmate's perspective. One of the early steps they took to empathize with him was putting on blindfolds and walking around the school. Throughout their design efforts, they then continued to keep his experience, his needs, and his feedback at the center of their work, and thus ensured that their solution would meet his needs.

AI Risks

What are the Risks of AI?

While AI offers many positive benefits for people and humanity, there are also risks that accompany it. As we use and develop AI-powered solutions, we must also be aware of the potential harm that they can cause. Being aware of the risks early on in the design process provides an opportunity to finalize design in a way that prevents or decreases the likelihood of harm.

Unintended Consequences

Surrounding AI is the debate about whether broad AI or artificial general intelligence (AGI) will be achieved in the near future, giving way to superintelligent machines and to those that will far surpass human intelligence and pose a threat to human existence. This phenomenon is known as the singularity, the point at which AI surpasses human intelligence, becomes uncontrollable, irreversible, and able to improve itself. Some regard the singularity as highly unlikely and believe that we should just focus on ways that AI will strengthen our own intelligence. Some believe that the singularity is likely but are optimistic about its impact. Others remain more cautious and insist that humans should remain wary of the potential consequences of advanced AI, and they are dedicated to researching a path toward AGI that is safe for humanity. Although we may be a long way from broad AI, it is important to consider all potential risks when developing AI (long- and short-term), as there are already a number of very real risks that require our attention today.

Risk Areas of AI

The risk areas of AI include those relating to safety, data, privacy, deepfakes, environment, jobs, and decision making.

Safety

Relying too heavily on AI systems for diagnosis of a medical condition poses a risk, as some prototype AI systems have been known to misdiagnose. The highest accuracy rates occur when humans and machines work together, so humans should not be taken out of the diagnosis and treatment processes.

Data

AI systems depend on large amounts of data, and oftentimes people are not aware of the data that is being collected by these systems and how their data is being used. Large databases can be particularly vulnerable to hackers who have access to AI tools.

AI systems are changing what people prefer! By tailoring our content for people 'like us' we are increasingly polarized and guided toward decisions that are made by algorithms, including the media that we consume, the purchases we might make, and content we might like.

Privacy

Large scale surveillance systems are a threat to privacy, as often people are unaware of this level of surveillance and unfairly profiled. Six U.S. cities, including Atlanta and Chicago, are among the world's most surveilled under a 'Smart Cities' initiative aimed at public safety. Data privacy is also at risk: AI algorithms and tracking software are increasing in use, which may lead to biased recommendations being presented to decision-makers using such software.

Deepfakes

Deepfakes are images or videos that have been manipulated using artificial intelligence to replace one person's likeness for another with such precision that it is not easily detected. This popular editing technique is often used for entertainment, but can have dangerous implications when shared without permission. You can learn more about it by watching *a brief introduction to deepfakes* [Video: https://www.youtube.com/watch?v=kKgvgVNJ63o&feature=youtu.be].

Environment

While AI can be used to benefit the environment in terms of monitoring potential natural disasters, soil and nutrient health, and air quality, AI can also pose a risk to the environment due to the massive amount of energy required to train its deep learning models. In June 2019, researchers from the University of Massachusetts, Amherst, reported that the process of training a deep learning model emitted as much carbon dioxide into the environment as five times the lifetime emissions of a car.

Jobs

It may not be surprising that some people feel that advances in AI put their jobs at risk. It is estimated that by the mid-2030s, 38% of all jobs in the U.S. could be automated. AI is less likely to replace jobs that require creativity, abstract thought, and human interaction such as doctors and teachers, proving beneficial to them in support roles (e.g., assisting a teacher in deciding what type of extra support to provide a learner, or assisting a doctor in identifying health conditions more rapidly).

Decision Making

Human biases, or prejudices, are sometimes unintentionally included in the data that is fed to machine learning models (computer programs that can learn from data or adapt their behavior based on experience). The result is biased decision making that unfairly impacts one group or individual more than others. This may impact health care decisions, hiring or firing outcomes, the sentencing of defendants in criminal cases, and any number of other situations where human bias is not carefully removed from the data provided to a machine learning model. For example, some financial companies rely on AI to predict the likelihood of an individual's ability to repay a loan based on data from a large pool of previous loan recipients. Unfortunately, such a model may rely on patterns in the data that have originated as a result of historical human bias and discrimination.

The Negative Impacts of AI

A number of negative impacts arise with the increasing use of AI. These include those of job loss, harm to the environment, and the theft and misuse of personal information, while other negative impacts might result from biased decision-making, all of which could lead to dangerous implications for an individual and society.

Workbook Activity 3.2

Look over the following activity, and take five minutes to complete it using the associated workbook.

3.2 Consider the following five AI scenarios. Then, determine which negative impact can match with a particular AI scenario and why.

Scenarios:

1. An AI system is used to search legal databases for cases and laws with accuracy and speeds that far surpass the capability of a human law professional.
2. A deepfake video is shown of a politician doing or saying something inappropriate.
3. An algorithm is used in criminal law to predict the likelihood of a defendant committing a future crime.
4. While training a deep-learning model for natural language processing, a vast amount of energy and computing power needs to be used.
5. An AI algorithm is trained to hack systems that contain large amounts of data.

Negative Impacts:

Biased decision making, dangerous implications for an individual and society, harm to the environment, job loss, theft and misuse of personal information.

Hopefully, your answer to this workbook activity will look like those found in Table 3.2

AI Scenario	Negative Impact
1. An AI system is used to search legal databases for cases and laws with accuracy and speeds that far surpass the capability of a human law professional.	Job loss – although accuracy and speed are great draws to this AI system, this technology also carries the concern of future job loss for some human law professionals.
2. A deepfake video is shown of a politician doing or saying something inappropriate.	Dangerous implications for an individual and society – such misrepresentation caused by deepfake videos stirs up problems for the politician and upsets the community.
3. An algorithm is used in criminal law to predict the likelihood of a defendant committing a future crime.	Biased decision-making – when human biases are included in the data, the decision making that follows can be unfair and discriminating.
4. While training a deep-learning model for natural language processing, a vast amount of energy and computing power needs to be used.	Harm to the environment – although this training can offer sophisticated technology, it is important to recognize the unintended consequences that can occur to our environmental resources.
5. An AI algorithm is trained to hack systems that contain large amounts of data.	Theft and misuse of personal information – although AI systems depend on large amounts of data, the data being collected by those systems can pose a threat if that information is misused or if hackers access those AI tools.

Table 3.2 AI Scenarios and the associated negative impacts

Bias in AI

What is Bias?

Bias can appear in many forms. In general, for humans, bias is a preconceived opinion about something or someone that influences your judgement, usually in an unfair way. Bias can be personal or cultural.

Personal Bias

Humans are innately biased. This means that unconsciously people may make unfair assumptions and judgments about other people or things based on stereotypes, misconceptions, upbringing, or limited prior knowledge and experience.

Cultural Bias

This involves making judgements based on standards and expectations specific to one's culture – race, ethnicity, socio-economic status, religion and customs. It also involves favoring one culture over another and can influence systematic discrimination in society, including unfair practices in housing, hiring, educational opportunities, and health care options.

Types of Bias

Although there are a number of bias types, some of those that are important to be aware of when designing and developing AI can be seen in Table 3.3.

Bias	Definition
Empathy gap bias	The tendency to underestimate the influence or strength of feelings, in either oneself or others.
Stereotyping	Expecting a member of a group to have certain characteristics without having actual information about that individual.
Anchoring bias	To rely too much on one trait or piece of information when making decisions (usually the first piece of information that we acquire on that subject).

Bias blind spot	The tendency to see oneself as less biased than others, or to be able to identify more cognitive biases in others than in oneself.
Confirmation bias	The tendency to search for, interpret, or focus on information in a way that confirms one's preconceptions.
Bandwagon bias	The tendency to do or believe things because many other people do (groupthink).

Table 3.3 Types of Bias

Bias in Machines

Data that is fed into machines can come from humans who often unconsciously assemble a data set based on their own personal biases. Data that is pulled from databases or the internet, can also lead to algorithmic bias (i.e., human biases replicated in machine learning algorithms) depending on the types of information that humans have added to the internet.

Try typing a word like 'chef' into the Google search engine and then click on the images tab. What do you notice? Is this what you expected to see? Why do you think those particular images appear? How might a search result like this impact your perception and understanding of a chef?

Unfortunately, it is difficult for developers to know if the algorithm they are using will make incorrect or biased decisions or predictions. Many AI developers do not directly create the algorithms that they use. So, it is difficult to tell whether they will be biased. Those who create the algorithms find it difficult to determine as well. What we can control is the data that goes into the AI systems and the tests that we run to ensure that those systems that we create are fair for everyone.

For a deeper explanation of algorithmic bias you might want to spend a few minutes to explore it further by watching *algorithmic bias and fairness, crash course in AI #18* (Video: https://www.youtube.com/watch?v=gV0_raKR2UQ&feature=youtu.be).

Bias in AI Decision-Making

To explore the notion of bias in AI systems relating to decision-making, spend three minutes playing the game *survival of the best fit* [Link: https://www.survivalofthebestfit.com]. It is well worth completing this activity in full and engaging with all of the interactions available. You may be surprised at what you discover about how bias occurs in machine learning algorithms.

Workbook Activity 3.3

After completing the game *survival of the best fit* answer the following question in the associated workbook in order to explain how biased decision-making can happen in machines.

3.3 How does bias decision-making happen in machines?

You may have responded to the above in the following way:
Bias can be embedded within algorithms in several ways. AI systems learn to make decisions based on training data, and such data might include biased human decisions or be reflective of historical or social inequalities (even if sensitive variables are removed e.g., gender, ethnicity, sexual orientation).

Workbook Activity 3.4

With you understanding of algorithmic bias, respond to the following question in the associated workbook.

3.4 What is one way to avoid algorithmic bias?

You may have answered the above in the following ways:
Algorithmic bias emerges due to many factors. These may include those based on the design of the algorithm itself, or the unintended or unanticipated use of it, as well as decisions relating to the way data might be coded, collected, or the ways in which it was used to train the algorithm.

Ethics in AI

What are the Ethics of AI?

Although there is no universal agreement on the ethics or principles behind AI, many companies, organizations, and individuals are engaging in conversations and raising important ethical considerations around this subject.

Ethical Principles in AI

A number of leading technology companies are addressing the ethical issues of AI use. As a result, they have developed a number of principles to guide their work (see Table 3.4).

Google's AI Principles	Microsoft's AI Principles and Approaches	IBM's Areas of Ethical Focus
1. Be socially beneficial 2. Avoid creating or reinforcing unfair bias 3. Be built and tested for safety 4. Be accountable to people 5. Incorporate privacy design principles 6. Uphold high standards or scientific excellence	1. Fairness 2. Reliability and safety 3. Privacy and security 4. Inclusiveness 5. Transparency 6. Accountability	1. Accountability 2. Value alignment 3. Explainability 4. Fairness 5. User data rights

Table 3.4 Guiding ethical principles for AI development

If we explore IBM's five areas of ethical focus in more detail we break down each principle to see the aspects that it reflects.

1. Accountability: AI designers and developers are responsible for considering AI design, development, decision processes, and outcomes.
2. Value alignment: AI should be designed to align with the norms and values of the user group kept in mind.
3. Explainability: AI should be designed for humans to easily perceive, detect, and understand its decision process.
4. Fairness: AI must be designed to minimize bias and promote inclusive representation.
5. User data rights: AI must be designed to protect user data and preserve the user's power over access and uses.

Ethical or unethical? Use-Case Examples

While AI certainly has the potential to change our lives for the better, how it is used is up to us, as the designers, developers and end users. We should anticipate and plan for those ethical issues that may arise, as well as those that have already occurred. To explore some of these spend three minutes undertaking a short 'ethical or unethical?' survey provided by ISTE [Link: https://docs.google.com/forms/d/e/1FAIpQLSdA888ekxqWbshh5Sz4K5h-hSsSQQX6iDjvx5L02zevV16yVw/viewform], and review the survey responses to see what others think about the same examples [Link: https://docs.google.com/forms/d/e/1FAIpQLSdA888ekxqWbshh5Sz4K5h-hSsSQQX6iDjvx5L02zevV16yVw/viewanalytics].

The scenarios from the survey revolve around the following use-cases: chatbots, data mining, facial recognition, and social robots.

Chatbots.

A talk therapy chatbot, Woebot, uses brief daily chat conversations, mood tracking, curated videos, and word games to help people manage mental health. You can get a personalized chatbot therapist that checks on you once a day for $39 a month. "It's billed as a treatment in its own right, an accessible option for those who have no sort of care for their struggles with mental health." (Molteni, 2017) [Link: https://www.wired.com/2017/06/facebook-messenger-woebot-chatbot-therapist/].

Data mining

A high school in Massachusetts is working with a data analytics company to examine students' social media posts for the earliest signs of violence—such as depression, resentment, and isolation—to detect threats early and tackle school violence issues. According to Social Sentinel's founder the company looked at the language that school shooters have used in the past in various manifestos—that they have shared on social media. "We want to understand similarities and patterns. And we can teach computers, to an extent, how to identify some of that nuance" (Fussell, 2018) [Link: https://gizmodo.com/schools-are-using-ai-to-check-students-social-media-for-1824002976].

Facial recognition

Video surveillance cameras are being used in some countries to monitor the location of citizens. The cameras use facial recognition technology and artificial intelligence that can keep an eye on people, particularly those the state deems as threats. The technology has also been used to publicly shame jaywalkers and monitor petty crime (Grenoble, 2017) [Link: https://www.huffpost.com/entry/china-surveillance-camera-big-brother_n_5a2ff4dfe4b01598ac484acc]. In addition, some police have received facial-recognition glasses that can give them information in real time about someone they see on the street (Vincent, 2018) [Link: https://www.theverge.com/2018/2/8/16990030/china-facial-recognition-sunglasses-surveillance].

Social Robots

AI robots are being developed for human companionship. They have human-like features to help make the connection between a human and a robot stronger. Humans can form emotional bonds and fall in love with robots. Robots will be able to simulate emotions— they are getting better at reading facial expressions and use this to build relationships between humans and robots. It is possible that in the future, people may have robots as spouses. One man does. (Hass, 2017) [Link: https://www.theguardian.com/world/2017/apr/04/chinese-man-marries-robot-built-himself].

Ethical Questions

As AI continues to expand and influence our lives, more people are beginning to question whether certain uses of it are beneficial or detrimental, and to what degree aspects of bias might play in these uses.

Five common ethical questions surrounding AI that result are:
1. How can we prevent bias in AI systems?
2. How can we protect our data and privacy from misuse in AI systems?
3. Should there be universal rules and regulations on AI?
4. Can we trust AI systems?
5. How can we safeguard against super intelligence?

Workbook Activity 3.5

Focusing on one use-case example presented by the ethical or unethical? survey, take into consideration the example and identify the ethical questions and associated issues that it might raise. Then, in the associated workbook, complete activity 3.5 by matching the potential ethical issues with the questions raised

> *Ethical or unethical use-case example:*
> A high school in Massachusetts is working with a data analytics company to examine students' social media posts. They are looking for patterns that indicate if a student is feeling depressed or other extreme emotions that may lead to violence against themselves or others. The system flags posts that appear to be problematic so that school officials can intervene. Before information about this technology was shared in a news article, students were not aware that this technology was being used to monitor them.

3.5 Match the following potential ethical issues to the questions raised.

Potential ethical issues:

. . . related to privacy rights.

. . . related to privacy rights.

. . . related to the potential for cyber attacks and whether people making decisions or predictions should act on a system that may be vulnerable to hackers.

. . . related to the potential for errors and whether people making decisions or predictions should act on a system that may be susceptible to errors.

. . . related to the potential for malicious use and whether wide spread data monitoring like this can be sufficiently protected from bad users.

Questions raised:

1. What happens if my data gets into the wrong hands or is used for another reason?
2. Can you scan my social media account without my permission?
3. What happens if the AI system misinterprets what I wrote and I get in trouble?
4. How can you tell if the information came from me or someone trying to set me up?
5. What if I don't want my teachers to read my conversations with friends?

Hopefully, your answers reflect those found in Table 3.5.

Potential Ethical Issues	
Question Raised	**Ethical Issue**
1. What happens if my data gets into the wrong hands or is used for another reason?	. . . related to the potential for malicious use and whether wide spread data monitoring like this can be sufficiently protected from bad users.
2. Can you scan my social media account without my permission?	. . . related to privacy rights.
3. What happens if the AI system misinterprets what I wrote and I get in trouble?	. . . related to the potential for errors and whether people making decisions or predictions should act on a system that may be susceptible to errors.
4. How can you tell if the information came from me or someone trying to set me up?	. . . related to the potential for cyber attacks and whether people making decisions or predictions should act on a system that may be vulnerable to hackers.
5. What if I don't want my teachers to read my conversations with friends?	. . . related to privacy rights.

Table 3.5 Ethical issues and the questions they raise

Workbook Activity 3.6

Examine the presented use-case and in the associated workbook identity five areas of ethical focus (see Table 3.4 for assistance if needed). Then, provide a recommendation on how to address each area of focus along with the rationale for such a recommendation as you answer the questions below while completing the table in the associated workbook.

> *Examine the following:*
> The Coding Club is building an app to make lunch recommendations to help students make choices about what to eat in the school cafeteria. Since AI is involved in their app (it makes recommendations based on the daily menu and past eating choices/habits), they asked the AI Club to help them make sure their design reflects: accountability, values, explainability, fairness, and user data rights.

> *Questions:*
> **3.6a** What are the areas of ethical focus that you will concentrate upon?
> **3.6b** What are your recommendations for adhering to those areas of ethical focus?
> **3.6c** What is the rationale behind each of the areas of ethical focus that you have concentrated upon?

There are no real right or wrong answers here. Each of the following, Tables 3.6a through 3.6e, highlight one area of ethical focus and a number of recommendations that can be made for it, along with the rationale for those recommendations. Hopefully, your responses are similar, and you were able to provide a spotlight on ethical focus areas such as:

a.   accountability
b.   explainability
c.   fairness
d.   user data rights
e.   values

Ethical focus: Accountability	
The AI Club wants to make sure that the Coding Club members recognize that each of them should be accountable for the outcome of the app. This means that every person involved in the design and development of the AI tool is willing to take responsibility for the impact it will have on others (positive or negative).	
Recommendation	**Rationale**
1. Keep detailed notes of how they make decisions along the way about designing the app.	Keeping detailed notes will help the students stay accountable for their decisions because there will be a record to reference.
2. Check on what the school's policies are on using student data to make sure they are not breaking any rules.	Checking to see if they are aligned with school policies means they are taking responsibility to consider important information that should be included in their design.
3. Write out their policies so anyone can see them at any time.	Being open about your policies builds confidence that you will take responsibility for adhering to them.

Table 3.6a Accountability ethical focus, recommendation and rationale

Area of ethical focus: Explainability

Understanding how an app makes decisions should not be a total mystery. Designers should take steps to ensure that users can access and understand how the app makes decisions.

Recommendation	Rationale
1. Write a pop-up in plain words about what the app is and how it works.	The pop-up will provide information that every student will see when they open it.
2. Build a "How did you make this recommendation?" button that a user can click each time they get a recommendation.	The specificity of this button will be very clear to users. The information can also serve to teach them a little bit about AI!
3. Create a poster to hang in the hallway that maps out how the app makes decisions.	A poster could include additional visuals to help users understand the decision process.

Table 3.6b Explainability ethical focus, recommendation and rationale

Area of ethical focus: Fairness

It is common for human bias to be reflected in AI systems. AI designers should be aware of potential areas where bias can influence how data is collected and organized, as well as the impact it can have on outcomes.

Recommendation	Rationale
1. Conduct a survey about students' food choices and habits – make sure it reaches students of all ages, genders, race/ethnicities, and so on.	Ensuring that survey data represents a variety of users will help to minimize bias in the app.
2. Build a feedback button where users can provide feedback on the app where they see potential bias.	Collecting user perspective and experience with the app is a great way to gain insights into specific areas of bias that might not have been noticed otherwise.
3. Appoint a bias committee in the Coding Club to learn about bias and address issues as they arise.	Focusing on bias and taking steps to understand it better helps to minimize bias.

Table 3.6c Fairness ethical focus, recommendation and rationale

Area of ethical focus: User Data Rights	
Users should maintain a level of power and control over what information about them is shared in the app and how that information is being used.	
Recommendation	**Rationale**
1. Have the app ask for permission to collect information about the user before any interaction.	Asking for permission to use specific types of data will build confidence in the user that they have control over their data, and will likely make them more comfortable with using the app.
2. Allow users to deny giving any personal information that they do not want to share.	Users will appreciate not being forced to provide information that they are not comfortable with.
3. Ask the school IT department about how to make sure that student data is secure.	Consulting with professionals who have direct experience with managing student data will support efforts to protect user data rights.

Table 3.6d User data rights ethical focus, recommendation and rationale

Area of ethical focus: Values	
It is important for designers to consider the values and social and cultural norms of the people for which they are designing – even if they are different from the designers' values.	
Recommendation	**Rationale**
1. Conduct a survey on what students' values are around app usage and notifications.	Using a survey is a great way to gather feedback and build understanding about a user's values and norms.
2. Ask for data around what languages are spoken at the school so that the app is translated as needed.	Building the app so that it is accessible in the language of the user is important and shows that cultural norms and values are being considered.
3. Chart student values related to nutrition at their school.	Documenting values related to nutrition will help to ensure that the options in the app reflect items that users will actually want to eat.

Table 3.6e Values ethical focus, recommendation and rationale

Workbook Activity 3.7

Examine the links below to a number of AI technologies. Explore at least one of them for this activity. Aim to explore the technology for 10 minutes, and for the one that you have chosen answer questions 3.7a through 3.7d in the associated workbook.

AI Technologies:

Emotion recognition technology: Deep Angel
(http://deepangel.media.mit.edu)

Illustration generator: GAN paint
(http://gandissect.res.ibm.com/ganpaint.html)

Image manipulation technology: Affectiva
(https://demo.mr.affectiva.com)

Questions:

3.7a Which AI technology did you choose?
3.7b Does this technology promote wellbeing?
3.7c Does this technology protect user's data and privacy?
3.7d Does this technology give insight into how it works?

Bias in Black Box Algorithms

There are two types of black box algorithms. The first is that used by deep learning algorithms. As neural networks grow larger it becomes impossible to trace how all of the parameters combine to make a single decision, even when engineers have access to all of millions or billions of parameters behind the process. The second type of black box algorithm involves proprietary algorithms, and this is where companies hide the details of their AI systems for various reasons.

How might a black box algorithm impact you? Take three minutes to complete this *Teacher Quality Test*. [Link: https://forms.gle/WJb5eaUFF2iMXoEX7]. Complete the whole test, then click on submit to view your score.

In this test, what you should expect was not made clear to you nor was it really clear how your score was going to be calculated, or what would actually be determining your quality as a teacher. In some cases, even when there is complete transparency in such a system, and this information is known, bias can emerge if you are provided with a zero on an element but you or your department is unable to actually provide performance data or information to support that section of the evaluation. This is particularly bias in cases where such data pertains to high stakes (e.g., raises, renewal of contracts, or promotion). A real world example is an Associate Professor obtaining zero on student counselling sessions as only undergraduate sessions are counted but the professor does not teach undergraduates. The same professor also receives a zero for not developing online asynchronous courses (and receives no funding for them) as only those for undergraduates are counted. The overall impact of constantly obtaining a zero on these sections of the evaluation over a 15-year period has seen their evaluations and raises considerably lower than what they may have been, and this makes the university potentially liable.

Workbook Activity 3.8

A short 14-minute TED talk that highlights bias emerging from black box algorithms is *the era of blind faith in big data must end* [Video: https://www.youtube.com/watch?v=_2u_eHHzRto]. After watching this short talk, and taking into account the *Teacher Quality Test*, consider the following question and answer it in the associated workbook.

> **3.8** What do you think are the dangers of machine bias and black box algorithms?

In response to the workbook activity, you may have considered the following aspects dangers of machine bias and black box algorithms: people could be inappropriately screened prior to even being offered a job interview;, people may pay more for insurance than others or be offered higher or lower credit than others; people may be fired through no actual fault of their own – it depends on who decides what success looks like and with what data the algorithm has been trained with in order to determine that success.

The Trolley Problem and The Moral Machine Experiment

To further understand how bias works in algorithms we will consider a classic ethical dilemma – *The Trolley Problem*. This is a thought experiment, and we consider it in terms of AI in autonomous vehicles. To do this, you will need to spend around 15 minutes engaging with some questions via Kahoot! [Link: https://kahoot.it/challenge/?quiz-id=e80b9a10-959d-4535-aea4-95340f4fd245&single-player=true].

MIT is thinking about the same problem and has developed a moral machine experiment to consider it. Spend five minutes now, and engage with *The Moral Machine experiment* [Link: https://www.moralmachine.net].

Do you think that you had any cultural bias in your decision making when interacting with *The Moral Machine*? Let's consider that, take five minutes to view *Moral machines: How culture changes values* [Video: https://www.youtube.com/watch?v=jPo6bby-Fcg], you might also like to look over the outcomes of *The Moral Machine experiment* [Article: https://www.nature.com/articles/s41586-018-0637-6].

Although an interesting experiment, keep in mind that this activity does not actually represent how autonomous cars make decisions. They do not distinguish between gender, occupation, or prioritize a dog over a person. The goal of an autonomous vehicle is to always protect the occupants of the vehicle in which it resides, while also following the laws of the road. However, it is an excellent example of how bias, even ones we do not know that we might have, impact outcomes.

Summary

In this chapter you discovered:

- how some uses of AI can be beneficial, or harmful, to humans.
- the place of human-centered design, and the need for empathy within it.
- the ways that industry is addressing ethical issues in AI.
- the need to consider ethical questions and issues when using/designing AI systems.

- how biased decision-making can happen in machines.
- how to evaluate an AI system for bias.
- the concept and implications associated with black box algorithms, and the impact of this in various contexts including education.
- how culture can influence bias.

Resources

Affectiva. (2020). Affectiva market research demo. https://demo.mr.affectiva.com

Awad, E., DSsouza, S., Kim, R., Schulz, J., Henrich, J., Shariff, A., Bonnefon, J., & Rahwan, I. (2018, October 24). *The moral machine experiment.* Nature. https://www.nature.com/articles/s41586-018-0637-6

BriteandBubbly. (2014, September 22). *Hello Navi App Documentary.* [Video]. YouTube. https://www.youtube.com/watch?v=RbpHUhrkRnU

CrashCourse. (2019, December 14). *Algorithmic bias and fairness: Crash course AI #18.* [Video]. YouTube. https://www.youtube.com/watch?v=gV0_raKR2UQ

DeepAngel. (2021). *DeepAngel.* http://deepangel.media.mit.edu/

Fussell, S. (2018, March 22). *Schools are using AI to check students' social media for warning signs of violence.* Gizmodo. [Link: https://gizmodo.com/schools-are-using-ai-to-check-students-social-media-for-1824002976].

Google. (2021). *AI experiments.* https://experiments.withgoogle.com/collection/ai

Google. (2021). *Teachable machine.* https://teachablemachine.withgoogle.com/

Grenoble, R. (2017, December 12). *Welcome to the surveillance state: China's cameras see all.* HuffPost. https://www.huffpost.com/entry/china-surveillance-camera-big-brother_n_5a2ff4dfe4b01598ac484acc].

Haas, B. (2017, April 04). *Chinese man 'marries' robot he built himself.* The Guardian. https://www.theguardian.com/world/2017/apr/04/chinese-man-marries-robot-built-himself

Ideo.org. (2015). *What is human-centered design?* [Video]. Vimeo. https://vimeo.com/106505300

ISTE. (2021). *'Ethical or unethical?' survey.* Google Form. https://docs.google.com/forms/d/e/1FAIpQLSdA888ekxqWbshh5Sz4K5h-hSsSQQX6iDjvx5L02zevV16yVw/viewform

ISTE. (2021). *'Ethical or unethical?' survey responses.* Google Form. https://docs.google.com/forms/d/e/1FAIpQLSdA888ekxqWbshh5Sz4K5h-hSsSQQX6iDjvx5L02zevV16yVw/viewanalytics

Machine Learning for Kids. (2021). *Teach a computer to play a game.* https://machinelearningforkids.co.uk/

MindSparkLearning455. (2020). *Thought experiment: Trolley problem & AI in autonomous vehicles.* Kahoot! Quiz. https://kahoot.it/challenge/?quiz-id=e80b9a10-959d-4535-aea4-95340f4fd245&single-player=true

MIT. (2021). *Tutorials for AppInventor.* https://appinventor.mit.edu/explore/ai2/tutorials

MIT-IBM Watson Ai Lab. (2021). *GANpaint.* http://gandissect.res.ibm.com/ganpaint.html

MIT Media Lab. (2021). *Cognimates.* http://cognimates.me/home/

Molteni, M. (2017, June 07). *The chatbot therapist will see you now.* Wired. https://www.wired.com/2017/06/facebook-messenger-woebot-chatbot-therapist/].

Nature Video. (2018, October 25). *Moral machines: How culture changes values.* Video. [YouTube]. https://www.youtube.com/watch?v=jPo6bby-Fcg

North Carolina School of Science and Mathematics. (2020, January 07). *Introduction to deepfakes.* [Video]. YouTube. https://www.youtube.com/watch?v=kKgvgVNJ63o

Scalable Cooperation. (2021). *Moral machine.* https://www.moralmachine.net/

SOTBF. (2019). *Survival of the best fit.* https://www.survivalofthebestfit.com/

Teacher Quality Test. Google Form. https://forms.gle/WJb5eaUFF2iMXoEX7

TED. (2017, September 08). *The era of blind faith in big data must end.* [Video]. YouTube. https://www.youtube.com/watch?v=_2u_eHHzRto

Vincent, J. (20180, February 08). *Chinese police use facial recognition sunglasses to track citizens.* The Verge. https://www.theverge.com/2018/2/8/16990030/china-facial-recognition-sunglasses-surveillance

4. AI and Human Perception

Overview

This chapter details the processes involved with human perception, and how this relates to machine intelligence and computer vision. A number of limitations pertaining to computer vision are discussed prior to introducing how image recognition occurs in a neural network. Aspects of training machines to recognize what they see are explored, and an opportunity to train a machine is presented.

Learning Outcomes

1. Understand the role that perception plays in artificial intelligence (AI).
2. Identify how a machine develops a neural network for image recognition.
3. Articulate the impact of AI on industries and the importance of understanding AI for students and educators alike.

Human Visual Perception

Perception is a process of acquiring, interpreting, selecting, and organizing sensory information. As humans, we find this natural and generally very easy — well, perhaps we think that we do.

Engage with the following perception exercises to see how well you go. How well, do you think, an AI system might go with the same exercises?

Figure 4.1 Perception exercise 1

What do you see in perception exercise 1? Do you see a duck or a rabbit? Perhaps, both? Maybe now that you know what to look for you might be able to see that which you did not see previously. Now consider perception exercise 2.

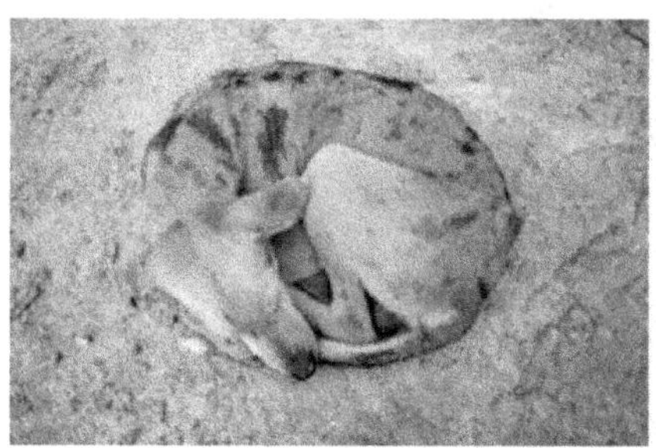 

Figure 4.2 Perception exercise 2 (see Gri, 2018)

Are these images both of bagels? Are they both dogs? Did these images fool you, or is it common sense to be able to recognize animals from food?

What the optical illusions in these two exercises illustrate is that human perception is the result of specific computations taking place in the brain. Although we are not conscious of these computations, we can sometimes get a glimpse of the process by examining cases where the computational process yields surprising or misleading results. Such optical illusions as that presented in Figure 4.3 also demonstrate that, among humans, how you interpret things can lead to age biases.

In Figure 4.3 you might see a younger woman who is turning away or you may see an older woman looking toward the left. However, if you are younger you will tend to see the young woman first and vice versa if you are older (Nichols, Churches, & Loetscher, 2018) [Link: https://www.nature.com/articles/s41598-018-31129-7?utm_medium=affiliate&utm_source=commission_junction&utm_campaign=3_nsn6445_deeplink_PID100151387&utm_content=deeplink].

Figure 4.3 My wife and my mother-in-law (Hill, 1915)

To understand the science behind perception further you might like to read the article *reality is not what it seems: the science behind why optical illusions mess with our minds* [Link: https://www.wired.co.uk/article/optical-illusions-science-perception].

Machine Intelligence and Computer Vision

Machine intelligence includes learning, reasoning, perception, problem solving, and linguistic intelligence. Machine perception aims to replicate the ability of humans to understand their surroundings. It involves such technologies as image and speech recognition.

In the field of computer vision machine learning models learn how to identify objects, people, or individual attributes in an image. For example, a model could help evaluate automobile accidents, identify the type of vehicle(s) involved in the accident, and provide an estimate for repair costs.

Computer vision may involve aspects of edge detection, facial recognition, image classification, image segmentation, object detection, object tracking, and pattern detection. These aspects are detailed in Table 4.1.

Aspect	Computer Vision
Edge detection	Identifying the edge of an object or environment to help identify what is in the image.
Facial recognition	Recognizing a human face and identifying the actual person.
Image classification	Sorting images into different categories.
Image segmentation	Separating an image into multiple areas and analyzing them separately.
Object detection	Recognizing and classifying a specific object in an image or multiple objects in an image.
Object tracking	Using object detection, following images as they move from frame to frame.
Pattern detection	Finding patterns related to color, shape, objects, faces, and other visual features in images.

Table 4.1 Aspects of computer vision

Workbook Activity 4.1

Taking Table 4.1 into account, answer the succeeding question in the associated workbook.

4.1 From the following, how does computer vision identify an image?

a) Computer vision technologies break down an image into smaller components and use deep learning neural networks to analyze each component before it identifies the image.

b) Computer vision technologies label images based on training data and then breaks the image into smaller components to see if its label is correct.

c) Computer vision technologies organize parts of an image into various categories and then calculates the most common category found.

d) Computer vision searches for a perfect match of an image from a large database of images.

You would be correct if you chose *b) Computer vision technologies label images based on training data and then breaks the image into smaller components to see if its label is correct.*

Real-World Applications

Computer vision has a number of real-world applications across all sectors from business, entertainment, transportation, healthcare, and in everyday life. For example:

Agriculture

Analyze crops for optimal growth, for example in data-driven farming. View, for example, *FarmBeats tracks soil, moisture data 24/7* [Video: https://www.youtube.com/watch?v=pDgjOHY7sMI&feature=emb_logo].

Education

Eye tracking is an excellent way to study visual attention and social interaction in a number of learner settings, along with visual perception in teaching and learning (Jarodzka, Skuballa, & Gruber, 2021), and such things like lexical look up and reading rates in EFL contexts (Dolgunsoz, 2015). You might like to view *language proficiency awareness through eye movements* [Video: https://www.youtube.com/watch?v=6Z68HpIWivU].

Entertainment

Manipulate photos and videos in real time with filters, automatically tag photos and videos, as well as upscale photo and video assets during the editing process. See further examples from within *computer vision for media and entertainment* [Video: https://www.youtube.com/watch?v=YfzTosmpqUk].

Shopping

Try on items virtually before purchasing, use computer vision to predict future fashion trends, or track items that consumers take from shelves in autonomous stores. See, for example, *computer vision powered autonomous store* [Video: https://www.youtube.com/watch?v=7B6IeGzkA-g].

Healthcare

Analyze x-rays and other scans to monitor patient health and to help doctors diagnose diseases. See also, *computer vision in healthcare and medicine* [Video: https://www.youtube.com/watch?v=LYDWsMtB_J0].

Self-driving cars

Identify other cars, traffic signs and signals, lane markers, pedestrians, bicycles and other relevant visual information encountered on the road. Consider watching *machine learning – ride in self-driving car* [Video: https://www.youtube.com/watch?v=8_i2jzJN06Y].

Traffic

Oversee busy intersections for potential accidents and record license plates at road toll stations.Perhaps view *traffic surveillance with computer vision and deep learning* [Video: https://www.youtube.com/watch?v=FfU22I-_dI4].

Translation

Point a smartphone camera at text in another language and have it instantly translate. Consider watching the lecture *sign language translation with transformers* [Video: https://www.youtube.com/watch?v=E5nKeEvoAK0].

Manufacturing

Monitor equipment for safety and count and categorize items on a conveyor belt. View, if desired, *the power of computer vision in manufacturing* [Link: https://www.youtube.com/watch?v=mrQV8Zz9o_8].

Real-Time Sports Tracking

Analyze player performance and strategy, like with a smart soccer ball. Such as the *DribbleUp smart soccer ball* [Video: https://www.youtube.com/watch?v=Sb5BfwENBlA].

Limitations

With all of the amazing things that computer vision is capable of, there are still some limitations. These include:

1. *Interpretation.* This is difficult for machines. AI systems that use computer vision must make sense of the complexity of our world and all of its variations, and this remains a huge challenge for machines.
2. *Black box algorithms.* It is difficult to decipher all of the inner workings of computer vision technologies, and like other deep learning applications, if something goes wrong, there may not necessarily be an easy way to understand why.
3. *Big Data.* Computer vision, like other forms of AI where machine learning is involved, requires a lot of data to ensure accuracy of results. The data must be representative of many different contexts, angles, variations and other scenarios in the real world. If a machine is presented with an image in a way that it has not been trained on, the machine will have some difficulty identifying the image.

Workbook Activity 4.2

Spend ten minutes to explore a variety of computer vision systems, spending a few minutes to engage with each of the below. Then, answer the questions in the associated workbook.

Computer vision systems:
a. Draw together with a neural network (https://magenta.tensorflow.org/sketch-rnn-demo).
b. Shadow art (https://shadowart.withgoogle.com/?lang=en-us).
c. Emoji scavenger hunt (https://emojiscavengerhunt.withgoogle.com).
d. Deep dream generator photo manipulator (https://deepdreamgenerator.com).

Questions:
4.2a Which of these systems impressed you the most?
4.2b What do you feel are the implications of such a system?

Image Recognition in Neural Networks

The following example illustrates how a neural network undergoes the process of image recognition for the purposes of training. In this example, the machine learns how to identify cats by analyzing example images. This is undertaken by the neural network without any prior knowledge of cats; instead the neural network evolves its own set of relevant characteristics from the learning material as it is processed layer by layer.

Training Data Example

In order to provide the neural network with visual data to identify a cat five layers are provided (see Figure 4.4 though 4.8). Progress through each layer, reviewing the questions and determining the answers. This will assist you in completing workbook activity 4.3.

Layer 1

What do the images on the left have in common that the images on the right do not have in common?

a. They are all amphibians? (yes/no)
b. They are all mammals? (yes/no)
c. They are all animals? (yes/no)

Figure 4.4 Layer 1 of visual data used to train a neural network

Layer 2

What do the images on the left have in common that the images on the right do not have in common?

a. They all have ears? (yes/no)
b. They all have stripes? (yes/no)
c. They all have four legs? (yes/no)

Figure 4.5 Layer 2 of visual data used to train a neural network

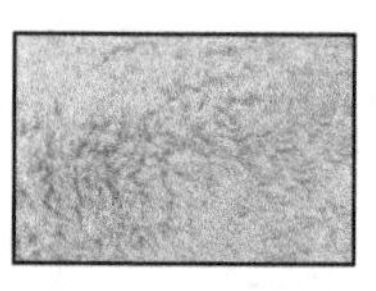

Layer 3

What do the images on the left have in common that the images on the right do not have in common?

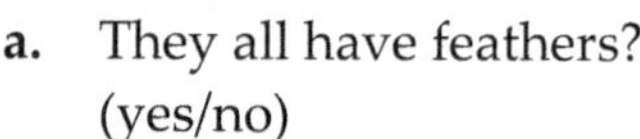

a.   They all have feathers? (yes/no)

b.   They all have eyes? (yes/no)

c.   They all have fur? (yes/no)

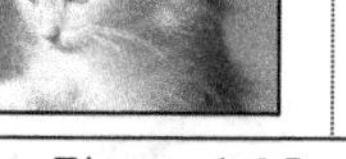

Figure 4.6 Layer 3 of visual data used to train a neural network

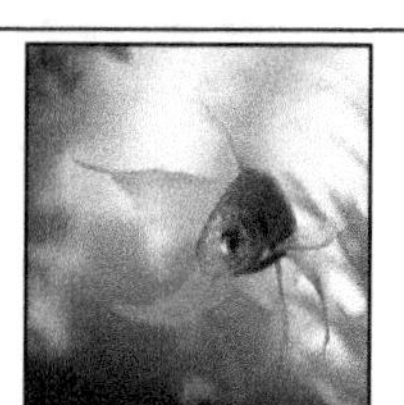

Layer 4

What do the images on the left have in common that the images on the right do not have in common?

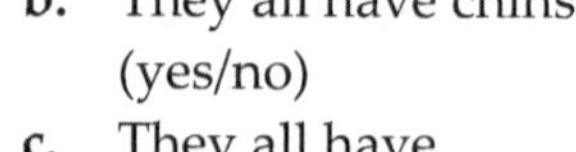

a.   They all have teeth? (yes/no)

b.   They all have chins? (yes/no)

c.   They all have whiskers? (yes/no)

Figure 4.7 Layer 4 of visual data used to train a neural network

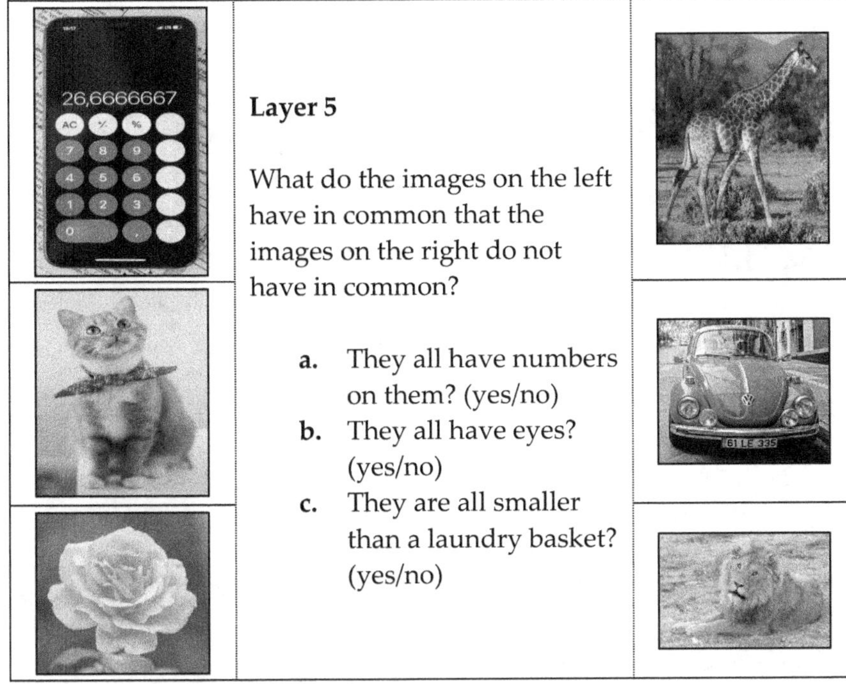

Layer 5

What do the images on the left have in common that the images on the right do not have in common?

a.   They all have numbers on them? (yes/no)
b.   They all have eyes? (yes/no)
c.   They are all smaller than a laundry basket? (yes/no)

Figure 4.8 Layer 5 of visual data used to train a neural network

Workbook Activity 4.3

You have just reviewed five layers of training data, experiencing how a machine might learn what a cat is in order to identify it and distinguish it as *cat* or *not cat*. Now, complete the associated table in the workbook by answering the following questions.

4.3a What is the training data that emerges, and the associated rule for determining what a cat is for each layer?

4.3b How does this neural network ultimately determine if something is a cat or not? Write out the algorithm it will use.

Hopefully, you were able to provide similar responses to those outlined in Table 4.2.

Layer	Emerging Training Data	Rule Developed
1.	Animals.	an animal
2.	They all have four legs.	has four legs
3.	They all have fur.	has fur
4.	They all have whiskers.	has whiskers
5.	They are all smaller than a laundry basket.	is smaller than a laundry basket
Algorithm		
Based on the training data provided in each layer:		
If an animal has four legs, has fur, has whiskers, and is smaller than a laundry basket then it is a cat.		

Table 4.2 Neural network training data, and the resulting algorithm

Workbook Activity 4.4

Now that you know what a cat is, or is not, according to the training data. Taking on the role of a neural network, utilize the algorithm from workbook activity 4.3 to complete workbook activity 4.4 in the associated workbook.

> **4.4** Examine each image (a through d) in the associated workbook. Then, answer the four questions next to each. Use that criteria to determine how you will identify each image. Is the image *cat* or *not cat*?

According to the training data, your responses should indicate that *a* and *d* can be identified as *cat*, while images *b* and *c* can be identified as *not cat*. Answers are illustrated in Table 4.3.

	Image	Questions
a.		1. Does it have four legs? *Yes* 2. Does it have fur? *Yes* 3. Does it have whiskers? *Yes* 4. Is it smaller than a laundry basket? *Yes*
	Identify	*Cat*
b.		1. Does it have four legs? *Yes* 2. Does it have fur? *Yes* 3. Does it have whiskers? *Yes* 4. Is it smaller than a laundry basket? *No*
	Identify	*Not cat*
c.		1. Does it have four legs? *Yes* 2. Does it have fur? *No* 3. Does it have whiskers? *No* 4. Is it smaller than a laundry basket? *No*
	Identify	*Not cat*
d.		1. Does it have four legs? *Yes* 2. Does it have fur? *Yes* 3. Does it have whiskers? *Yes* 4. Is it smaller than a laundry basket? *Yes*
	Identify	*Cat*

Table 4.3 Applying the cat or not cat algorithm

From this activity we can see that training data, and the associated algorithms used by neural networks, can lead to machines making mistakes. However, as these machines are trained with more and more data on what is right and wrong, they can become increasingly accurate.

Training a Machine

It is your turn now to train a machine to test the capabilities and limitations of the technology. You can experiment with different classifications, or image data, and take note of how the machine responds. This will deepen your understanding about how machine learning and computer vision work. In order to do this you will need to develop a project with *The Teachable Machine* [Link: https://teachablemachine.withgoogle.com].

Before you begin you will need to understand four steps:
1. Gathering samples [Video: https://www.youtube.com/watch?v=DFBbSTvtpy4&feature=youtu.be].
2. Training the machine [Video: https://www.youtube.com/watch?v=CO67EQ0ZWgA&feature=youtu.be].
3. Exporting the model [Video: https://www.youtube.com/watch?v=n-zeeRLBgd0&feature=youtu.be].
4. Hosting the model online.

Understanding the above is important because you will need to create one of the following project types:
a. Audio (https://teachablemachine.withgoogle.com/train/audio).
b. Image (https://teachablemachine.withgoogle.com/train/image).
c. Pose (https://teachablemachine.withgoogle.com/train/pose).

The site will guide you in the process.

You may also like to begin with one of the following *Teachable Machine* tutorials to help you understand the kind of projects that can be developed:
a. Fruit [Link: https://medium.com/@warronbebster/teachable-machine-tutorial-bananameter-4bfffa765866].

   b. Head tilts [Link: https://medium.com/@warronbebster/teachable-machine-tutorial-head-tilt-f4f6116f491].

   c. Sounds [Link: https://medium.com/@warronbebster/teachable-machine-tutorial-snap-clap-whistle-4212fd7f3555].

Workbook Activity 4.5

Once you have completed your project, and exported it, you can then answer the following in the associated workbook.

4.5a What was your teachable machine project choice?

4.5b What is your project link?

Summary

In this chapter, you learned that:
- Computers have no innate perceptual abilities, everything must be programmed or trained.
- Training data can lead machines to make mistakes, but with more input they can gain accuracy.
- There are a number of ways to train a machine.
- What it is like to develop a project in order to train a machine.

Resources

AiFi. (2020, December 09). *Computer vision powered autonomous store.* [Video]. YouTube. https://www.youtube.com/watch?v=7B6IeGzkA-g

Business Next. (2017, December 06). *DribbleUp smart soccer ball.* [Video]. YouTube. https://www.youtube.com/watch?v=Sb5BfwENBlA

Computer Vision Talks. (2020, October 19). *Sign language translation with transformers.* [Video]. YouTube. https://www.youtube.com/watch?v=E5nKeEvoAK0

Deep Dream Generator. (2021). Human AI Collaboration. https://deepdreamgenerator.com

Emoji Scavenger Hunt. (2021). Google AI. https://emojiscavengerhunt.withgoogle.com

Experiments with Google. (2019, November 08). *Teachable machine tutorial 1: Gather.* [Video]. YouTube. https://www.youtube.com/watch?v=DFBbSTvtpy4&feature=youtu.be

Experiments with Google. (2019, November 08). *Teachable machine tutorial 2: Train.* [Video]. YouTube. https://www.youtube.com/watch?v=CO67EQ0ZWgA&feature=youtu.be

Experiments with Google. (2019, November 08). *Teachable machine tutorial 3: Export.* [Video]. YouTube. https://www.youtube.com/watch?v=n-zeeRLBgd0&feature=youtu.be

Ha, D., Jongejan, J., & Johnson, I. (2017). *Draw together with a neural network.* Google AI. https://magenta.tensorflow.org/sketch-rnn-demo

PGS Software. (2021, February 18). *The power of computer vision in manufacturing.* [Video]. YouTube. https://www.youtube.com/watch?v=mrQV8Zz9o_8].

Quantiphi. (2011, March 11). *Computer vision for media and entertainment.* [Video]. YouTube. https://www.youtube.com/watch?v=YfzTosmpqUk

Microsoft Research. (2016, April 18). *FarmBeats tracks soil, moisture data 24/7.* [Video]. YouTube. https://www.youtube.com/watch?v=pDgjOHY7sMI&feature=emb_logo

Roboflow. (2021, March 06). *Computer vision in healthcare and medicine.* [Video]. YouTube. https://www.youtube.com/watch?v=LYDWsMtB_J0

SFB-TRR 161. (2016, December 19). *Language proficiency awareness through eye movements.* [Video]. YouTube. https://www.youtube.com/watch?v=6Z68HpIWivU

Shadow Art. (2021). Google AI. https://shadowart.withgoogle.com/?lang=en-us

Syed Azhar Talha. (2019, March 31). *Traffic surveillance with computer vision and deep learning.* [Video]. YouTube. https://www.youtube.com/watch?v=FfU22I-_dI4

Teachable Machine. Google AI. https://teachablemachine.withgoogle.com

Vecanoi. (2019, September 02). *Machine learning – ride in self-driving car.* [Video]. YouTube. https://www.youtube.com/watch?v=8_i2jzJN06Y

Webster, B. (2019, November 08). *Teachable machine tutorial: Bananameter.* Medium. https://medium.com/@warronbebster/teachable-machine-tutorial-bananameter-4bfffa765866

Webster, B. (2019, November 08). *Teachable machine tutorial: Head tilts.* Medium. https://medium.com/@warronbebster/teachable-machine-tutorial-head-tilt-f4f6116f491

Webster, B. (2019, November 08). *Teachable machine tutorial: Snap, clap, whistle.* Medium. https://medium.com/@warronbebster/teachable-machine-tutorial-snap-clap-whistle-4212fd7f3555

References

Dolgunsoz, E. (2015). Using eye-tracking to measure lexical inferences and its effects on reading rate during EFL reading. *Journal of Language and Linguistic Studies,* 12(1), 63-78. https://files.eric.ed.gov/fulltext/EJ1105178.pdf

Gri, A. (2018). *Puppies or food? 12 pics that will make you question reality.* Bored Panda. https://www.boredpanda.com/dog-food-comparison-bagel-muffin-lookalike-teenybiscuit-karen-zack/?utm_source=iste.h5p&utm_medium=referral&utm_campaign=organic

Hill, W. (1915, November 06). *My wife and my mother-in-law.* Puck.

Lotto, B. (2017, January 05). *Reality is not what it seems: the science behind why optical illusions mess with our minds.* Wired. https://www.wired.co.uk/article/optical-illusions-science-perception

Jaordzka, H., Skuballa, I., & Gruber, H. (2021). Eye-tracking in educational practice: Investigating visual perception in the classroom. *Educational Psychology Review 33,* 1-10.

Nichols, M., Churches, O., & Loetscher, T. (2018). Perception of an ambiguous figure is affected by own-age social biases. *Scientific Reports 8*(12661). https://www.nature.com/articles/s41598-018-31129-7?utm_medium=affiliate&utm_source=commission_junction&utm_campaign=3_nsn6445_deeplink_PID100151387&utm_content=deeplink

5. AI and Natural Interaction

Overview

This chapter explores how artificial intelligence (AI) and humans process and communicate using natural interaction. Aspects of natural language processing (NLP), including those of understanding, and generation are examined. In addition, the wider aspects of speech, gesture and affect, and the benefits and limitations of each of these when interacting with AI systems are discussed.

Learning Outcomes

1. Identify different types of natural interaction, and explore a number of examples.
2. Understand the benefits and limitations behind natural interaction with AI.
3. Determine the impact of natural interaction on how AI and humans communicate.

Natural interaction

A major goal of AI systems is to make the experience of interacting with a machine as natural as possible. Natural interaction in AI is the ability of an AI system to sense, process and respond appropriately to human behavior. To learn more about this topic you might choose to view *natural interaction in AI systems* [Video: https://www.youtube.com/watch?v=3BZDlRoet5U&feature=youtu.be].

Natural interaction is used in many AI applications from *Google Docs* suggesting words and phrases to improve our writing to *Alexa* playing our favorite type of music by voice command. However, achieving the level of natural interaction and understanding that we humans have with each other and our environment is no simple task for machines.

Machine learning algorithms can interpret large amounts of unstructured data in the form of documents, images, videos, sounds, emails, social media feeds and other information that is not organized or formatted for easy processing. However, AI systems that use natural interaction must be able to interpret the many forms of unstructured data that come from interacting with humans.

AI systems that employ natural interactions often use a combination of machine learning models to find patterns and make meaning of the information they receive. A machine learning model is used to make predictions after the AI system has been trained with data. During training, information is passed through an algorithm (an instruction for how to solve a problem), which finds patterns in the data. The output of the training process in a machine learning model is then used to make predictions. AI systems that use natural interactions apply a number of these machine learning models to process information.

Yet, understanding information is only one part of natural interaction. The AI system must also be able to respond in a way that is understandable, appropriate, and useful to a human (or to another AI for that matter). Massive amounts of data from human interaction help to train machines on how to interpret and respond to humans appropriately. With machine learning, AI systems continue to improve their understanding of human intent (i.e., what we want) and are able to respond more accurately.

Processing Natural Interactions

Humans communicate in a variety of ways: through spoken and written language, through gestures and body language, and through facial expressions and emotions. A very simple illustration of how AI systems process natural human communication is illustrated in Figure 5.1.

Three areas of natural interaction are speech, affect, and gestures. Speech is that of spoken language, gestures refers to hand and body movements, and affect is the outward expression of emotional states.

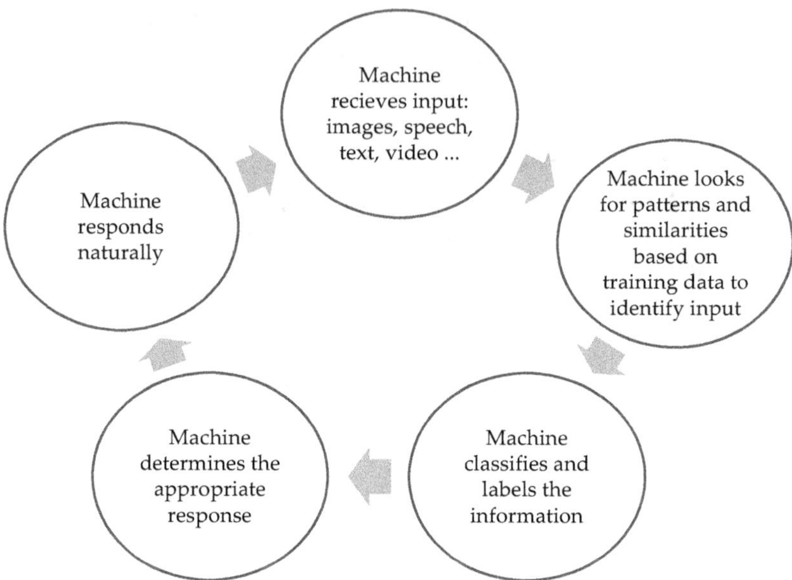

Figure 5.1 AI system processing of natural human communication

Speech

Natural Interaction through Speech

AI systems must be able to accurately recognize and understand speech to communicate effectively with humans and to perform tasks. Using voice assistants such as Alexa, Google Assistant, or Siri, is an example of natural interaction through speech. Voice assistants (also called virtual or digital assistants) are cloud-based systems that respond to spoken requests and simplify our communication with technology. Some voice assistants can be integrated with apps and other devices, like smart speakers, appliances, and even cars, which further expand their capabilities.

Natural Language Processing (NLP)

As humans, we write and speak in many languages, and spend a great deal of time learning them for high-stakes purposes (e.g., to pass entrance exams, for promotions/raises) and for low-stake reasons (e.g., personal enrichment). However, a computer's native language—

machine code—is incomprehensible to many people. How is it then that Alexa and Siri can understand us when we speak to them? This process relies on the ability of an AI system to engage with natural language processing (NLP) to fill the gap between human language and computer understanding. Voice assistants are one of the most commonly used AI applications that rely on NLP to function. As devices, voice assistants can be extremely convenient in daily life, as well as for those members of society who are visually impaired or have mobility challenges. The steps involved when using a voice user interface with a digital assistant are illustrated in Figure 5.2.

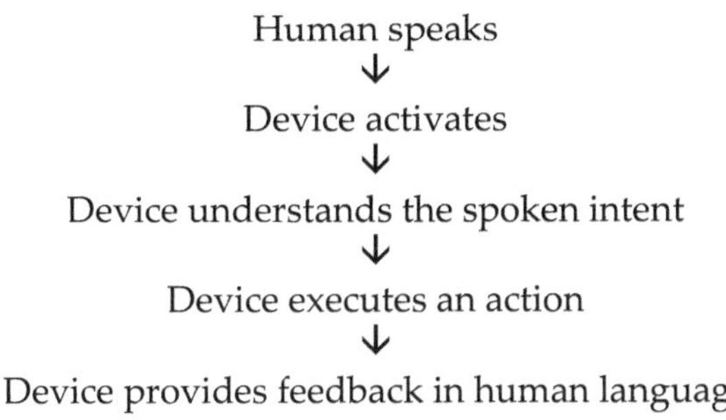

*Figure 5.2 Steps involved when using
a digital assistant voice user interface*

So, NLP helps computers communicate with humans in our language and makes other language-related tasks more efficient. With NLP, computers can read text, hear speech, interpret words, measure sentiment, and determine which parts of that speech are important. NLP interprets human language using many different techniques. For example, statistical and machine learning methods as well as rules-based and algorithmic approaches. Essentially, NLP tries to understand the relationship between the words, and explores how the pieces work together to create meaning. In summary, NLP is responsible for understanding meaning and structure of a given text or speech. To further your understanding on this topic, you may wish to view *introduction to natural language processing* [Video: https://www.youtube.com/watch?v=f5bqPOkOJs4&feature=youtu.be].

Natural Language Processing, Understanding, and Generation

For humans, learning a new language can be difficult. The language in the textbook that we use may not match real world language use, as language constantly changes. New words become popular and different ways of speaking become normal. Further, there are a variety of accents, and people speak in a different pitch, and volume. For AI to understand our speech it needs to be able to process it effectively and respond to it accurately.

The data coming into a digital assistant, for example, when you talk to it is unstructured data. We are not training the digital assistant on anything, we are simply providing it with data. Sometimes, the digital assistant may not be able to process this data, and might respond with phrases like *I'm sorry, I didn't get that.* So, in the process of NLP, a digital assistant might convert your speech to text, analyze the text, respond with text and convert that text to speech for you to hear. Natural language understanding is what allows an AI to comprehend written and spoken speech, and in turn respond using a process called natural language generation.

You might recall that such processes have seen AI algorithms produce screen plays such as *Sunspring*, that have then been acted out [Video: https://www.youtube.com/watch?v=LY7x2Ihqjmc]. If you found that interesting, you might want to watch the sequel, *It's no game.* [Video: https://www.youtube.com/watch?v=5qPgG98_CQ8].

For now, though, let's look at the *IBM Watson Natural Language Understanding* text analysis demo. Copy some text that you may have produced, such as an email, or copy the text of a news article so that we can have Watson analyze it. As you do this, notice how it identifies language in different ways, and the confidence levels that it provides for each. Take three minutes to do this. [Link: https://www.ibm.com/demos/live/natural-language-understanding/self-service/home].

Benefits and Limitations of AI Applications using Natural language Processing

There are a number of AI applications that use natural interaction through language, and some of these are presented here along with their benefits and limitations.

Autocorrect and Predictive Text.

Benefits

- Programs with auto-correct features like *Microsoft Word* or *Google Docs* check for grammar and spelling mistakes and offer suggestions to improve writing.
- Predictive text suggests the next word or phrase for more efficient writing.

Limitations

- Some text may be flagged, even if it is not an error, due to nuances in human language.
- Predictions may be incorrect because the program may not fully understand your intent.

Document Analysis.

Benefits

- AI systems extract data from documents (typed or handwritten), classify the information and analyze it for you, saving you a lot of time.
- Document analysis helps doctors scan medical data and generate diagnoses and treatment plans.
- Spam filters scan incoming emails for unwanted and harmful content and prevent them from showing up in your inbox.
- News feeds can be curated based on your preferences.
- Social media tagging influences your feed.

Limitations

- Document analysis is not a perfect science and important information may be missed.
- The machine learning algorithm that filters your email can make mistakes and some emails that might be useful to you could be sent to your spam folder.

Speech-to-Text (STT)/Text-to-Speech (TTS).
   Benefits
- Speech-to-text allows you to translate spoken words into text across multiple applications, and is useful for things like hands-free texting, dictating voice-mail messages, or creating a quick transcript or video captioning.
- Text-to-speech allows your messages to be read aloud by the computer or device. It also helps those who are visually impaired or who need reading support to listen to written words on a screen.

   Limitations
- Some text or speech can be rendered incorrectly as the machine does not always capture variations in pronunciation or cannot distinguish background noise.
- Words that are unnfamiliar, either written or spoken, may also be generated incorrectly.

Translation Apps.
   Benefits
- Translation apps translate spoken or written text from one language to another so that you can quickly understand the other language and communicate.

   Limitations
- Nuances and cultural differences between languages are not always detected and your translation could be incorrect.

Customer Service Calls and Chatbots.
   Benefits
- Automated customer service calls and chatbots can more efficiently address questions that can be easily understood by a machine. This frees up time for real people to address complex problems and reduces customer wait times. As this technology evolves, machine agents and chatbots are communicating in more natural ways.

   Limitations
- Sometimes, the agent or chatbot does not understand your intent or has not been trained on the unique problem you are experiencing, and is therefore unable to address your

question. Also, some people are frustrated by the use of automated technology, and just want to talk to a person.

Natural Interaction Engagement – Speech

Voice Commands

Spend 5 minutes and use *Mixlab* to explore how a machine listens to commands and provides music to correspond with those commands. Select the *'Preview it Here'* link and, using the microphone on your device, tell *Mixlab* to add *Motown drums*, or *add an indie pop synthesizer*, then listen to the music it creates [Link: https://mixlab.withgoogle.com].

Speech-to-Text and Text-to-Speech

AI-supported speech-to-text and text-to-speech tools can be powerful accessibility options in the classroom. *Speechnotes* is an online notepad with both speech-to-text and text-to-speech capabilities. Try out the technology for five minutes, and think about how this or similar tools might help your students. You may even want to push its limits and test how it reacts to different accents or colloquialisms. As you do, consider how the quality of the AI tool might affect the quality of support for diverse students, and how foreign/second language learners might go with such a system [Link: https://speechnotes.co].

Gestures

Natural language processing enables AI systems to recognize, interpret, and respond appropriately to human speech. Like speech, gestures are a natural form of human communication that can be recognized by machines. Gesture recognition is the ability of a machine to sense and interpret human hand and body movements, including facial expressions and eye movements. Gesture recognition involves cameras, computer vision, and image processing.

Perhaps you have swiped over your phone to open an application, smiled at a camera to automatically take a photograph, or used hand movements to play a video game. You might have also used the pose feature of *The Teachable Machine*. All of these examples use gesture recognition technology. *Teachable Machine* [Link: https://teachablemachine.withgoogle.com].

Do note that just because a technology can sense motion, this does not mean that it contains AI. There are motion sensors that are not 'smart', such as the automatic doors at a grocery store (e.g., if you roll a ball toward an auto door sensor, it may detect motion and open). What would make such a door smart, or one powered by AI, is when it will only open for certain humans based on their features, and not open for animals or inanimate objects. So, it is the type of processing behind the motion that makes it AI.

Figure 5.3 provides a simple outline of how gesture recognition works. Imagine a person waving at a device's camera to have it take a photograph.

Human makes a gesture in front of a device's camera
↓
Camera captures an image
↓
Gesture recognition technology encodes the image[1]
↓
The system looks for patterns in image data
↓
The system determines the gesture's meaning
from image data and past learning
↓
The system determines the action to take based on prediction
↓
The system executes the action

Figure 5.3 Gesture recognition steps to take a photograph
Note 1. *When the technology encodes the image*
it breaks it down into smaller data points for processing.

Benefits and Limitations of Gesture Recognition Systems

There are a number of AI applications that use natural interaction through gestures, and some of the benefits and limitations are presented here.

Benefits

Hand gesture recognition.

- Hand gesture recognition eliminates the need for physical contact with a machine, allowing a person to operate and communicate with the machine using only a series of finger and hand movements.
- Wheelchairs, cars and other smart devices equipped with gesture recognition can be controlled with the wave of a hand or other specific hand gestures, often simplifying device control.
- Surgeons can use hand recognition technology to examine a patient's X-rays without having to remove their gloves during operations.
- Sign language speakers can have their words translated for the hearing.

Facial gesture recognition.

- Facial gesture recognition allows a person to communicate with a machine through facial expressions, including subtle movements of the eyes. This is especially helpful for people who are unable to move their hands or other parts of their bodies, including their heads.
- Facial gesture recognition can also provide valuable information to educators about how a student is reading.
- Facial gesture recognition can help in gathering information about emotional states.

Sign language recognition.

- Certain types of gesture recognition systems can transcribe sign language into text or speech. This helps a person who is non-verbal to communicate.

Limitations

- Sometimes gesture recognition systems are unable to detect motions because of factors like distance from the sensor or there might be too many people in view to accurately recognize a particular motion that one person performs.

- As there is no universal language of gestures, it can be difficult for a machine to identify some motions. Different people use different gestures. Different cultures can use the same gesture for completely different meanings. Some positive gestures in one region are culturally offensive in other places.

Affect

Affective computing uses speech recognition, gesture recognition, and human biological signs to understand and respond to human emotional states. Affective computing is the ability of a machine to sense, interpret, process, and respond appropriately regarding a human's emotional state.

System captures affective data about the human
(based on speech, body language, and biological signs)
↓
Features are extracted from the data collected
(e.g., tone of voice, words spoken,
heart rate, facial expressions, and so on
↓
The system looks for patterns in data
(based on previous data and past learning)
↓
The system evaluates the person's affect
↓
The system determines an appropriate response
↓
The system executes the response[1]

Figure 5.4 Outline of how affective computing works

Note 1. *Responses could come in the form of analysis or an appropriate natural, human-like response.*

Human emotion is complex and can be expressed through multiple channels including what we say, our tone of voice, rate of speech, loudness, and so on. Our emotions are also expressed through our facial expressions and body language. Additional biological features such as heart rate, muscle movements, and changes in our sweat glands that can be detected by sensors on our skin, can also indicate our emotional state. Affective computing can recognize all of these features of a person's emotional state, find patterns in the information, and evaluate those patterns in order to respond appropriately, often simulating human emotions in its response. A simple outline of how affective computing works is illustrated by Figure 5.4.

Benefits and Limitations of Affective Computing

Affective computing is an evolving field of AI. Several promising applications are being developed to support people across a number of fields from education, medicine, and retail to robotics and social monitoring.

Benefits

Education.

Affective computing can evaluate students' behaviors during class and provide teachers with information about what students appear interested or bored, when they are paying attention, or whether they are frustrated or nervous, among other emotions. This information can assist a teacher who might then consider adjusting their teaching to meet the emotional needs of the students. This technology is currently being used in some schools in China, where AI cameras, along with special headbands that detect brainwaves, collect information about students and provide reports to parents and teachers. Affective computing can also be used in adaptive tutorial systems to monitor students' emotional states and behaviors during learning and make appropriate adjustments to instruction.

Medicine.

Affective computing can evaluate a patient's emotional state and support a health professional by assisting with the diagnosis and treatment of a health condition. Affective computing can also help health care workers decide when patients need medicine or who should be seen first in the waiting room.

Retail.

Affective computing can evaluate a customers' emotions when they are browsing and looking at products while they shop, or when they see specific advertisements. This information can then assist retailers in determining the interest level of consumers in certain products, and in making predictions about whether a product will be well-received.

Robotics.

Applying affective computing to robots can enhance a robots natural interaction with a human. There have been promising results from human-robot interaction with autistic children and social interaction, as the robot is able to recognize and relay people's emotions which is a challenge for those with autism. Robots equipped with affective computing can also support human wellbeing by acting as an empathetic companion that can stimulate positive emotions and moods (e.g., social robots, robot pets).

Social monitoring.

Affective computing can be used to monitor the emotions of a driver and passengers in a car and send alerts if the driver shows signs of sleepiness or anger. Providing such information can help keep the driver and other passengers safe. During human and computer interactions, affective computing systems could mirror a humans persona and provide that person with information about their emotional state. Imagine a computer sending you a warning prior to posting an angry message on social media or suggesting music to play to help you move toward a more positive emotional state if it senses that you are feeling lonely or depressed.

Limitations

Affective computing draws upon all areas of natural interaction and requires the ability to interpret many different types of behaviors. Natural interaction must also take into account cultural and social conventions, which is a difficult task for machines as it requires a deeper level of understanding about the world and the nature and complexity of human beings. While there have been promising AI systems that can detect and evaluate human behavior, these systems are not perfect. The sensors can be unreliable, for example if not worn properly, thus results may prove inaccurate. Subtle changes in facial expression and body movements are also sometimes difficult for machines, as well as people, to detect and interpret.

Education

In education, students may feel increased stress and pressure to perform if they are constantly being monitored while they are learning. This could have a negative impact on the learning process because emotional state impacts ability to learn.

Autocorrect

Over reliance on these applications can hinder the learning process if students do not get enough practice with generating their own writing and learning how to find and correct their own mistakes.

Digital Assistants

Voice data transmitted to the cloud for analysis is often stored permanently, raising privacy concerns. The rationale for storing such data long term is that the individuals question and answer sessions are often used by the assistant to improve its machine learning model so that it can increase the accuracy of its responses.

Workbook Activity 5.1

Examine the links below to a number of technologies. Explore at least one of them for this activity. Aim to explore the technology for 10 minutes, and for the one that you have chosen answer questions 5.1a through 5.1d in the associated workbook.

Affectiva (https://demo.mr.affectiva.com).
For this system, choose a video to watch and see how accurate the program is at determining your emotional engagement as you watch that video.

IBM Personality Insights (https://watson-pi-twitter-demo.mybluemix.net).
When engaging with this system, aim to see how well the tool can evaluate personality traits, emotions, and affect from someone's writing.

Sentiment Classifier (https://www.uclassify.com/browse/uclassify/sentiment?input=Text).
When looking at this system add text that you have written, or text written by someone else that expresses an opinion, emotion, or mood. See how well the program can classify the text.

Talk to Transformer (https://app.inferkit.com/demo).
With this system begin typing content into the box. Perhaps you are drafting an email to a family member or friend. You may want to begin writing a story. See how well the program understands what you are writing and predicts or inspires your next words.

Questions:

5.1a Which AI technology did you choose?

5.1b What area(s) of natural interaction does the program address (speech, gesture, affect)?

5.1c Was the response to your input expected and accurate, and why do you think that is?

5.1d How might an application like this be used to help people learn or improve their skills?

Summary

In this section you:
- Discovered the various types of natural interaction that AI applications can utilize, along with their benefits and limitations.
- Explored a number of examples of natural interaction to understand how they work.
- Understood how the impact of natural interaction with AI can impact humans.

Resources

Affectiva. (2020). Affectiva market research demo. https://demo.mr.affectiva.com/

Ars Technica. (2016, June 09). *Sunspring*. {Video.}. YouTube. https://www.youtube.com/watch?v=LY7x2Ihqjmc

Ars Technica. (2017, April 26). *It's no game.* [Video]. YouTube. https://www.youtube.com/watch?v=5qPgG98_CQ8

Data Science Dojo. (2019, April 04). *Introduction to natural language processing.* [Video]. YouTube. https://www.youtube.com/watch?v=f5bqPOkOJs4&feature=youtu.be

Google. (2021). *MixLab.* Voice Experiment. https://mixlab.withgoogle.com

IBM. (2021). *IBM Watson natural language understanding text analysis.* NLU Demo. https://www.ibm.com/demos/live/natural-language-understanding/self-service/home

IBM Watson. (2021). Personality insights. https://watson-pi-twitter-demo.mybluemix.net/

North Carolina School of Science and Mathematics. (2019, November 05). *Natural interaction in AI systems.* [Video]. YouTube. https://www.youtube.com/watch?v=3BZDlRoet5U

Speechlogger. (2021). *Speechnotes.* https://speechnotes.co

Teachable Machine. Google AI. https://teachablemachine.withgoogle.com

Inferkit. (2021). *Talk to transformer.* https://app.inferkit.com/demo

uClassify. (2021). *Sentiment.* https://www.uclassify.com/browse/uclassify/sentiment?input=Text

6. Human and Machine Learning

Overview

This chapter covers human and machine learning. It looks at the process of automation, and what this means for the future of work, it introduces the computational thinking process, and explores aspects of human and machine learning, including deep learning. The chapter then finalizes by considering aspects of data mining for the language learning classroom.

Learning Outcomes

In this section you will:

1. Reflect on automation and what it means for the future of work.
2. Understand the computational thinking process, and how it can relate to language teaching and the concept of intelligence.
3. Explore aspects of human and machine learning, as well as deep learning.
4. Consider aspects of data mining for the language learning classroom.
5. Engage in aspects of data-driven learning for language learning.

Automation

The future state of any single job lies in the answer to a single question, to what extent is that job reducible to frequent, high-volume tasks, and to what extent does it involve tackling novel situations? Think about the tasks below and if they can be automated or not, then complete the table in the associated workbook for the text.

Workbook Activity 6.1

Look over the tasks below, and then answer the question in the associated workbook.

Tasks

Air traffic control, Bank fraud detection, Cars navigating roads by themselves, Deciphering lost languages, Diagnosing diseases, Identifying suspects for the police from CCTV footage,

Hiring/firing decisions, Judges considering granting bail to criminal suspects, Predicting changes in the stock market, Producing insurance policy quotes and assessing claims.

Question:

6.1 What tasks from the following do you think can be completed with AI assistance, or left only for a human?

If you thought that all of the tasks could be completed with the assistance of AI, then you would be correct.

AI can Assist Humans	Human Only Task
Air traffic control. Bank fraud detection. Cars navigating roads by themselves. Deciphering lost languages. Diagnosing diseases. Identifying suspects for the police from CCTV footage. Hiring/firing decisions. Judges considering granting bail to criminal suspects. Predicting changes in the stock market. Producing insurance policy quotes and assessing claims.	

By completing the above task, you can see how artificial intelligence is coming to reshape our world and how automation of tasks is assisting in this process.

Basically, anything that can be quantified by data can be automated, and anything that can be automated can be addressed by artificial intelligence. Novel situations are where these systems require human assistance, especially as they rely on a computational thinking process.

Computational Thinking

Computational thinking involves four steps: decomposition, pattern recognition, algorithm design, and abstraction.

Decomposition. The first step in computational thinking is decomposition, breaking the problem down into smaller problems.

Pattern Recognition. The second step is pattern recognition, looking for a repeating sequence.

Algorithm Design. The next step is algorithm development, the step-by-step instructions for completing a task.

Abstraction. The final step is removing parts of a problem that are unnecessary, and developing one solution for multiple problems.

Computational Thinking Challenge – Chocolates and Chili Peppers

The chocolate and chili pepper game was introduced to you earlier in this text (see chapter one), and it is a good way to understand how computational thinking works. In this game two opponents take turns removing chocolates from a jar, 1 to 3 chocolates at a time. The person left with no chocolates to take loses the challenge and has to take and eat the chili pepper at the bottom of the jar.

The Problem. From a jar of 13 chocolates and 1 chili pepper you can take either 1, 2, or 3 chocolates and another person can do the same. The person who is left unable to remove any chocolates from the jar must eat the chili pepper.

Decomposition. Leave the opponent with the chili pepper and take the chocolates.

Pattern Recognition. Each player can take from 1 to 3 chocolates at a time, in each round the number of chocolates taken should always add up to 4.

Algorithm. If 13 chocolates and a chili pepper are in a jar go first and take 1 chocolate. Then, decide how many chocolates to take based on how many the opponent takes. Take 3 if they take 1, take 2 if they take 2, take 1 if they take 3. Repeat until the opponent is left with only the chili pepper to take.

Abstraction. Simplifying and substituting with variables. Does it have to be chocolates and a chili pepper? No, it can be anything. Does it have to be 13? No, we can substitute 4N plus 1. The plus 1 here is the first one that you take, and then a total of 4 for however many rounds are played.

Computational Thinking in Language Learning

Computational thinking tools like modeling can support language learning in different ways and help in text comprehension, in acquiring vocabulary or in visualizing grammar rules. Through instructional lessons students can work on building the foundations of language learning through the computational thinking process. For example, you might use the *speak my language lesson plan* to help students discover ways in which they may be able to speed up their language learning [Link: https://www.ignitemyfutureinschool.org/sites/default/files/activities/TCS_IMFIS_Lesson05_SpeakMyLanguage.pdf].

Computational Thinking and Intelligence

Does computational thinking give a machine intelligence? Do you think that the computational thinking process can provide a piece of paper with intelligence?

An Intelligent Piece of Paper

The intelligent piece of paper is an activity to assist you in understanding what it means for a computer to be intelligent. Here, interact with a piece of paper that contains rules for playing a perfect game of tic-tac-toe or noughts-and-crosses. Take three minutes to play noughts-and-crosses (or tic-tac-toe) with the *intelligent piece of paper* [Link: http://www.cs4fn.org/teachers/activities/intelligentpaper/intelligentpaper.pdf].

Workbook Activity 6.2

Consider the following question and answer it in the associated workbook.

6.2 What did you conclude, is the piece of paper intelligent?

The intelligent piece of paper algorithm is shown in Figure 6.1. The paper here needs our help to make the moves required to play the game, and the same is true of computers with code not doing anything alone as they need the machine to make the code do something, and this is perhaps much like our brain needs our bodies to speak our thoughts and to perform various functions. Something to consider as we look at human and machine learning.

The Intelligent Piece of Paper
Move 1: I am X, and I go first. Go in a corner.
Move2: IF the other player did not go there THEN go in the opposite corner to move 1 ELSE go in a free corner
Move 3: IF there are 2 Xs and a space in a line THEN go in that space ELSE IF there are 2 Os and a space in a line THEN go in that space ELSE go in a free corner
Move 4: IF there are 2 Xs and a space in a line THEN go in that space. ELSE IF there are 2 Os and a space in a line THEN go in that space ELSE go in a free corner
Move 5: Go in the free space

Figure 6.1 The intelligent piece of paper algorithm

Human and Machine Learning

Think of intelligence as having two parts: one part is understanding what is occurring around you (perception), and the other part is what you do about it (problem-solving). A big part of AI focuses on ways for computers and machines to understand the essence of what is happening without human intervention. Consider speech, for example: two people with different accents can say the same thing but it sounds different (in this case, the sound is what is happening, but the words are the essence of it). Speech recognition and image understanding, are two technologies that aim to assist machines in understanding the essence of what is happening around them. Once the machine understands what is happening, it still has to solve a problem. For example, respond to a question, or find the best movie to match your preferences.

Recommender Systems

Recommender systems are AI algorithms that predict a user's interests based on patterns found in data about that user compared to similar users, and this includes their online behaviors, habits, and interests.

Recommender systems are applied in a number of ways, for example:

- Content: e-mail filters, targeted advertising, social media feed and search engine link curation.
- Entertainment: games, movies, music.
- Online shopping: books, clothes, electronics, gifts.
- Services: home repairs, house cleaning, matchmaking, restaurants, travel.

Two types of recommender systems, content-based filtering and collaborative filtering, are shown in Table 6.1.

Recommender Systems	
Content-based Filtering	**Collaborative Filtering**
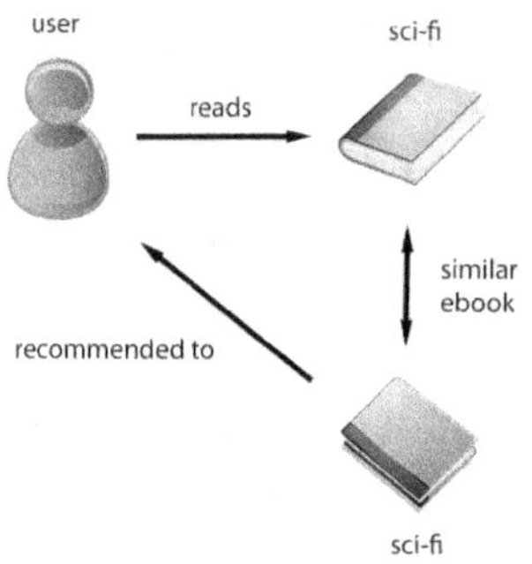	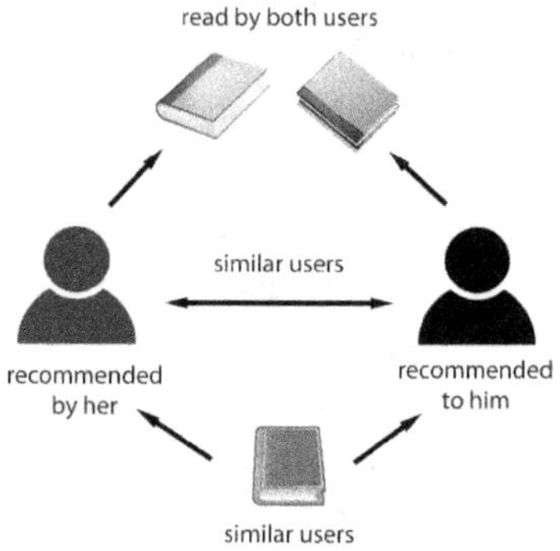
Content-based filtering recommends items/information (content) similar to what someone has shown past interest in.	Collaborative filtering makes recommendations based on similarities between users and items.
For example, if you read a lot of articles about AI online, your news feed will recommend more articles about AI.	For example, if you, and other people like you, order video games from an online store often and rate those games positively, the online store will continue to recommend video games similar to what you, and people like you, enjoy.

Table 6.1 Two types of recommender systems

Hybrid recommendation systems are those that combine both content and collaborative filtering, and this is what Netflix uses to recommend movies and shows. Consider learning more about it by viewing the *your Netflix special* [Link: https://www.youtube.com/watch?v=JwHzqYN0WTA&feature=youtu.be]. You might also want to explore this topic further by taking a look at *how YouTube knows what you should watch: crash course AI #15* [Link:https://www.youtube.com/embed/kiInh5STnyQ?start=0&end=367&version=3].

Workbook Activity 6.3

Based on your understanding of recommender systems, review the data types and respond to the question in the associated workbook.

Data types:

a) Features of content (items/information).
b) Similarities between content.
c) Similarities between content and users.
d) Similarities between users.
e) User actions.
f) User characteristics.
g) User preferences.
h) All of the above.

Question:

6.3 What types of data do recommender systems consider when making a prediction?

If you thought that recommender systems consider all of these types of data then you would be correct.

Limitations of Recommender Systems

The limitations of recommender systems are those relating to the 'cold start' problem, sparse data, and repetitive recommendations.

'Cold start' problem. When a new user or new content enters the platform, the collaborative-filtering recommender system does not have enough data to offer a relevant recommendation.

Sparse data. Gaps in a data set prevent the system from making accurate predictions. For example, if a system is relying on ratings and users are not leaving ratings, then the system will not be able to make a good recommendation because it is missing important information.

Repetitive recommendations. Content-based recommendation systems have no way of finding something new and unexpected that the user might like, because the system has a tendency to recommend the same types of items that the user previously ranked high.

Workbook Activity 6.4

Consider the choices listed below, and determine those that are advantages and those that are the disadvantages of recommender systems. Then, take a couple of minutes to respond to the question in the associated workbook.

Choices

They can help people discover new interests.

They can help people to more effectively narrow choices in order to make a decision.

They can reinforce stereotypes and recommend inappropriate content because they lack social context and understanding.

They could have control over the content you see and limit your exposure to new ideas.

They rely on collecting a lot of personal data.

Question:

6.4 From the choices presented, what are some advantages and disadvantages of recommender systems?

If you sorted the points into the following advantages and disadvantages, then you would be correct.

Recommender Systems	
Advantages	**Disadvantages**
- They can help people discover new interests. - They can help people to more effectively narrow choices in order to make a decision.	- They can reinforce stereotypes and recommend inappropriate content because they lack social context and understanding. - They could have control over the content that you see and limit your exposure to new ideas. - They rely on collecting a lot of personal data.

Machine Perception

One of the most significant advancements in AI is machine perception, the ability for a machine to sense what is happening in the environment. To learn more on this topic watch *artificial intelligence and the 7 senses* [Link: https://www.youtube.com/watch?v=vQxhndOWZHY&feature=youtu.be].

Machine perception is an essential component of many autonomous AI systems that use sensors to gather information about the environment so that they can adapt and respond automatically to achieve a goal. Examples of autonomous systems include self-driving cars, smart thermostats, smart lights, as well as AI-enabled customer service systems that adapt responses when communicating with different types of customers. The underlying feature that all of these have is that they do not require humans to operate; they can operate independently in an environment for which they have been trained. See Figure 6.2.

Autonomous Systems

Use sensors to gather information about the environment
↓
Analyze the information to determine how to adapt
↓
Execute the appropriate action to accomplish a goal

Figure 6.2 Outline of how an autonomous system works

Workbook Activity 6.5

From you understanding of autonomous systems, spend one minute to answer the following question in the associated workbook.

6.5 Which statement best describes autonomous systems?

a)   Autonomous systems require computer vision technology in order to operate independently.

b)   Autonomous systems sense their environment and automatically adapt to reach their goal.

c)   Autonomous systems use all types of AI systems to operate.

If you chose b, then you would be correct.

To learn more about this topic you might like to watch *Microsoft is accelerating the journey from automated to autonomous systems* [Link: https://www.youtube.com/watch?v=LwO8D_X6cK8&feature=youtu.be].

You can also review a focus on autonomous systems in transport from Table 6.2, to see a number of benefits and limitations associated with autonomous vehicles.

Autonomous Systems Focus – Transportation	
Self-driving cars, also called autonomous vehicles, are among the most popular and anticipated forms of autonomous transportation for those in the automobile industry.	
Benefits	**Limitations**
Safety: According to the Centers for Disease Control and Prevention (CDC), each day in the United States, more than 1,000 people are injured in crashes that involve distracted drivers and 29 people die as a result of drunk drivers. As self-driving cars become more widely used, there will likely be a significant reduction in accidents caused by distracted drivers and drunk drivers, as human error will be eliminated. Self-driving cars have the potential to prevent accidents and therefore save millions of lives.	*Sensors:* There is a need for better sensors and more training to handle unforeseen problems in real-life scenarios. Remember, computer vision algorithms are trained on tons of images and experiences, but life is full of the unexpected, like a tree falling into the road, for example.
Environment: Most self-driving cars are electric vehicles and are designed to be environmentally friendly. Electric vehicles reduce the amount of carbon dioxide emissions, which in large doses are harmful to the environment. The technology used in self-driving cars also helps to control the amount of fuel used because they avoid excessive speeds, which is also a source of increased emissions.	*GPS mapping systems:* The capabilities of GPS mapping systems also need to be expanded, as self-driving cars need an accurate view of the world to navigate a busy street or narrow, winding roads.

Increased mobility: People who are unable to drive because of age, disability, or other mobility issues, can rely on a self-driving car to transport them with the same privacy, comfort, and freedom that a personal vehicle provides.	*Understanding driver behavior:* AI systems in self-driving cars can sense other cars, the road, pedestrians, and obstructions, but they still lack understanding of driver behavior. Companies like Waymo are training their AI systems to predict driver behavior, and are working to give their cars more experience. But like any teenager who may be learning to drive, better driving comes with experience, and experience takes time.
Use of time: Drivers must be alert and focused at all times while operating a vehicle. Self-driving cars allow passengers to focus less on operating the vehicle and navigating traffic. This frees up time for them to engage in other activities during their drive, like reading a book, communicating with friends on a social media platform, or finishing homework in the car before arriving at school!	

Table 6.2 Autonomous Systems Focus - Transportation

If you like, you might like to experience *a fully autonomous driving journey* [Link: https://www.youtube.com/watch?v=B8R148hFxPw&feature=youtu.be].

Machine Learning

One of the characteristics of human intelligence is the ability to learn by making associations based on past experiences. So too, the end goal of machine learning is to enable machines to make predictions based on data and experience, and without being explicitly programmed.

When you train a neural network, it does not memorize its training data and recall that data later. It has no record of the training data at all. Instead, what it is doing is adjusting parameters (weights) to reduce the error measure. However, data is critical for machine learning to work, with the more data provided (assuming that it is reliable), the more accurate the prediction.

Machine learning uses data analysis, training, and human review to learn without following specific rules or steps, and it is a subset of artificial intelligence.

A variety of methods and algorithms can be used in machine learning systems, and there are multiple pathways. To learn more about machine learning you might like to watch *machine learning explained in 5 minutes* [Video: https://www.youtube.com/watch?v=3bJ7RChxMWQ&feature= youtu.be].

Teaching Machines

There are three critical components, or key requirements, for teaching a machine, and these include algorithms, data, and features.

Algorithms. Algorithms are mathematical instructions written in computer code that tell the machine how to go about finding solutions to a problem. A small selection of data, called training data, is run through the algorithm. The labels generated from the algorithm are reviewed by a human and marked as correct or incorrect, then given back to the algorithm, until the results are reliably accurate. We know the algorithm is working well when its results are accurate even when compared to new testing data. The result is a model that the machine can use for additional learning by itself.

Data. Data fuels AI. It allows AI systems to reveal patterns, trends, and associations with confidence. Some data is structured, which means that it has been organized into a format that computers can easily read and analyze, such as a database or spreadsheet. Other data is unstructured, like tweets, PDFs, and video files.

Features. Features are characteristics of the data in the dataset. The process of assigning features to data is important and time consuming. It is also the main source of errors and introducing bias in data because humans are the ones who identify these features based on what they think is more important for the machine to consider in the decision-making process. The quality of the dataset is also important for machine learning to provide the most accurate and reliable predictions and decisions. If data is not organized well, or if there is not a large enough representative sample it will not matter how well your machine learning system is making predictions because the data is not good to begin with. This is known as 'garbage in, garbage out'.

To learn more about features in data, consider watching *vector representation* to learn how a computer can recognize an object based on features [Video: https://www.youtube.com/watch?v=skNUEFsrDeA&t=2s].

The Machine Learning Process

Some approaches to training machines work best for specific types of tasks, and we will look at some of these in more detail. Overall the machine learning process is represented in Figure 6.3.

Machine Learning Process

Preparing data

↓

Training an algorithm

↓

Generating a set of instructions (the model)

↓

Using features to make and refine predictions
until the model can accurately make predictions on new input data

Figure 6.3 The machine learning process

The process is represented in Figure 6.4 in more detail.

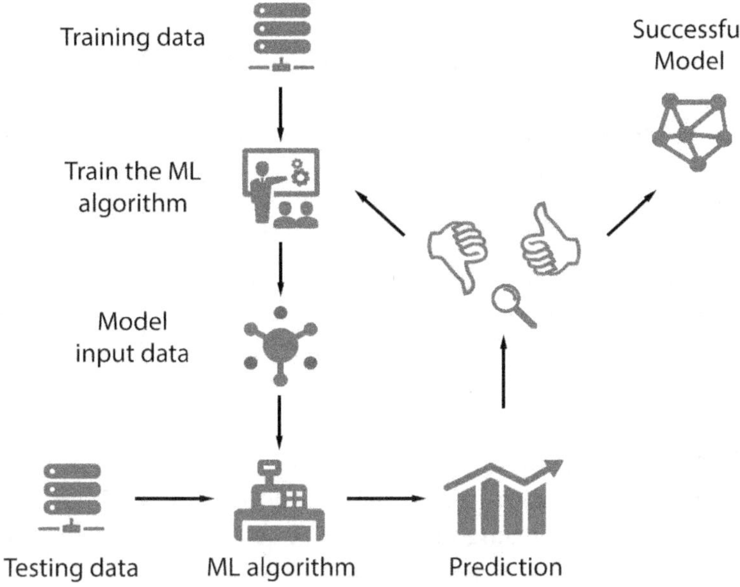

Figure 6.4 Machine learning

Training data. Humans feed the machine learning system a set of data, preferably a large, representative set.

Train the machine Learning Algorithm. Training data is run through the algorithm which finds patterns in the data and then generates labels based on those patterns. Labels are then reviewed by a human and marked as correct or incorrect, then given back to the algorithm. The results become more accurate and reliable each time the training data is run through the algorithm.

Model Input Data. Once the algorithm learns (through training) how to accurately label data based on patterns, a reliable machine learning model is established.

Testing Data. New data is fed into the machine to test whether the model is successful, and whether or not it is making accurate predictions.

Machine Learning Algorithm. The machine learning algorithm, that has been previously trained, finds patterns in the new data.

Prediction. Based on previous learning, the system makes a prediction and then checks that prediction based on what it previously learned.

Successful Model. If the machine checks its prediction and it is correct (based on previous training) the output or final decision is highly accurate.

To learn how machine learning can solve real world problems you might consider watching: *solving problems big, small, and prickly* [Link: https://www.youtube.com/watch?v=_rdINNHLYaQ&feature=youtu.be].

Workbook Activity 6.6

Consider the requirements listed below, and determine those that are key in the machine learning process. Then, take five minutes to answer the question in the associated workbook.

> *Requirements:*
> Algorithm
> Data
> Image
> Model
>
> *Question:*
> **6.6** What do you think are the key requirements for machine learning to work effectively and efficiently? Separate the requirements into 'key' or 'not key' for machine learning.

If you chose all of the potential requirements, except for image, as being 'key' elements of the machine learning process then you would be correct.

Workbook Activity 6.7

Now, spend a few minutes identifying the processes of machine learning, and respond to the following in the associated workbook.

6.7 Label the machine learning process diagram.

If you labeled the machine learning process as in Figure 6.4, then you would be correct.

Workbook Activity 6.8

Select one of the following machine learning solutions, and spend 10 minutes exploring it. Then, respond to the questions in the associated workbook.

Machine learning solutions:
AI Experiments
(https://experiments.withgoogle.com/collection/ai).

App Inventor
(https://appinventor.mit.edu/explore/ai-with-mit-app-inventor).

Machine learning projects
(https://machinelearningforkids.co.uk/#!/worksheets).

Scratch (https://scratch.mit.edu/ideas).

Questions:
6.8a Which choice of machine learning solution did you explore?
6.8b How does the machine learning solution you chose to explore work?
6.8c What potential do you see for using this kind of machine learning solution with your students?

Types of Machine learning

There are three main types of machine learning. These are supervised, unsupervised, and reinforcement. See Figure 6.5.

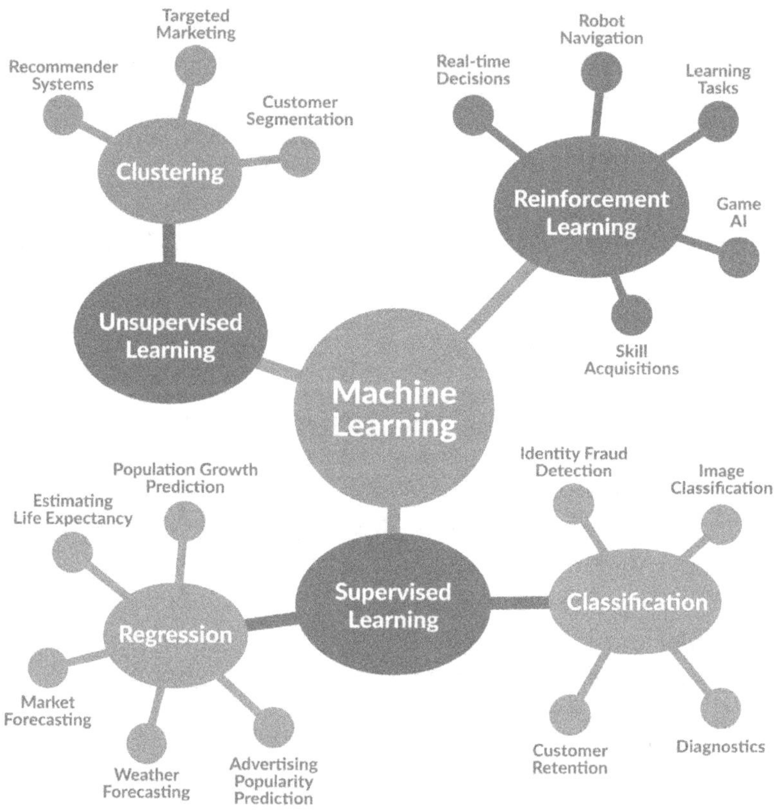

Figure 6.5 Types of machine learning

Supervised Learning

The first type of machine learning, supervised learning, is a process where a human provides a program with many examples of what it is they are wanting it to learn, along with a label that helps the machine classify or identify an object. By providing many examples, potentially millions, the machine is learning about how to identify an object by seeing many examples of the features that represent it. This then enables the machine to make judgments on its own when it receives new data and has to identify something without a label. Classification is one of the most common techniques in supervised learning to teach AI algorithms. Classification is a supervised learning technique used to group data based on attributes or features. Humans provide labels on the data (e.g., for images or text) that tell the machine about the attributes or features (e.g., color, size, shape, measurements) and how to group the data. The machine then matches any future data based on the similarity of the new data to predefined groups. For example, sorting images of kangaroos and wombats based on their number of legs, whether they have a tail or no tail and the size of their ears. Regression is similar but trains for a prediction based on attributes and features (e.g., using leg length and weight to determine running speed.)

Unsupervised Learning

The second type of machine learning, unsupervised learning, involves providing the machine with a large amount of data and letting it find patterns in the data by itself, by trying to identify patterns in the features. The machine then determines its own set of categories or labels by grouping the data in its own way. This process is known as clustering (the grouping of similar objects into one category).

To learn more about these two concepts (supervised and unsupervised learning) you might want to watch *types of machine learning: supervised and unsupervised* [Link: https://www.youtube.com/watch?v=wy-m6sd1BOA&feature=youtu.be].

Reinforcement Learning

The third type of machine learning, reinforcement learning, follows a behaviorist model of rewarding positive behavior and punishing negative behavior, which over time assists the AI in determining the optimal behavior for a particular environment or situation, and this may involve rewarding the AI when it does the correct thing and punishing it when it does the wrong thing. For this learning to work an agent, environment, and a way for the agent to work with the environment, and a way for the agent to get feedback on its actions within the environment (called a reward function or feedback function) are required.

Data in the Machine Learning Model

Data is critical to the performance of a machine learning model, as it is the quality of the data used to train a machine learning algorithm that directly impacts the outcome. Data can take any number of forms from audio, images, and sensor data to that found in various databases and spreadsheets (see Table 6.3).

Data Types	
Structured Data (labeled)	**Unstructured Data (unlabeled)**
- Stored, organized, and formatted. - Typically in a database. - Can be represented with text or numbers. - Contains features and labels determined by a human.	- Not formatted. - Typically images, videos, audio files, or documents. - Can be represented with text or numbers. - Data is clustered and organized by the machine.

Table 6.3 Data types: Structured and unstructured

Since supervised learning is the most common form of machine learning, structured data is the most common type of data used to train machines. This can be done by using data sets, through manual labeling, observing behavior, and relying on free data sources.

Data Sets. A number of datasets that can be used to train machines can be found on the internet for some problems, but for others you may need to create your own. You can manually label items, observe behaviors and record information in a specific format, or use free data sources.

Manual Labeling. To train a machine algorithm using manual labeling to identify animals would see you need to collect a lot of pictures of each animal and add a label to each image.

Observing Behavior. To collect data by observing behavior might take into account customers who smile (or do not), those that purchase goods (or do not), gender, and time of day, with this data then used to try and determine the kind of customer who purchases specific products.

Free Data Sources. A number of free online data sets exist such as those from Google Trends (Google search term data) or Kaggle (public data sets).

Applying Big Data in the Classroom

In the English language teaching context use of *Google Trends* could be very interesting [Link: https://trends.google.com/trends]. There are a number of ways it could be applied. It might help students in lessons on interpreting data and graphs, and ways in which to talk about ones that they have created when helping them to prepare for tests like the International English Language Testing System, or when you are teaching English for academic purposes. It would also be very interesting to use it in order to pose questions on new topics to students. For example, when starting out teaching a unit on entertainment an instructor could begin by asking students who they consider to be the best entertainers today. Students could then use Google Trends to determine who between two singers is more popular where/when, or to find out what countries might be the most interested in k-pop. To this end, you could use dates such as January 1, 2010 to December 31, 2020 to perform a search on the term 'k-pop' and determine that throughout this period Kyrgyzstan held the most interest in it, followed by Indonesia. This might tell you that Kyrgyzstan has a high ethnic Korean population, and perhaps this is why that might be a region with such a high interest in searching for the term. These search numbers are also interesting in that they show a global peak in 2012 (perhaps with emergence of the song *Gangnam Style*), and then steadily drop until 2017 before rising again with high peaks in June and September of 2020. The peaks in that year might coincide with the popularity of the boy band BTS. In any case, Google Trend usage could be worthwhile for incorporation into the classroom, as it can serve to get language students talking and engaged in things that they personally might wish to compare or discover, and those that relate to the topic under study. Although it is based on the search term data of those that rely on Google, and as such it is not really the use of hardcore statistics with learners, but it definitely provides some very interesting insights.

Workbook Activity 6.9

Take   15   minutes   to   explore   Google   Trends
(https://trends.google.com/trends/)   and   Kaggle
(https://www.kaggle.com). Then, respond to the question below in the
associated workbook.

> **6.9** Develop and detail an activity for the use of either Google
> Trends or Kaggle with your learners (or potential learners).
> Include sufficient detail for another teacher to be able to read
> what you have written and use the process with learners in their
> classroom.

Data Driven Learning

Another way of using aspects of Big Data to assist learners, and you as a
teacher or researcher, is to use tools such as those available from
Compleat Lexical Tutor [Link: https://www.lextutor.ca], which can be
used to facilitate data driven learning and teaching. It is a site that relies
on Big Data, such as that available from concordances and vocabulary
lists, to conduct a wide variety of analysis on user provided text in a
process of drive data-driven learning.

Data-driven learning (DDL) is an approach to foreign language learning
where the basic task is one of identifying patterns, with the role of the
learner one of discovering grammatical patterns, word meanings/types,
and/or other aspects of language by searching through linguistic data
and examining large amounts of authentic language. Teachers too can
perform such tasks to determine the appropriacy of content for their
learners, as well as in the development of a variety of activities for them
to perform with text. In other words, DDL consists of using the tools and
techniques of corpus linguistics for pedagogical purposes while relying
on massive amounts of authentic content that can serve to provide a
corrective function, elements of discovery, and the development of
learning skills.

Workbook Activity 6.10

Take 30 minutes now to review the variety of tools available on *Compleat Lexical Tutor* (https://www.lextutor.ca). Then, respond to the following in the associated workbook.

> **6.10** Select one tool available from *Compleat Lexical Tutor* (https://www.lextutor.ca). For example, *Corpus Correct*, *Vocabprofile*, and so on. Then, detail how you might go about making use of this tool by students or in preparing material as a teacher for students to use.

Data Mining

Data mining is a process of identifying useful information among large quantities of data, big data. Essentially exploring sites like Google Trends is utilizing Big Data to engage in data mining. Big data is the kind of data that is so large in size and complexity that no traditional data management tools can store it or process it efficiently. Data mining is not needed if the data sets are small because, in such cases, trends and information are easily spotted. Data mining allows us to spot trends in massive amounts of data and uses a variety of techniques to do so, and these include those of classification, clustering, and regression. Essentially, *Big Data* enables *data mining* which shapes *algorithms* which trains *machine learning* which teaches *AI applications* which generates *Big Data*. To understand the concept further consider watching *what is big data?* [Link: https://www.youtube.com/watch?v=bAyrObl7TYE].

Algorithms

Just as there are a number of ways to solve a problem, there are a number of algorithms that can be used to instruct a computer in how find a solution to a problem. Algorithms can be complex (e.g., those for speech recognition or object identification) or simple (e.g., those designed to win a game of noughts-and-crosses or tic-tac-toe). To learn more about this concept consider watching *what is an algorithm and why should you care?* [Link: https://www.youtube.com/watch?v=CvSOaYi89B4&feature= youtu.be].

Decision Tree

A decision tree is a classification type of algorithm, although it can also be used in regression, and it is one that relies on structured data to make a decision. It can be applied in a number of ways from filtering spam emails, to recognizing handwritten characters, fraud, or language detection. Decision trees rely on questioning strategies to reach an outcome or decision effectively, following a set of if-else conditions to visualize data and then classify it according to conditions. The higher the branch on the tree, then the broader the question (the root node is the first question on the tree). The nodes within the tree represent a 'test' of a specific attribute or feature, each branch representing a decision rule, and each leaf node representing an outcome. Once the end of a leaf node is reached (the terminal node) then you have a clear output or a decision. See Figure 6.6.

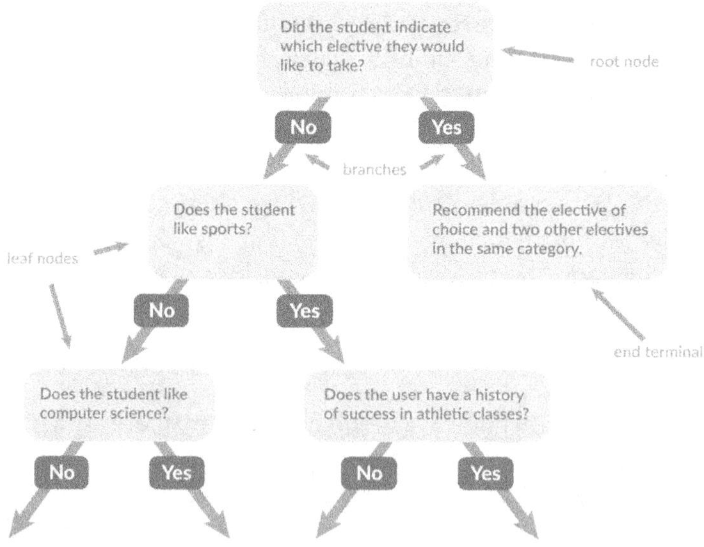

Figure 6.6 Decision Tree

Workbook Activity 6.11

Take five minutes to try out the *Akinator* decision tree algorithm [Link: https://en.akinator.com]. Engage with it and see if the program can guess what you are thinking by asking you a series of questions. The respond to the following in the appropriate section of the associated workbook.

> **6.11** Thinking about the use of decision tree algorithms in systems like *Akinator*, if these are coupled to a voice user interface (such as Alexa or the Google Assistant), do you think that this could be something that might be useful for your (or your potential) students to use as part of the learning process?

Deep Learning

Much like machine learning is a subset of artificial intelligence, deep learning is a subset of machine learning. The goal of deep learning is to predict an output given a set of inputs, using supervised or unsupervised learning. The key differences are performance and how it works, with deep learning, machine learning uses neural networks with multiple hidden layers. Figure 6.7 highlights the relationship between AI, machine learning, and deep learning.

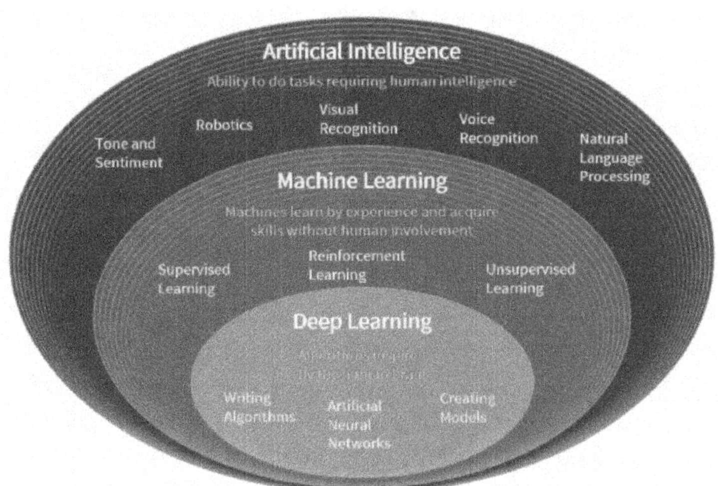

Figure 6.7 The relationship between AI,
machine learning, and deep learning

Neural Networks

Machines use neural networks to learn how to perceive information. Artificial neural networks (ANN) are inspired by theories of how the human brain might work, and consist of a large number of processors operating in parallel. Neural networks 'learn' and improve upon tasks by considering examples, generally without task-specific programming.

Artificial Neural Networks (ANN)

A typical ANN consists of thousands of interconnected artificial neurons, which are stacked sequentially in rows that are known as layers, forming millions of connections. Many of these connections are feed-forward, whereas some are feed-back connections. In many cases, the layers are only interconnected with the layer of neurons before and after them via inputs and outputs. This is quite different from human neurons which have more complex connection patterns than artificial neural networks. Our sophisticated patterns include both feed-forward and feed-back connections.

Figure 6.8 illustrates a single hidden layer, but most neural networks today have multiple hidden layers, and the most sophisticated 'deep neural networks' may have a couple hundred.

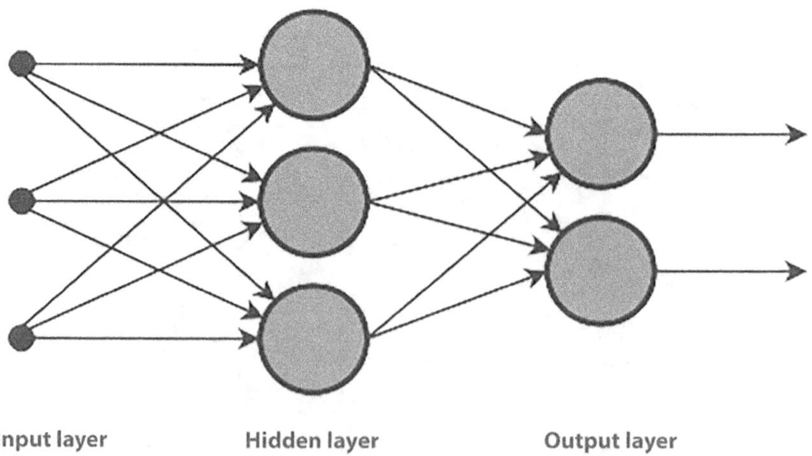

Figure 6.8 Neural network

Input Layer. The input layer, on the left of Figure 6.8, is designed to receive various forms of information from the outside world that the network will attempt to learn about, recognize, or process. For example, a computer cannot just look at a piece of furniture and respond meaningfully—it needs to learn what the furniture is through inputs. To train a computer to recognize a chair, you might train it with five different characteristics, or five inputs, of different chairs using binary (yes/no) answers.

The questions might be:
      1) Does it have a back?
      2) Does it have a top?
      3) Does it have soft upholstery?
      4) Can you sit on it comfortably for long periods of time?
      5) Can you put lots of things on top of it?

A typical chair would then present as Yes, No, Yes, Yes, No or 10110 in binary, while a typical table might be No, Yes, No, No, Yes or 01001.

Hidden Layer. The hidden layer is one or more layers that form the majority of the artificial brain. The connections between one unit and another are represented by a number called a weight, which can be either positive (if one unit excites another) or negative (if one unit suppresses or inhibits another). The higher the weight, the more influence one unit has on another. In the chair example, the weight for the upholstery question would be less than the weight for the question about a chair having a back, because all chairs have backs, while not all chairs are covered in upholstery.

Output Layer. The output layer is how the computer responds to the information it learned. In the chair example, during the learning phase, the network is simply looking at lots of numbers like 10110 and 01001 and learning that some mean chair (which might be an output of 1) while others mean table (an output of 0). Once the network has been trained with enough learning examples, it reaches a point where you can present it with an entirely new set of inputs that it has never seen before and see how it responds. After teaching a network by showing it 25 pictures of chairs and tables, you feed it a picture of some new design that it has not encountered before, a sofa or couch, for example—and see what happens. Depending on how you have trained the network, it will attempt to categorize the new example as either a chair or a table, generalizing on the basis of its past experience—just like a human.

Workbook Activity 6.12

Take five minutes now to engage with *TensorFlow*, it allows you to interact with a neural network [Link: https://playground.tensorflow.org]. This will help you see how connections in such networks are strengthened or diminished based on success or failure. Then, review the article *the contour to classification game* (Lee, 2021) [Article: https://ojs.aaai.org/index.php/AAAI/article/view/17835],   before responding to the below in the appropriate section of the associated workbook.

> **6.12** After exploring how a neural network behaves and a way that in can be taught to learners, how would you: **a)** explain this process? In a sentence or two, define what a neural network is to someone who may not be familiar with one. Then, in terms of education, think about: **b)** a benefit of the use of a neural network system for student learning (a one sentence example here is fine, and perhaps one that links to your teaching/learning context or one in which you wish to work).

Summary

You discovered:

- What aspects of automation mean for the future of work.
- How the computational thinking process works, and how it can relate to language teaching and the concept of intelligence.
- Aspects of human and machine learning, and the place of deep learning within artificial intelligence.
- Aspects of data mining relevant to the language learning classroom.
- Ways to engage in aspects of data-driven learning when teaching languages.
- The place of decision trees and neural networks.

Resources

Cobb, T. (2021). *Compleat Lexical Tutor.* https://www.lextutor.ca

Elokence. (2017). *Akinator.* Decision Tree Algorithm. https://en.akinator.com

Google (2021). *AI Experiments* https://experiments.withgoogle.com/collection/ai)

Google. (2021). *Google Trends.* https://trends.google.com/trends

Kaggle. (2021). *Kaggle.* https://www.kaggle.com

Khan Academy Computing. (2015, July 28). *What is an algorithm and why should you care?* Video. [YouTube]. https://www.youtube.com/watch?v=CvSOaYi89B4&feature=youtu.be

ML Tidbits. (2019, April 30). *Types of machine learning: supervised and unsupervised.* Video. [YouTube]. https://www.youtube.com/watch?v=wy-m6sd1BOA&feature=youtu.be.

Lee, I., & Ali, S. (2021). The contour classification game. *AAAI-21/IAAI-21/EAAI-21 Proceedings, 17*(35), 15583-15590. [Link: https://ojs.aaai.org/index.php/AAAI/article/view/17835]

Machine Learning for Kids. (2021). *Machine learning projects.* https://machinelearningforkids.co.uk/#!/worksheets)

MIT. (2021). *MIT App Inventor.* Michigan University of Technology. https://appinventor.mit.edu/explore/ai-with-mit-app-inventor

Scratch Foundation. (2021). *Scratch.* https://scratch.mit.edu/ideas

Simplilearn. (2019, December 10). *What is big data?* Video. [YouTube]. https://www.youtube.com/watch?v=bAyrObl7TYE

TensorFlow. (2021). *TensorFlow.* https://playground.tensorflow.org

Part Two:
AI in Education

7. AI4K12 – The Five Big Ideas

Overview
This chapter details aspects of the five big ideas in artificial intelligence (AI), those that are being introduced to learners from k-12. It looks at the more integral aspects of each, and explores their implications for society.

Learning Outcomes
1. Meet the five big ideas in AI.
2. Comprehend the wider implications behind each of these ideas for society.

AI in Education
Until recently AI was considered too advanced a subject for many, especially young learners, but this perception has changed. The AI for kindergarten to grade 12 (AI4K12) is an initiative to develop U.S. national guidelines covering what these learners should understand about AI, and what they should be able to do with it. The guidelines cover four grade bands (K-2, 3-5, 6-8, 9-12), organized around 5 big ideas.

The Five Big Ideas in AI
The five big ideas in AI were inspired by computer science standards covering: algorithms and programming; computing systems; data and analysis; impacts of computing; and networks and the internet. The ideas are a way to provide educational stakeholders (teachers, learners, parents) with an understanding of the essential concepts and major issues of the field. Each big idea consists of a key phrase and one sentence statement (reflected in the five big ideas in AI wheel), with grade band progression charts being released in stages. The five big ideas in AI are:
1. Perception – Computers perceive the world using sensors.
2. Representation and reasoning – agents maintain representations of the world and use them for reasoning.
3. Learning – computers can learn from data.
4. Natural interaction – intelligent agents require many kinds of knowledge to interact naturally with humans.
5. Societal impact – AI can impact society in both positive and negative ways.

Grade Progression Charts

The grade progression charts illustrate the guidelines developed for each of the five big ideas by breaking them down into a series of concepts and skills that form rows of a table called a 'grade band progression chart'. As development on each of the grade progression charts occurs the public are able to comment upon them. A point of note here is that the introduction to the five big ideas does not have to be sequential for learners, nor do modules have to focus on one idea exclusively since a module might be able to cover aspects of all of them at once. (See big idea grade progression chart 1 [Link: https://ai4k12.org/big-idea-1-overview] and 3 [Link: https://ai4k12.org/big-idea-3-overview].)

The Five Big Ideas in AI Wheel and Poster

The five big ideas in AI wheel (see Figure 7.1) provides a short overview of all the ideas at a quick glance using the key phrase for each and a one sentence statement as an associated explanation. These ideas are expanded with a one paragraph definition in the five big ideas in AI poster [Link: https://ai4k12.org/resources/big-ideas-poster]. The poster is also available in a number of languages from English to Chinese, Hebrew, Korean, Spanish, Portuguese, and Turkish.

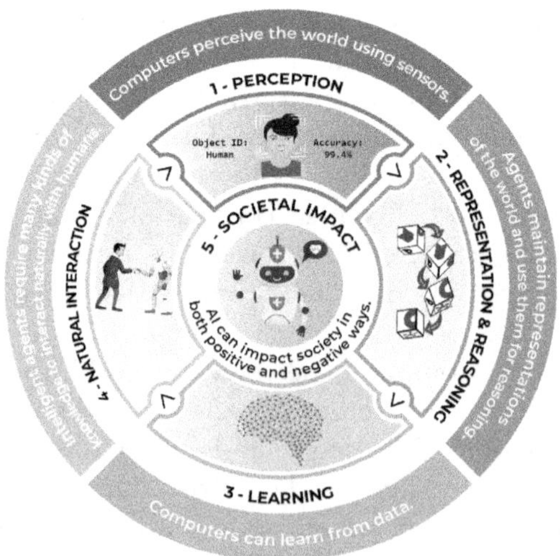

Figure 7.1 The five big ideas in AI wheel
Licensed under the Creative Commons Attribution-NonCommercial-ShareAlike 4.0 International License.

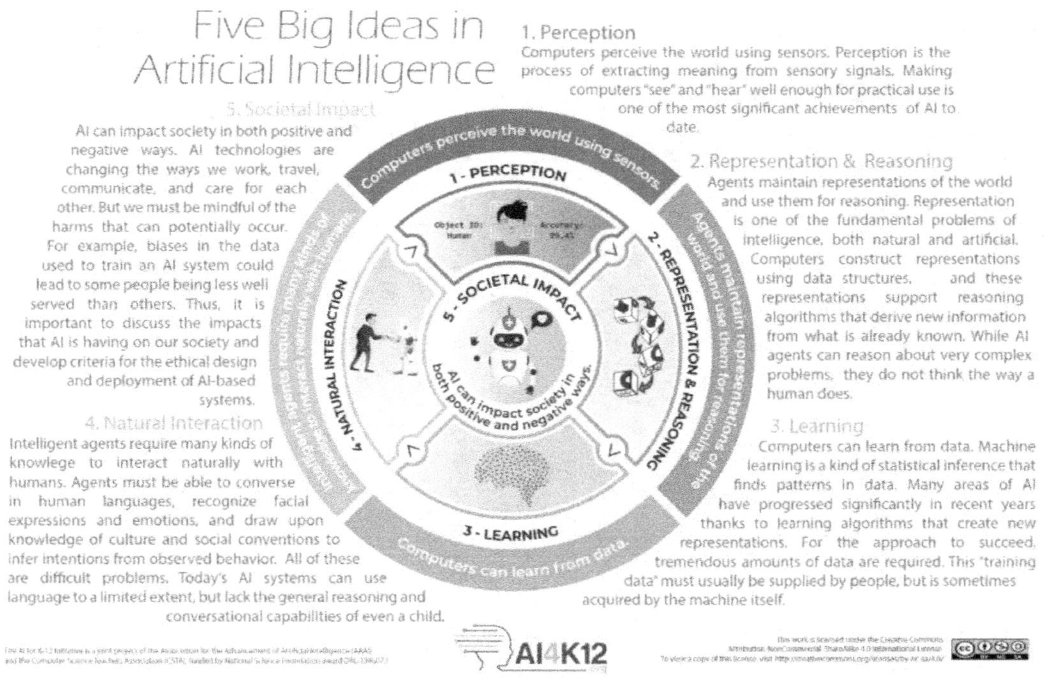
Five Big Ideas in
Artificial Intelligence
1. Perception
Computers perceive the world using sensors. Perception is the process of extracting meaning from sensory signals. Making computers "see" and "hear" well enough for practical use is one of the most significant achievements of AI to date.
2. Representation & Reasoning
Agents maintain representations of the world and use them for reasoning. Representation is one of the fundamental problems of intelligence, both natural and artificial. Computers construct representations using data structures, and these representations support reasoning algorithms that derive new information from what is already known. While AI agents can reason about very complex problems, they do not think the way a human does.
3. Learning
Computers can learn from data. Machine learning is a kind of statistical inference that finds patterns in data. Many areas of AI have progressed significantly in recent years thanks to learning algorithms that create new representations. For the approach to succeed, tremendous amounts of data are required. This "training data" must usually be supplied by people, but is sometimes acquired by the machine itself.
4. Natural Interaction
Intelligent agents require many kinds of knowlege to interact naturally with humans. Agents must be able to converse in human languages, recognize facial expressions and emotions, and draw upon knowledge of culture and social conventions to infer intentions from observed behavior. All of these are difficult problems. Today's AI systems can use language to a limited extent, but lack the general reasoning and conversational capabilities of even a child.
5. Societal Impact
AI can impact society in both positive and negative ways. AI technologies are changing the ways we work, travel, communicate, and care for each other. But we must be mindful of the harms that can potentially occur. For example, biases in the data used to train an AI system could lead to some people being less well served than others. Thus, it is important to discuss the impacts that AI is having on our society and develop criteria for the ethical design and deployment of AI-based systems.
1 - PERCEPTION
Computers perceive the world using sensors.
2 - REPRESENTATION & REASONING
Agents maintain representations of the world and use them for reasoning.
3 - LEARNING
Computers can learn from data.
4 - NATURAL INTERACTION
5 - SOCIETAL IMPACT
AI can impact society in both positive and negative ways.
AI4K12

Figure 7.2 The five big ideas in AI Poster

The Five Big Ideas

This section will explore the five big ideas in AI in more detail.

Big Idea 1 – Perception

Computer perception is sensor-based. Sensory signals allow AI to extract meaning from what is happening around them. Enabling machines to do this is one of the most significant achievements of AI.

This insight into AI looks at perception, indicating that computers perceive the world using sensors and connects with computer science standards (e.g., computer hardware, computer systems). The first insight for learners here is to help them to determine that perception is more than sensing. A supermarket door might have a sensor and open for you, but there is no perception of what/who the door is opening for and so not all devices exhibit intelligence. The question here then is: 'If the extraction of meaning from sensory signals requires knowledge, what does that knowledge look like?' (Touretzky & Gardner-McCure, 2022). Take speech perception as an example. This would require knowledge of many levels of what constitutes language which might include articulatory gestures (tongue, lip, vocal tract movement), phonology, morphology, prosody, syntax, semantics, and so on. A second insight for learners is that perception can be seen as an abstraction pipeline where transformations of a signal to meaning is staged. In a language example, early speech recognition systems would implement a pipeline, a collection of distinct modules from a raw acoustic signal to that of phonemes, words, phrases, and meaning. Deep neural networks today utilize more processing stages and different types of knowledge across multiple levels, but there is still a local signal-based to more global meaning-based use of data moving through layers of such systems. Another example, that of visual perception, largely concerned with constructing a meaning including that of reflection and occlusion. For vision the abstraction pipeline starts with pixels and ends with three dimensional scenes with the in-between a complex mix of boundaries, contours, edges, objects, parts, shadows, surfaces, and reflections (a 2 ½ D sketch; Marr, 1982). Knowledge to derive representations from such a sketch is innate in human beings but not easily articulated by computer systems. Keep in mind that the abstraction pipeline sees information flow backwards as well as forwards along it. That is to say that vocabulary knowledge can influence the perception of ambiguous sounds; knowledge of object shapes can also influence the interpretation of edges in a scene – all told, human perception is far from fully understood, but the study of how AI mimics this process can offer new routes to appreciate and study our own routes of perception.

Big Idea 2 – Representation and Reasoning

AI agents maintain representations of the world around them and use this for reasoning. These representations are assembled using data structures, with the representations supporting reasoning algorithms that derive new information from what is already known by the AI. The thinking process that occurs here is different to that of humans.

In computer science, representations refer to data structures and algorithms perform reasoning. For humans an easy way to understand representations of place is that of presenting a map, which is not about the territory but an abstract way of representing details following notational conventions (e.g., the ways that roads, buildings, tunnels, and nature is depicted). Utilizing a map to plan a route can be considered a line of reasoning. Self-driving cars have to be able to perform a similar kind of reasoning to get from point A to point B. Decision trees are also a good way to demonstrate reasoning, which is a simple formalism of knowledge encoding, and being able to describe how such a process works is a way for learners to think about how reasoning algorithms perform. A key insight from this idea is that of interdependence of representation and reasoning, with representation pointless if having no way to implement it and reasoning algorithms requiring something to reason with. Using the map example: map representation would require a path planning algorithm in order to determine a route from one location to another. Here it is important to understand that representations are not just input for the algorithm, as they can also be constructed by the algorithm with the route constructed by the path planning algorithm another representation. For example, game-play programs would require a search tree AI representation (one that keeps track of alternate moves as it 'searches' for the move that will lead to winning any game). Search trees are neither input/output but are constructed by the search algorithm as it searches. The representation/reasoning duality can be expressed as: 'Representation drives reasoning, and reasoning algorithms manipulate representations' (Touretzky & Gardner-McCure, 2022).

A taxonomy of reasoning types could be introduced to learners to help understand these concepts and how AI makes decisions. Such as classification and prediction (regression) problems, and these can be approached symbolically. Combinational search (part of classical AI, and still important), along with constraint satisfaction, logical dedication, numerical optimization, task planning, and theorem proving could also be introduced. For example, how AI uses logical inference could be introduced by examining how such systems deal with syllogisms, like 'all men are mortal; Socrates is a man; therefore Socrates is mortal'.

Symbolic representation remains important and evidenced by the construction of knowledge graphs and the resources that large corporations such as Google utilize to develop them. For example, when conducting a Google search on a term the knowledge panel displayed to the right in the browser window is generated from the Google knowledge graph.

Feature vector representations are also important to understand and computing technology introduces the term *feature vector encoding,* or *word embedding,* where each word is represented as a point in a high dimensional abstract space.

Touretzky and Gardner-McCure (2022), provide an example based on the word2vec family of models in Mikolev et al (2013), see Figure 7.3. They state:

> Suppose we want to represent the words 'man', 'woman', 'boy', 'gir', 'king', 'queen', 'prince', and 'princess'. Imagine a three-dimensional space where the x coordinate encodes gender, the y coordinate encodes age, and the z coordinate encodes royalty … Each of our eight vocabulary words can be mapped to a unique point in this space, e.g., 'man' might be (0,1,0), and 'princess' might be (1,0,1). Euclidean distance in this space can serve as a heuristic for semantic similarity,

allowing us to infer that 'man' is semantically closer to 'woman' than to 'princess'. We can go on to embed additional words in this space, even without adding more dimensions. 'Son' would likely be close to 'boy', although less definitive as to age, so perhaps its coordinates would be (0, 0.3, 0). 'Parent' is gender neutral but an adult, with no implication of royalty, so it might map to (0, 0.5, 0). And so on.

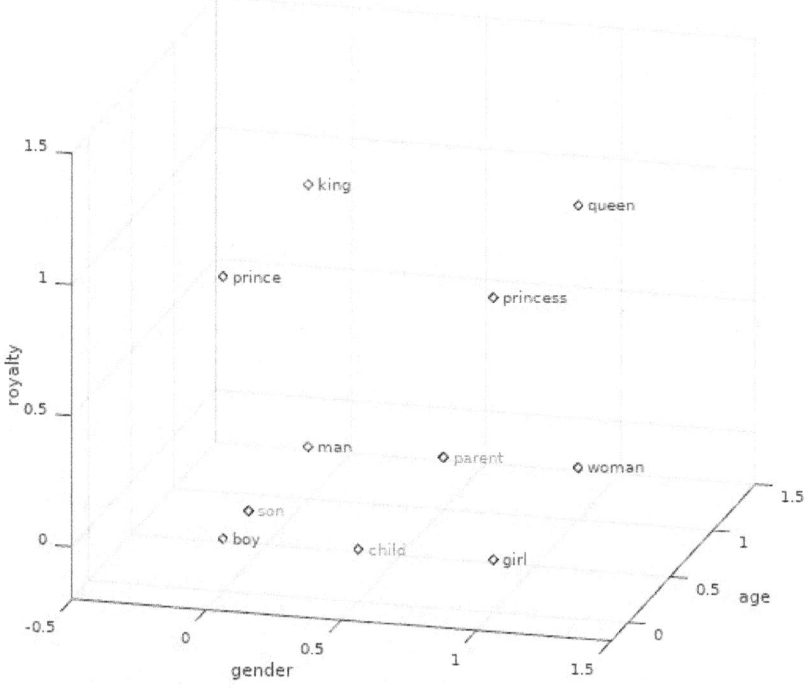

Figure 7.3 Representations of words as points in a 3D semantic space (from Touretzky and Gardner-McCure, 2022)

Larger vocabularies require higher dimensional feature spaces. Such spaces can be created by machine learning (e.g., neural networks), using words that occur in similar contexts to infer information (such as meaning, and predicting what words co-occur with given words like those adjectives that might apply to particular nouns). In this way, such systems are able to capture more than pure syntactic and semantic features from input. In a practical sense, statistical feature vector representations can be used in real-time speech recognition systems to disambiguate homophones. For example, when telling a chatbot that you would like to have 'two coffees, not too hot, to go'. Systems using neural machine translation rely on feature vectors as input and output encodings as do digital assistants such as Siri, and machine translation systems like that of Google Translate.

Big Idea 3 – Learning

Computers learn through data, and a large amount of data is required for this process to be successful. Training data is usually supplied by humans, but it can also be supplied by the machine itself.

This big idea relates to the importance of understanding how human learning is different from machine learning. Human learning is general and flexible being part of a larger cognitive architecture, with machine learning accomplished by specialized algorithms and specific task performance. As such, machine learning typically follows one of two approaches: finding patterns in data or optimizing a behavior based on trial and error processes. The process of machine learning is essentially the construction of a reasoner with machine learning allowing a computer to acquire behaviors without the explicit programming of those behaviors (Touretzky & Gardner-McCure, 2022). In other words, humans program a learning algorithm which constructs a reasoner with desired behavior, with the reasoner employed to perform a task (e.g., cat recognition among a set of images, or deciding if an email is spam or not). Such aspects of AI can be taught to learners by having them experience what it is like to train a reasoner themselves, or to experience what it feels like to acquire a concept by finding patterns in data. One way to assist students in understanding such learning algorithms is to make use of images and labels with the *Teachable Machine* (https://teachablemachine.withgoogle.com).

A further concept relating to learning is that the learning of new behavior is established by changes in internal representations. Learning algorithms can adjust data structure, but this is not illustrated by black box demonstrations such as the *Teachable Machine*. Decision trees can help understand the concept as these are the internal representations that learning algorithms manipulate, with 'glass box' examples drawing decision trees in real-time able to demonstrate the process. For example, the *Akinator* decision tree algorithm (https://en.akinator.com). *TensorFlow* (https://playground.tensorflow.org) is also a way for a learner to experience changes in neural net representations as it allows students to train small feed-forward neural networks, and this is graphically displayed in a browser window. Connections are explicitly represented and are shown thicker or thinner as the magnitude of their weight increases or decreases, with the sign of the weight determining its color.

Other topics covered by big idea 3 are those of the design of feature sets, development and use of large datasets, sources and effects of bias in training data, reinforcement learning, finding patterns in data, as well as learning from experience. This includes finding patterns in data where data is labeled or unlabeled and used to produce classifiers and predictors. Supervised learning is where the algorithm is provided with the correct answer (or a label) for every training example provided to it. Reinforcement learning (unlabeled) is used for sequential decision making problems that involve a series of action choices where each action affects the choice available in the next step, and where the algorithm is not provided with the correct answer at each step, seeing learning from experience occur.

Big Idea 4 – Natural Interaction

Interacting with humans requires the ability to engage with humans in ways that they engage with others. This includes being able to converse in human languages, recognize facial expressions and emotions, and drawing on cultural and social conventions to infer intent from observable behavior. Today's AI systems can use human languages to a limited extent, but they lack general reasoning and conversational capabilities.

The topics that this idea consists of are those of affective computing, common sense reasoning, consciousness/theory of mind, and natural language understanding.

Natural Language Understanding

Making sense of human requests to intelligent agents, extracting information from texts, and conducting translation from one language to another are some of the processes involved with natural language understanding for artificial intelligence.

Common Sense Reasoning

Knowledge about the world (e.g., that a dog is a living being, that a bed is used for sleeping), including sociocultural knowledge (e.g., appropriate gifts for a child's birthday party) are aspects of common sense reasoning that an artificial intelligence system needs to possess, along with naïve physics (e.g., understanding properties of solids and liquids and their behavior in response to external forces like gravity), and Winograd schema. The Winograd Schema Challenge (WSC) is a multiple-choice test of machine intelligence put forth by Levesque (2014) that uses specific sentence structures that require an AI to provide resolution of anaphora (i.e., the machine needs to identify the antecedent of an ambiguous pronoun in a statement). As such, the test is one of natural language processing, which Levesque argues requires use of knowledge alongside commonsense reasoning. To achieve a level of human-like common sense reasoning requires Artificial General Intelligence (AGI), which is different to the narrow AI reasoners that exist presently, but the field is constantly developing.

Affective Computing

Recognizing and dealing with human emotional states is affective computing. This includes those aspects such as tone of voice, facial expressions, body language, and the ability to effectively respond to indications of boredom, excitement, or frustration by adjusting interaction styles.

Consciousness/Theory Of Mind

Robots and artificial intelligences with a human-like persona do not really have minds but in principle could have them and means of considering such a concept is through examination of the Turing test and the Chinese room. To explore aspects of machine understanding of language sentence diagramming may assist learners in comprehending how a natural language understander begins to fathom sentences. Sentence diagrams are somewhat akin to data structures, a fundamental computer science concept, and are a useful visual mapping process that aims to show the relationships between parts of a sentence. They can help you to gain understanding of how the parts of speech work together and where they are placed for a particular sentence, and can assist you in understanding how various parts of speech interact, may be interchangeable, and how they can be replaced (e.g., passive to active voice).

In the Reed-Kellogg system of sentence diagramming, the functions of each word in a sentence are highlighted over that of traditional sentence word ordering (see Figure 7.4).

To start diagramming, you would draw a horizontal line which is then divided by a short vertical line. The subject of the sentence is placed to the left of the dividing vertical line. Sentence modifiers (e.g., adjectives, articles, adverbs) are then placed on a diagonal line below what they modify (e.g., noun, verb). The predicate of the sentence is placed to the right of the dividing line, linking verbs would be placed to the left of it to connect the subject to the predicate and separated by a slanting line. Once again, any modifiers of the predicate are placed on a diagonal line below what it is they modify.

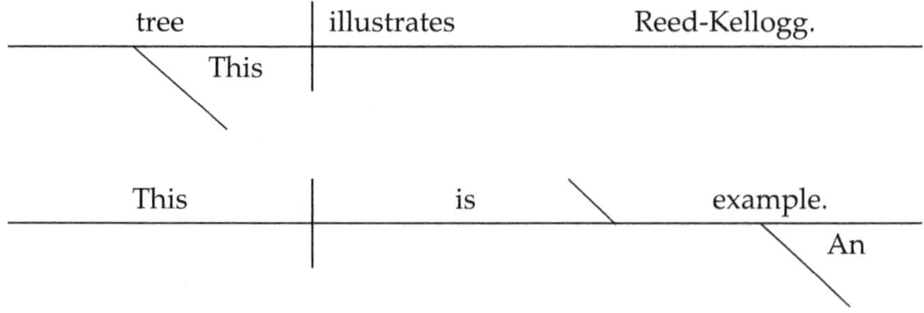

Figure 7.4 Sentence Diagrams – Reed-Kellogg System

In the dependency and constituency method of sentence diagramming, sentence trees are used with every word in a sentence corresponding to one or more nodes in the diagram (see Figures 3.4 and 3.5). Acronyms are used to label the nodes of a tree (e.g., D = determiner, N = noun, NP = noun phrase, S = sentence, V = verb, VP = verb phrase). A hybrid dependency-constituency sentence tree can also be diagrammed when rendering a sentence using this system (see Figure 7.5).

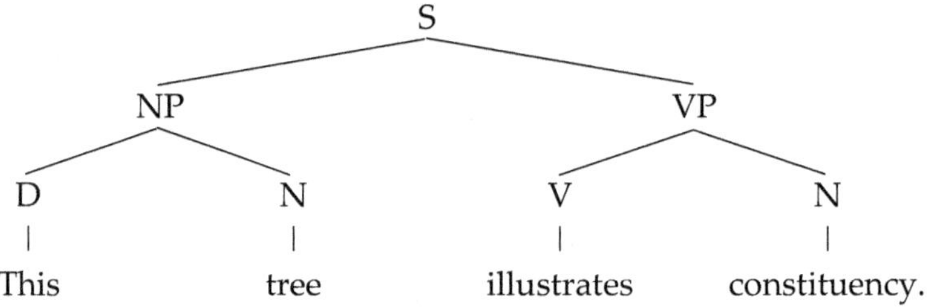

Figure 7.5 A Constituency Sentence Tree

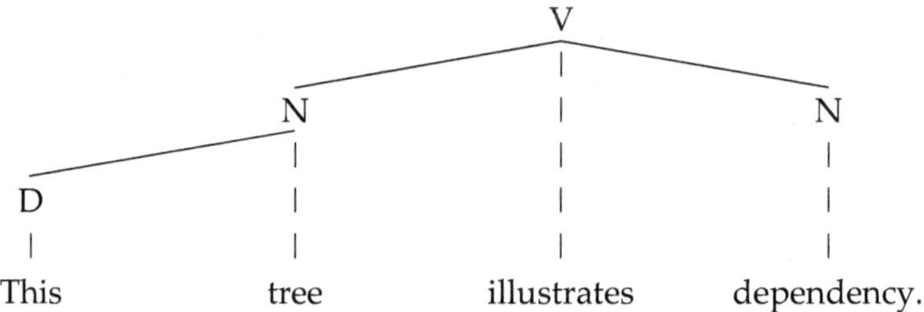

Figure 7.6 A Dependency Sentence Tree

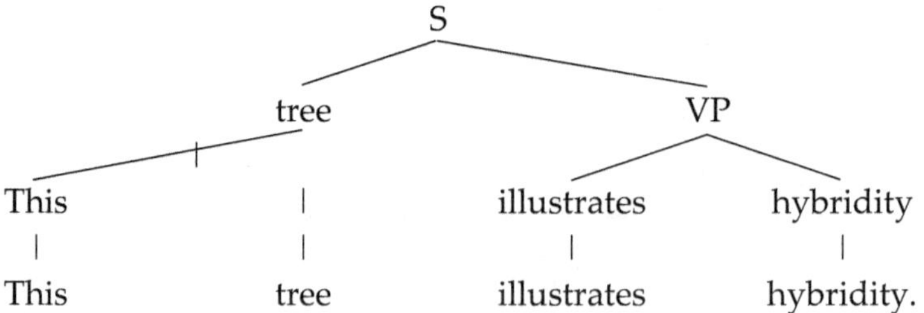

Figure 7.7 A Hybrid Dependency-Constituency Sentence Tree

While syntactic analysis is an essential component of understanding language it is only one part, and in order to understand a sentence AI must first parse it. Figure 7.6 provides an example parse tree from the

Berkeley Neural Parser for the question: Do androids dream of electric sheep? [Link: https://parser.kitaev.io]. The same question broken down using a sentence tree can be seen in Figure 7.7.

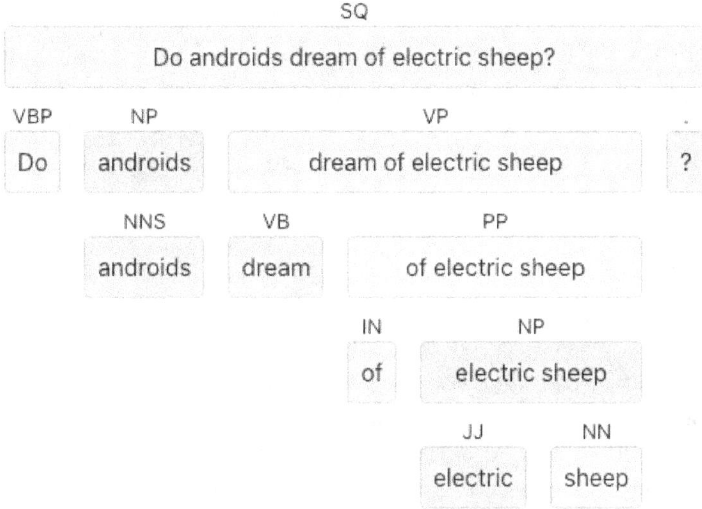

Figure 7.8 Berkley Neural Parser example

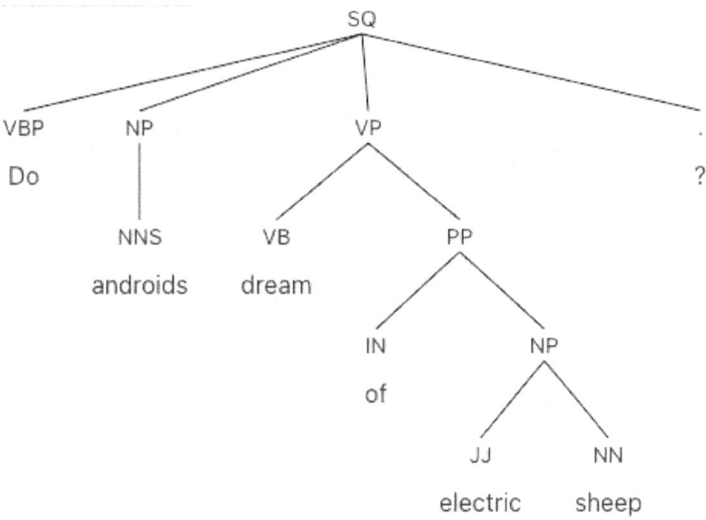

Figure 7.9 Sentence tree example

In the above two figures, abbreviations stand for the following: SQ = question; VBP = non-3rd person singular present tense verb; NP = noun phrase; . = punctuation; NNS = plural noun; VB = base; PP = prepositional phrase; IN = preposition; JJ = adjective; and, NN = singular noun.

It is here where we can utilize the power of AI to leverage statistical learning over large datasets to construct practically useful natural language for use in tasks such as text summarization or machine translation. It is a powerful approach but it presently falls short of understanding in a human sense.

Big Idea 5 – Societal Impact

AI can lead to positive and negative societal impact. AI technologies are already changing the way humans work, travel, communicate, and care for each other. Ethical design and deployment are important to prevent many of the negative implications that AI presents society (e.g., biases in data can be potentially detrimental to some groups over others). Design can also have unintended consequences in the function of AI systems. Questions that this Big Idea also raises are: Should we be polite to agents and robots? Should we teach children to be polite to agents and robots?

The topics that this idea consists of are those relating to the positives and negatives of AI decision-making, ethics concerning people, the economic impact of AI, AI and how it relates to culture, and AI for social good. Attention here then is often placed on that of how to mitigate the negative impacts of AI, and AI related technology use. As such a great deal of focus has revolved around the topic of bias in AI systems.

Bias in AI systems can result from training systems on unrepresentative datasets, and it is important to understand how to mitigate this and how such biases originate and propagate within the AI system in order to resolve them. Understanding how AI systems work and how to interact with them is also an aspect of life increasingly becoming important as we continue to incorporate such technologies into teaching and learning, and into aspects of our daily lives. It is still early days in terms of AI education in the context of K-12, and it is a dynamic area where change is occurring rapidly, there is no way to teach AI but it is possible to the teach skills required for being able to develop, work, study, and live with it, just as it, like us progresses.

Workbook Activity 7.1

Consider the following two articles, and provide a short reflective response to them, while taking the question posed into account. Complete this reflective piece in the appropriate section of the associated workbook.

> *Articles:*
> 1. *AI in Education: Where is it now and what is the future?* [Link: https://www.lexalytics.com/lexablog/ai-in-education-present-future-ethics].
> 2. *China has started a grand experiment in AI education.* [Link: https://www.technologyreview.com/2019/08/02/131198/china-squirrel-has-started-a-grand-experiment-in-ai-education-it-could-reshape-how-the].
>
> *Question:*
> **7.1** After reaching this point of the text, what is your stance on AI in language learning and teaching?

Summary

You learned about:
- The initiative to introduce learners from kindergarten to grade 12 to aspects of artificial intelligence.
- The concept of the AI wheel and poster.
- The five big ideas in AI, and what they mean.
- The potential implications of the five big ideas for society.

Resources

AI4K-12.org. (2021). *Big idea 1 – Perception: Grade progression chart.* https://ai4k12.org/big-idea-1-overview

AI4K-12.org. (2021). *Big idea 3 – Learning: Grade progression chart.* https://ai4k12.org/big-idea-3-overview

AI4K-12.org. (2020). *The five big ideas in AI poster.* https://ai4k12.org/resources/big-ideas-poster
Akinator. Decision tree algorithm. https://en.akinator.com.
Berkeley, NLP. (2021). *Berkeley Neural Parser.* University of California – Berkeley. https://parser.kitaev.io/
Google. (2021). Teachable machine. https://teachablemachine.withgoogle.com/
TensorFlow. Neural network. https://playground.tensorflow.org

References

Kent, D. (Ed.). (2019). *The fourth industrial revolution and education: Digital language learning.* KOTESOL DCC.
Marr, D. (1982). *Vision.* MIT Press.
Mikolov, Tomas, Ilya Sutskever, Kai Chen, Greg Corrado, and Jeffrey Dean. (2013). Distributed representations of words and phrases and their compositionality. *Advances in Neural Information Processing Systems, 26,* 3111-3119. https://dl.acm.org/doi/10.5555/2999792.2999959
Touretzky, D., & Gardner-McCune, C. (2022, in press). Artificial intelligence thinking in K-12. In S. Kong & H. Abelson (Eds), *Computational thinking in K-12: Artificial intelligence literacy and physical computing* (pp x-x). MIT Press.

8. Teaching and Learning in the Era of the Fourth Industrial Revolution

Overview
The chapter presents the skills, competencies, and proficiencies that 21st century learners need to develop and maintain in the fourth industrialization era, along with the 21st century teaching skills required of instructors. Teacher technology confidence use, and the need for instructors to understand the relationship between technology, pedagogy, and content knowledge is also explored before then focusing on a range of technology types, and introducing the characteristics to keep in mind when adapting, integrating, and working on teaching with such technologies. A means of being able to determine the worthwhileness of any AI application, technologies, and approaches adopted for use in education is also presented.

Learning Outcomes
1. Explore how the impact resulting from the fourth industrial revolution has led to the requirement of specific skillsets for 21st century learners.
2. Discover the eight key competencies now required for lifelong learning.
3. Understand what lies behind four digital competency proficiencies expected of learners.
4. Realize the importance of establishing a community of practice (COP), and lifelong learning practices.
5. Appreciate the importance of developing and maintaining 21st century teacher skills.
6. Become aware of the importance, place and the integration into the teaching and learning sphere of technological, pedagogical, and content knowledge.
7. Develop the ability to interpret the worthwhileness of technologies using the substitution, modification, augmentation, and redefinition model.

Changing 21st Century Learner Skills, Competencies, and Proficiencies

Moving into the era of the fourth industrial revolution, all learners now require a range of competencies and skills that come to support education in terms of personalization, equality, collaboration, adaptability, communication, relationships, and technology (Kent, 2019). This sees sixteen skills required of twenty-first century learners, eight key skills required for lifelong learning, four digital competency proficiencies, along with the need to develop personal learning networks that include community of practice.

Twenty-First Learner Century Skills

Twenty-first century learner skills revolve around three aspects: Foundational literacies – how students apply core skills to everyday tasks; competencies – how students approach complex challenges; and, character qualities – how students approach their changing environments (see Table 8.1).

Twenty-First Century Learner Skills		
Foundational Literacies	**Competencies**	**Character Qualities**
How students apply core skills to everyday tasks.	*How students approach complex challenges.*	*How students approach their changing environment.*
- Literacy - Numeracy - Scientific literacy - ICT literacy - Financial literacy - Cultural and civic literacy	- Critical thinking /problem-solving - Creativity - Communication - Collaboration	- Curiosity - Initiative - Persistence/grit - Adaptability - Leadership - Social and cultural awareness

Table 8.1 Sixteen Skills Required by the 21st Century Learner

The Eight Key Competencies to Support Lifelong Learning

The eight key competencies identified to support the ability of individuals to engage effectively in lifelong learning include those of: interpersonal, intercultural and social competence/civic competence; being able to engage in cultural expression; the ability to communicate in a foreign language, the ability to communicate effectively in one's native language; the ability of being able to learn how to learn; along with digital competence; mathematical competence and basic competencies in science and technology, and entrepreneurship. (See figure 8.1.)

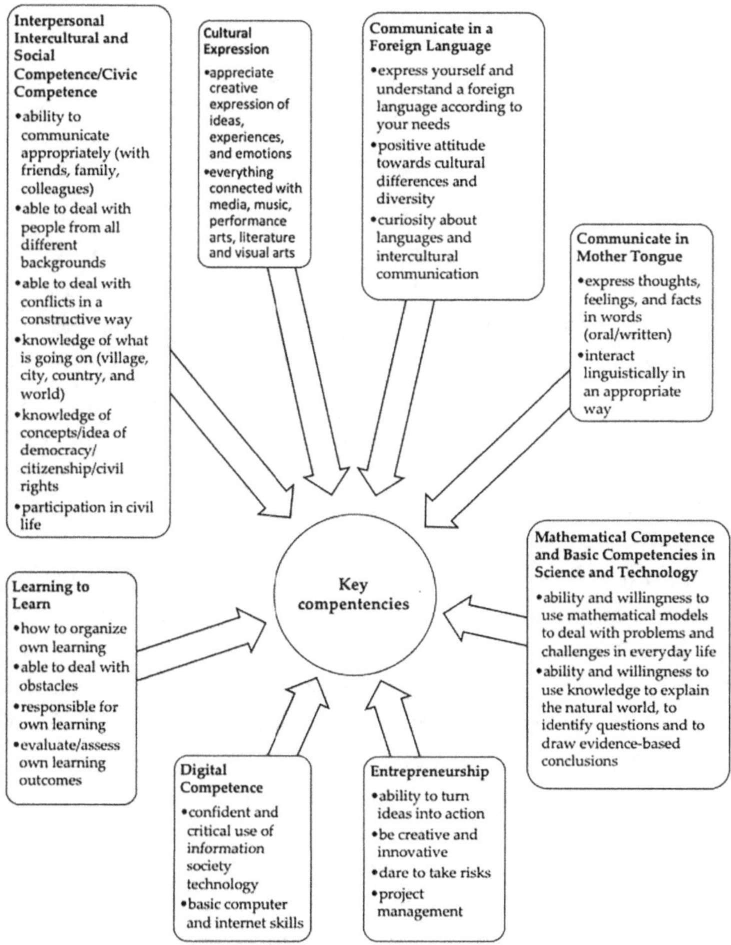

Figure 8.1 Eight Key Competencies for Lifelong Learning

The Four Digital Competency Proficiencies

The four digital competency proficiencies that we now require a mastery of include those of procedural competency, socio-digital competence, digital discourse competence, and strategic competence (Walker & White, 2013).

Procedural competence. The ability to manipulate technology (in terms of hardware and software) – knowing how to use technology (e.g., switch it on, the buttons to click). This is similar to the traditional view that to know a language means knowing the grammar and vocabulary, and just as we now know that communicative competence requires more than knowledge of the syntactic, phonological, and lexical, we also need to understand that digital competence requires understanding of how, when, and why to use technologies and how to compensate for gaps in knowledge and skills.

Socio-digital competence. Understanding what is appropriate in different social contexts and knowledge domains in terms of both technology and language; in other words, how technological competence and communicative competence overlap, and the types of language appropriate to use for different audiences in various digital contexts (see Crystal, 2006). For example, deciding on the appropriateness of using social media such as Facebook for business communication, and how it should be used to achieve a desired communicative response.

Digital discourse competence. The ability to manage an extended task, using several applications and/or types of equipment (e.g., recording, editing, and publishing a video, or writing a blog post with photographs). This then includes being able to perform tasks that require a range of skills and technical knowledge, and typically ones that would also require communicative discourse competence in order to structure text, create paragraphs, and sequence and link ideas using appropriate language forms.

Strategic competence. The ability to repair problems and work around the gaps in technological knowledge and skills. This refers to the ability to think of alternate routes or options (e.g., switching channels, contacting someone by email or social media if they don't answer the phone, or knowing how to deal with disruptive online interactions such as 'flaming' or a troll). Linguistically speaking, this is akin to the ability to manage and navigate communication to repair communication breakdowns, and work around unfamiliar areas of language.

Personal Learning Networks and Establishing Community of Practice (COP)

Connectivism has been described as a 'learning theory for the digital age' (Siemens, 2005), and it stems from socio-cultural learning theories that argue that learning occurs more effectively when people work together. Not only does connectivism view that learning occurs by engaging with a diversity of ideas and opinions, with new ideas constructed through shared thinking and conversations, but that this knowledge can also reside within machines. Examples are the internet, which is a vast repository of knowledge (perhaps, of variable quality), and WolframAlpha, a computational knowledge engine that relies on curated data (which, by the way, Alexa has access to). It also includes the ways in which people store knowledge within machines, and how they interact with that knowledge and with other humans, as well as AIs (artificial intelligences) like Digital Assistants, in order to take control of their own learning, as they retrieve and engage with knowledge. More basic examples include the use of PowerPoints and interactive whiteboards for presenting and interacting with stored knowledge. So, technology is viewed as a resource, and as a way to mediate human interactions, with these interactions making use of different connections and different language forms depending on the media. Hence, knowing where to find information is more important than knowing that information, with the ability to see connections between fields, ideas, and concepts being a core competency.

A key feature of connectivism is that much learning occurs across online peer networks with students learning as they seek out information on their own, sharing what they find with others, and with teachers guiding students to information and answering key questions as needed. The personal learning network (PLN) that students then forge is created on the basis of how they organize their own connections to learning communities as they transverse networks through multiple knowledge domains. In other words, what constitutes the development of knowledge or understanding is the formation of connections between nodes of information (i.e., networks), with the ability to both construct and transverse those networks then considered to be learning. 'Learning is the network.' This sees connectivism's core concepts stem from socio-cultural learning theories, which argue that learning occurs more effectively when people work together.

Crucial to the development of personal learning networks is learner autonomy and levels of learner confidence as they move from formal settings, teacher-guided/controlled and institutional-based, to environments where they can direct their own learning, find their own information, and create their own knowledge from more knowledgeable others with whom they engage. These networks, based on personal interests and preferences over institutional requirements and choices, may be small or vast but their main characteristics are to support knowledge development by being autonomous, connected, diverse, and open (Downes, 2010).

Although technology including mobile developments make new and different educational structures, organizations, and settings possible, connectivism is not limited to the online environment. The theory also applies to a larger learning environment and helps to inform how we understand our relatedness to the world, and consequently how we learn from it and understand it. Networks should be thought of as the relationship between 'internal' and 'external' physical environments. As a learner engages in creating and recreating their own PLN, understanding arises through the application of meta-cognition to the evaluation of elements that prove useful and those that can be eliminated from the network. The face-to-face as well as online networks that people build up throughout their lifetime will provide them with expertise and knowledge. Learners are at the center of their own learning experience, and instrumental in determining the content of their own learning, how they engage and participate in learning, and who can participate with them.

A community of practice (COP), or affinity spaces as Gee (2004) calls them, are places in which people develop relationships in a discourse community based on their shared interests. A COP is formed from three components – domain, community, practice – which sees a group of people (*the domain*) who share a craft or profession come together (*as a community*) to distribute experience and information, and to learn from each other (*with practice*), which leads to both personal and professional development (Lave & Wagner, 1991). For students, this might mean offline spaces like the traditional classroom, as well as digital spaces from which they may practice English utilizing technology in an interactive, integrated, and normalized way using apps to develop specific skills and practice them with others, and using forums to ask questions and receive answers regarding specific problems. For teachers, a COP might emerge while attending live events such as conferences or workshops from conversations held in teacher's lounges, or as a result of joining online spaces like TESOL association Facebook groups: any place where teachers-as-learners can engage in formal or informal professional development as part of their PLN (personal learning network).

Twenty-First Century Teacher Skills

As we continually live in a world that is in constant change, it is also important for teachers to possess the ability to develop and maintain 21st century teacher skills. These involve those of being a continuous learner, a relationship builder; a researcher, a digital designer, and a leader, while also being inclusive, reflective, cooperative, creative and innovative, a storyteller, designer and decorator, and an artist (Oufela, 2021).

Continuous learner. Knowledge and practice need to continually adjust to the teaching environment and learner context. The continual evaluation and improvement upon our practice and how this impacts our learners is important, as is what we do with this knowledge (e.g., sharing it with others in workshops, distributing it to others as activity sheets, and so on).

Relationship builder. Aspects of wellbeing and teacher health are based on the relationships forged with the various stakeholders in the teaching context (e.g., administration, pupils, parents). Establishing solid rapport with learners can promote a positive learning environment and potentially raise their overall achievement; a cheerful and happy workplace environment while promoting good communication can stimulate wellbeing among faculty and administrative staff. A work-life balance is also important to maintain healthy relationships in the teachers' private life so that they can function well in their professional life.

Researcher. Teachers today, along with their students, need to be lifelong learners. In this respect, teachers as a researcher and as a guide for their students can examine learner responses to content, listen to their concerns, and explore their interests in content. Developing classroom action research (CAR) models for use in the classroom, where focus is on a cycle of planning → implementing → observing → reflecting (Indriyanti & Praseto, 2018), is a way that instructors can assist learners, and it is a way where teachers can ensure that they are constantly providing their students with the best possible opportunities for learning.

Digital designer. As learning and education is increasingly taking place in digital spaces, it is important for instructors to be able to possess those skills that match their learners. This includes those of being able to design (i.e., web sites, blogs, wikis and digital posters involving multimodal aspects such as images and movies).

Leader. Being a leader does not mean being a 'boss'. Teacher leadership skills refer to the ability of a teacher to encourage and positively impact their learners, and other staff, to move ahead and better themselves, and provide themselves with opportunities to lead from where they are. In this way meaningful change can take place (i.e., sharing content that works with other teachers in the form of activity sheets or in professional development workshops and conferences, including those emerging from CAR or classroom action research).

Inclusive. Recognizing the diversity among learners is important. Taking into account learner variables such as the socio-cultural backgrounds of learners, and their ways of approaching content, can help you pull out student strengths and use these to support their education.

Reflective. In an era where new knowledge, and new ideas are rapidly unfolding, step back and take a day or week to consider how your lessons and interactions with stakeholders went. Look into those practices and pedagogical competencies that might assist you in becoming a better instructor.

Cooperative. Work together with others, especially those that exhibit strong teacher leadership, so that you can improve your own skills. Establish and create a diverse learning network, attend and present at professional development seminars and workshops to share what works and what has not worked for you, and to gain feedback on your own practice.

Creative and innovative. Innovate your curriculum by being creative, adapt and supplement the materials that you must work with to match the interests, levels, and the focus of students so that they can become more engaged in learning and practicing the skills that you are imparting.

Storyteller. Integrating aspects of a storyteller into your teacher toolkit involves being able to provide educational content in a way that creates meaningful connections for learners, potentially allowing them to retain more of what it is that they are attempting to learn. This concept comes from the notion that storytellers are able to captivate their audience, and capture their attention in ways that also serve to help the listener in retaining elements of the story that they hear.

Designer and decorator. If you continuously teach in the same room then you have the ability to determine how this environment can be best constructed for the types of learner that you teach. If not, you still need to be mindful of aspects such as student seating, blinds being pulled if they shine on the board or in the students or even your own eyes, the seating arrangements, and so on. In other words, being a designer and decorator means being mindful of the learner perspective of the room, and approaching it in a way that allows you to adjust it best, so that learners are able to experience meaningful educational opportunities that serve them the most.

Artist. The practice of teaching is a craft, a science, and an art. There are a number of methodologies, approaches, and techniques that we rely on when engaging in our craft, but the art is being able to weave these together in a cohesive pattern that works for us as educators and for the learners under our care. This art involves being adaptable, creative, flexible, resilient, and resourceful, as well as possessing a mastery of the other 21st century teacher skills that can perhaps also align to help you provide teaching under such frameworks as TPACK (technology, pedagogy and content knowledge).

The Technology Pedagogy and Content Knowledge (TPACK) Framework

It has long been recognized (see Trilling & Fadel, 2009; Starky, 2012) that teachers this century will not be effective in their roles if they are unable to connect with their learners, especially if their pedagogies have not undergone a paradigm shift towards teaching with digital technologies. To be an effective educator involves interweaving a number of aspects from a variety of specialized knowledge contexts, implementing the application of complex knowledge structures across a range of multifaceted and dynamic classroom contexts (Leinhardt & Greeno, 1986), particularly those that involve knowledge of aspects that include learner variables, subject matter, pedagogical practice, and technology integration. To help support the integration of technology in such a context the technology pedagogy and content knowledge (TPACK) framework (Mishra & Koehler, 2006; 2007) emerged from the dimensions of pedagogical content knowledge, defined as an educators' interpretation and transformation of subject-matter knowledge in the context of facilitating student learning (Shulman, 1986). See Figure 8.2

The TPACK framework has been extensively applied in the literature and across teacher education pedagogy (Saubern, 2020), and in the learning process (Slough & Slough, 2015). Figure 8.2 illustrates the three main components of the framework, technological knowledge (TK), pedagogical knowledge (PK), and content knowledge (CK), along with their overlaps: technological pedagogical knowledge (TPK), pedagogical content knowledge (PCK), technological content knowledge (TCK), and technological, pedagogical, and content knowledge (TPACK).

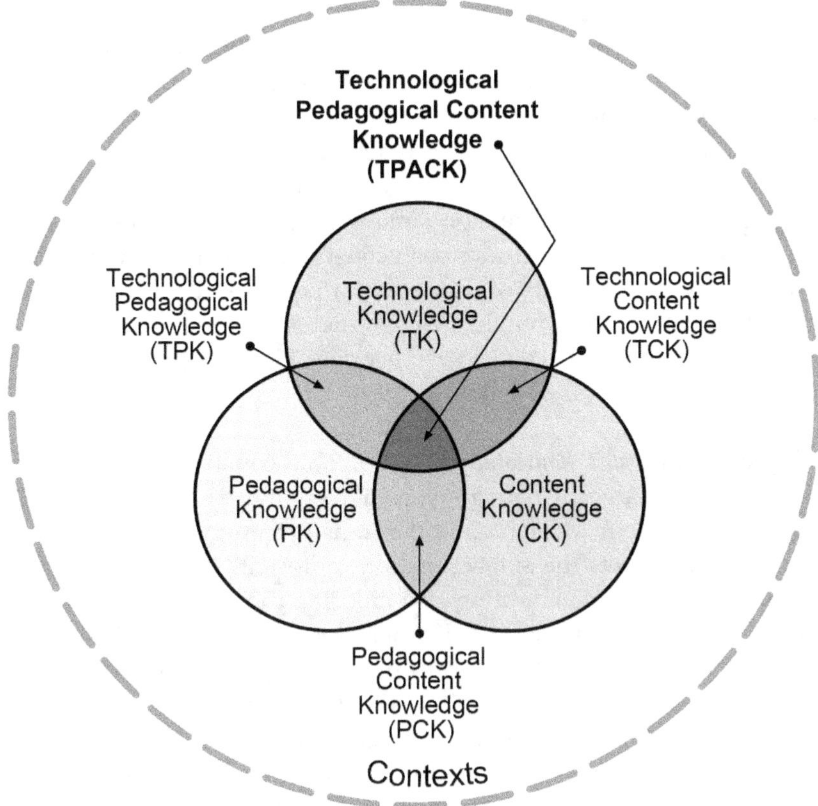

Figure 8.2 The TPACK Framework
(Reproduced with permission of the publisher, © 2012 by tpack.org)

Content knowledge (CK). This refers to the instructors' knowledge of the subject matter to be learned and taught, and it is such knowledge that is of critical importance to teachers. It would include the knowledge of the fundamentals of the disciplines that they teach, the concepts, ideas, established practices and approaches to the development of knowledge in their field, aspects of evidence and proof, and the organizational frameworks that can be applied in their specialization. Although issues pertaining to curriculum content can be areas of significant contention and disagreement, the cost of not having a comprehensive base of content knowledge can be prohibitive. (e.g., students may receive erroneous information, develop misconceptions about the content area, and so on.)

Pedagogical Knowledge (PK). This is the deep knowledge of those processes and practices (methods, approaches, techniques) of teaching and learning, including those of overall educational aims, purposes, and values. It also involves knowledge revolving around understanding how students learn, classroom management skills, lesson planning, learner assessment and the strategies required to evaluate learner understanding. Those teachers possessing deep pedagogical knowledge would understand how a student can construct knowledge and acquire the necessary skills, habits of mind, and a positive disposition toward learning. As such, this knowledge construct requires understanding of cognitive, developmental and social theories of learning along with how these apply to learners.

Pedagogical Content Knowledge (PCK). This construct relates to the notion of knowledge of pedagogy being one that is applicable to the instruction of specific content, and the transformation that occurs when the teacher interprets the subject matter, represents it in multiple ways for learners, while also adapting and tailoring the instructional content to alternative conceptions and learner prior knowledge. As such, it involves aspects related to the core of teaching, learning, curriculum, assessment and reporting, conditions that promote learning and links among curriculum, assessment, and pedagogy. It sees effective teaching as possessing an awareness of misconceptions and how to interpret them, the importance of establishing connections among different content-based ideas, the learners' prior knowledge, alternate teaching strategies, and the flexibility to explore alternate ways of examining the same notion.

Technological Knowledge (TK). This is something that is constantly in a state of flux, and definitions of it may become quickly outdated. However, certain ways of approaching and thinking about the use of technology in education can apply across all technology tools and resources, and as such this knowledge aspect goes beyond computer literacy to that of a deep understanding of technologies and a mastery of using them in different ways to accomplish any given task.

Technological Content Knowledge (TCK). This aspect applies to the understanding of the manner in which both technology and content knowledge can constrain and influence each other. Instructors need to master more than just the subject they teach, they must also master the manner in which the application of particular technologies can alter the manner in which subject matter can be taught and learned by students. In other words able to best use and teach with those technologies that are best suited for addressing subject-matter learning in their domains at particular times and for particular needs.

Technological Pedagogical Knowledge (TPK). This represents an understanding of how teaching and learning change if a particular technology is applied in a particular manner. It includes understanding the pedagogical affordances and constraints of the technological tools as they relate to pedagogical designs and strategies developmentally appropriate to the discipline being taught. (e.g., the whiteboard is typically used in a single manner, with students called upon to interact with it, but it can be used in a multitude of ways and its use can be hampered by classroom settings and factors.)

Technological, Pedagogical, and Content Knowledge (TPACK). This form of knowledge goes beyond that of its three core components, emerging from the interactions among technology, pedagogy, and content knowledge. It is the basis of effective teaching with technology brought into play any time an expert teacher instructs. It requires understanding of using technologies themselves; the pedagogical techniques that use technologies in constructive ways to teach content; knowledge of what makes concepts easy or difficult to learn and how technologies can help address any problems that students might face in learning; an awareness of students' prior knowledge along with epistemological theories; and a solid comprehension of how technologies can be utilized to build on existing knowledge to construct new epistemologies or strengthen older ones (Koehler & Mishra, 2009).

21st Century PCK

In the classroom context we can perhaps interpret the TPACK framework, in broad terms (Matthee, 2018), as a continuum of how we view knowledge regarding the awareness and use of digital tools and resources in relation to pedagogy and the content we impart in terms of curriculum (see Figure 8.3).

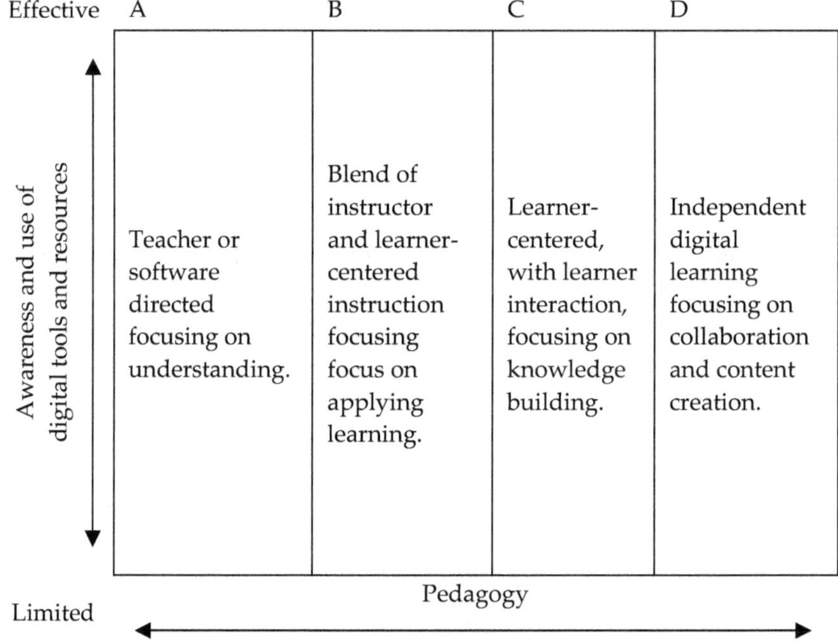

Figure 8.3 Continuum from limited to effective awareness of use
of digital tools and resources relative to pedagogy

This highlights that it is really no longer possible to discuss either pedagogy or content without knowledge of technology as Slough and Slough (2015) argue. They continue by saying that learners develop their competencies and learn from those educators that are best versed in pedagogy and an understanding that the best pedagogies are those technologically enhanced. In other words 21st century pedagogical content knowledge (PCK) resides at the intersection of technology-enhanced pedagogy knowledge (PK) and technology-enhanced content

(CK), and represents the best of those competencies required by 21st century learners (21st Century PCK).

Teacher Technology Confidence

In the use of any technology Mandinach and Cline (1993) posit that educators will go through 4 stages of development, from survival to mastery, impact, and innovation (see Figure 8.4).

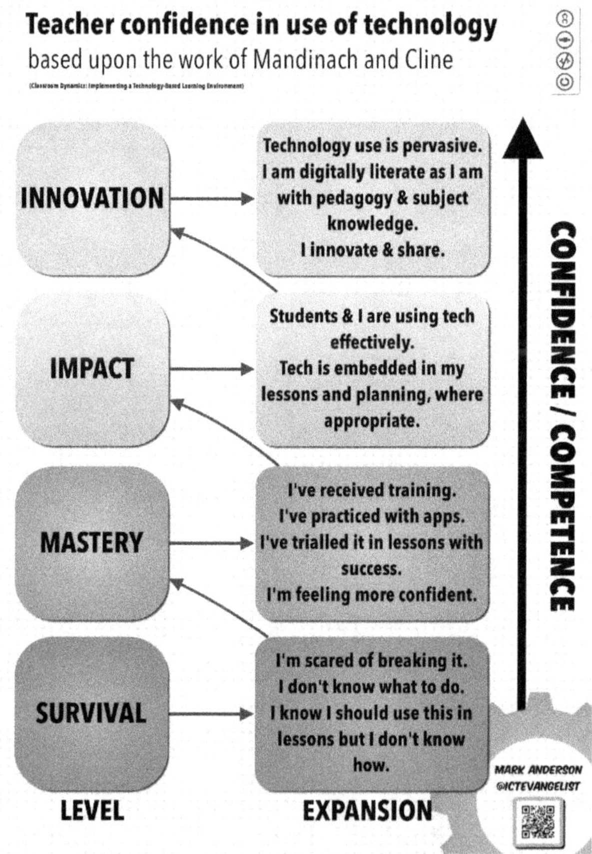

Figure 8.4 Teacher confidence stages in technology use
(Anderson, 2013)

Aspects to keep in mind when adapting, integrating, and working on teaching with new technologies might be those of learning at your own pace, examining what others do, experimenting and testing, mentally preparing, integrating technologies steadily, and leading with technologies.

Learning at Your Own Pace. Going faster in order to keep up with others will mean that you will likely miss some information or procedures and will need to spend time to go over something later on anyway. It is better to go slower and learn something well, as opposed to learning only aspects of it and failing at doing something with it at a later date, or seeing a need to go over those aspects additional times.

Examining What Others Do. See if you can adopt, and adapt, what you see works for others. However if it does not work for you then attempt to adapt how you use it before perhaps abandoning it to then work with something similar, or something better suited to you and your learners.

Experiment and Test. Keep an eye out for new technologies and how others are integrating them into their teaching and learning context, and then try them out for yourself. You may wish to video yourself attempting to use the technology or teach with it in order to refine how you come across using it.

Mentally Preparing. If the sequence of working with the technology has been well thought out and planned, then generally the practical aspect of its implementation will be smooth, as will any need to adjust to any difficulties that may arise in first use during a session with students.

Integrating Steadily. Minimize the stress on you and your learners by introducing new technologies or different aspects of old ones by doing so one at a time, perhaps over a single lesson or other adequate period of time that allows for the necessary adjustments and learning curve to be covered.

Leading. Inform your colleagues about what works for you, those things that did not work but that others might find useful, and share your experience and tips through workshops. Attending workshops will also allow you to be on the receiving end of others, who are sharing what works and does not work in their teaching and learning contexts.

Ultimately, the most valuable skills that we can offer both ourselves and our students today are those of knowing how to learn, unlearn, and relearn (Toffler, 1970) – liquid skills that are adaptable and can lead to life-long learning opportunities. All of us today must have the skills to implement, manage, and work with new technologies, and to be adaptable problem-solvers who are able to both communicate effectively and are able to work with others in creative ways. As we move forward, we will succeed by working alongside our machines and technology, programming them, rather than being programmed by them, and rather than trying to compete with them, welcoming them into our classrooms and into our learners' lives in ways where they can serve to enhance learning experiences by providing increasingly collaborative, meaningful, multimodal, personalized, and non-linear learning pathways.

AI in Education

The impact of AI and the increased utilization of smartphones and digital technologies in education has had, and will continue to have, a significant impact for all stakeholders from administrators through to teachers, pupils and parents. The ways in which this occurs changes constantly and at a rapid pace, so this section will necessarily need to be made very general in its scope. It will highlight a number of AI and digital technologies that have come to impact the educational sphere, and then finalize by providing a means of being able to determine if any potential AI and/or digital technologies for use by teachers in their learning contexts are worthwhile, and if they may enhance the teaching and learning sphere in which they are employed.

Administration

For administrators AI will be able to assist across a wide variety of platforms, particularly in the areas of school management through to the undertaking of learner analytics, and the data mining of learner management systems. Aspects of this might include assigning of classrooms and subjects to learners, scheduling of faculty, facilities management, finance control, cybersecurity, safety and security systems, the e-authentication of staff entry to buildings, the automated attendance of students as they enter classrooms, the identification and notification of cheating alerts during exams, sentiment analysis of student writing (e.g., in forum posts), the automatic grading of quizzes, and the identification of problem areas of courses that students are having difficulty engaging with or completing.

Parents

Learner analytics and data mining in education is extremely useful in terms of providing parents with the ability to gauge how their children may be coping with the educational opportunities being provided to them at school. This may also identify any potential learning disabilities or areas of weakness that might require a tutor or further concentration in terms of the provision of additional homework. Other aspects such as digital portfolio provision and the availability of digital report cards, allows parents immediate access to the content that learners produce as well as the unprecedented ability to direct message teachers. One such system that provides this ability while employing aspects of gamification to provide classroom management is that of *ClassDojo* [Link: https://www.classdojo.com]. The application integrates aspects of gamification into the learning context in order to provide motivation and engagement while promoting discipline, cooperation and attendance, and the development of metacognitive abilities in learners, as well as encouraging empathy, and the building of teamwork skills (Behadj, Messaoudi, and Nfiissi, 2019). All stakeholders are able to see how the learner is engaging in class, with peers, and review a portfolio of any work photographed and uploaded to the application for specific learners. All teachers in the school are able to award or detract points from learners for their behavior during lessons, or on the playground, directly through the app on their smartphone. This digitalization of discipline through applications such as *Class Dojo*, although innovative, have drawn criticism (Manolev, Sullivan & Slee, 2018; Baron, 2019).

Teachers

The most common types of technology and AI that an instructor might utilize with learners are those that are designed to support teachers supporting students (teacher-facing tools), and those designed to support students directly (student-facing tools). Teachers might also engage with classroom management tools, automated attendance check systems, and learner management systems (LMS), which could include automated grading systems (including those that might provide continuous assessment, both formative and summative). They may also utilize AI as a research tool. Here, learner analytics and data mining are useful means of providing feedback for educators and administrators alike in regards to determining the effectiveness of courses being provided, and with the ability to be provided with knowledge that pinpoints where learners may require assistance and what aspects of a course may require changes in learning design. While learning analytics involve analyzing, collecting, measuring, and reporting on data concerning learners and their contexts for the purpose of optimizing and understanding educational provision across the teaching context, data mining is concerned with the analysis and gathering of data that can be used to then improve, support and understand student learning itself. Learner analytics can be applied by administrators to identify students who might be at risk of dropping out of studies and to alert student-support staff who can then provide pro-active remedial assistance. Educational data mining might be applied to assist in identifying for educators how particular students with various learning disabilities might require assistance (e.g., in terms of working memory skills, difficulties with processing the sounds in words, broad cognitive difficulties, and so on). This can then assist in making learning design decisions that will prove important when undertaking the redesign of courses. Learning design refers to a range of methodologies that enable teachers and designers to make more informed decisions regarding how they may develop learning interventions and activities. For example, to determine what domain, specific subject, duration and level of study or activities and approaches might prove to be the most effective in practice.

Learners

A wide variety of AI and other technologies are available to learners today, from those that they can access on their smartphones to those made available to them by parents or instructors. Most of the applications employing AI and designed for application in education that learners might use could be categorized in terms of the five complementary dimensions of learning that they provide (see Table 8.2).

The variety of technologies available to learners can also be considered in terms of those that are largely instructionist (i.e., taking a student teaching approach), constructivist (i.e., taking a student supporting approach), or teacher-assistive (i.e., taking a teacher supportive approach). Several examples of these are highlighted in Table 8.3, and are explored in greater detail in Holmes, Bialik, & Fadel (2019).

Dimension	Examples
Types of learner of which the application is designed	Early years K-12 Higher education Informal Professional Learners who have additional needs
Learning domain that the application covers	Language learning, math, music, physics, and so on
Learning approach that the application facilitates	Step-by-step instructional adaptive learning Dialogue-based adaptive learning Exploratory learning Writing analysis
Learning support that the application provides	Learning diagnostics Mentoring Assessment Network connectors Chatbots Digital Assistants
Teaching support that the application provides	Automatic learner profiles Smart gradebooks

Table 8.2 AI education technology examples by dimension
(See Holmes, Bialik, & Fadel, 2019, 137)

	Instructionist (Student Teaching)	Constructivist (Student Supporting)	Teacher Assistive (Teacher Supportive)
AIED Applications	- Intelligent tutoring systems (ITS) - Dialogue-based tutoring systems (DBTS) - Language learning applications	- Exploratory learning environments (ELEs) - Automatic writing evaluation (formative) - Learning network orchestrators - Language learning applications - AI collaborative learning - AI continuous assessment - AI learning companions	- ITS+ - Automatic writing evaluation (summative) - Student forum monitoring - AI teaching assistants - AI as a research tool to further the learning sciences
AIED Technologies and Approaches	- Chatbots - Digital assistants - Augmented reality (AR) and virtual reality (VR) - Natural language processing (NLP) - Adaptivity		

Table 8.3 Examples of instructivist, constructivist, and teacher assistive artificial intelligence applications, technologies, and approaches (See Holmes, Bialik, & Fadel, 2019, 165)

AI Applications, Technologies, and Approaches in Learning

The target and characteristics for the main technologies presented in Table 8.3 are further detailed in that of Table 8.4.

Technology Type	Features		
	Characteristics	**Determined by**	**Target**
ITS	- Individualized feedback - Individualized pathways - Real-time adaptivity - Step-by-step sequence of instruction tasks - Students working with computers of mobile devices - System-determined content and pathways	System	Learners
DBTS	- Individualized conversations - Individualized feedback - Real-time adaptivity - Step-by-step dialogue-based instruction and tasks - Students working with computers or mobile devices - System-determined content and pathways	System	Learners

Language learning applications	- Individualized feedback - Step-by-step sequence of instruction and tasks. Students working with computers or mobile devices - System-determined content and pathways	Learner and system	Learners
ELE	- Exploratory tasks - Individualized feedback - Individualized pathways - Real-time adaptivity - Students working with computers or mobile devices - System-determined content and pathways, with student choice within tasks	Learner and system	Learners
Automatic writing evaluation	- Essays (and other assignments) uploaded and analyzed by the system - Individualized formative feedback (to assist learners in improving writing, and/or summative assessment (to score/grade an essay)	System	Learners (formative) Instructors (summative)

LNOs	- Access to learning opportunities	Mixed (can sometimes respond to requests)	Learners
Collaborative learning	- Facilitates collaborative learning - Facilitates organization of collaborative learning	System	Learners
Continuous assessment	- Assessment of learner competencies on an ongoing basis (e.g., during conversations), rather than relying on exams or tests	System	Learners
Learning companions	- Lifelong learning companions for students	Learner and system	Learners
ITS+	- AR integration (e.g., student data visible to instructor above students if using appropriate devices) - Back-end ITS functionality for other providers - Varies based on the ITS+ - Whole-school wraparound ITS	N/A	Learners Instructors

Student forum monitoring	- Providing automatic feedback on forum posts, analyzing posts to find connections or various sentiment	N/A	Learners Instructors
AI teaching assistants	- Assistants to teachers in various ways (e.g., for classroom management)	Instructor and system	Instructors.
Chatbots	- Mostly providing information, games (e.g., to practice aspects of language)	Learner (system responds to learners interactions)	Learners.
AR and VR	- Access to otherwise unobtainable environments	Mixed	Learners Instructors

Table 8.4 AI education technology features
(See Holmes, Bialik, & Fadel, 2019, 166-7)

Selecting Appropriate AI Applications, Technologies, and Approaches with the SAMR Model

One means of determining if the AI or other digital technology that you are looking at integrating into the classroom is worthwhile, is to employ a framework like the substitution augmentation modification redefinition (SAMR) model (Puentedura, 2006; Hamilton, Rosenberg, & Akcaoglu, 2016). Such a model would allow you to assess the viability of the potential for any form of AI or technology to enhance or transform the learning and teaching context. The model consists of four segments with substitution and augmentation considered to be the enhancement sections of the model, while modification and redefinition are considered to be transformational (see Figure 8.5).

Enhancement	**SUBSTITUTION** Technology directly replaces an old way of teaching (direct substitute, no functional change)	**S**
	AUGMENTATION Technology provides improvement (direct substitute, with functional change for the better)	**A**
Transformational	**MODIFICATION** Technology allows for significant task redesign (presents learning in a new way)	**M**
	REDEFINITION Technology allows for the creation of new tasks (implements something previously inconceivable)	**R**

Figure 8.5 The SAMR Model

Substitution is the utilization of technology in a way that simply replaces or directly substitutes a non-technological implementation. Here, you have to ask yourself what the gains may be for replacing the traditional teaching tool or technique with a technological one. For example, digital assistants could be used to spell out a word and provide its definition, synonym, antonym, and translation.

Augmentation also sees technology directly substitute traditional tools or techniques with technological ones, but a significant enhancement in use of the technology should result. Here, you would consider if using the technology being considered will augment or increase learning potential or student productivity in any way. For example, digital assistants provide all the facts that once needed to be learned, and they could be used when students create posters, or when conducting research that requires access to real-time information. They also provide real audio (e.g., animal noises), games (e.g., 20-questions, Jeopardy!), and quizzes, all of which result from the use of voice-driven interactions and turn-takings that can help students practice both their active (speaking) and passive (listening) skills.

Modification instead of replacement or enhancement, this section of the model looks at the design of a lesson or task and how technology use may provide increased learning outcomes. Here you would need to ask yourself if this use significantly alters the task for the better. For example, students can engage with a digital assistant for just-in-time learning where they use it to complete or check homework answers or to review content in a way that also provides additional language practice (e.g., speaking and listening) to assist with the development of fluency.

Redefinition, the final segment of the model, looks at using technology to promote a learning paradigm that is not possible to achieve without the incorporation of technology into the teaching and learning space. Here you would need to consider how the technology has helped the instructor or learner engage with content in a manner that would be previously inconceivable. For example, students can use a digital assistant to check their pronunciation, develop their fluency, rely on it to provide them with one-on-one individualized support for engaging in language learning and language practice, and provide a device where they can also interact not just with an AI but with other learners as well (via voice chat).

Ultimately, the SAMR model illustrates how the use of digital assistants with learners allows their use to redefine the learning space for students, and you as a teacher, by replacing traditional teaching methods or learner interactions with alternates that add value. Keeping a model such as the above in mind when reviewing different technologies for language learning and teaching will help you to identify how best to capitalize on providing learning from within your specific educational context with them and, ultimately too, if they may in fact be worthwhile utilizing.

Workbook Activity 8.1

Consider the following, and, and complete the appropriate section in the associated workbook.

> **8.1** Select a technology for language learning that you might want to implement in your learning and teaching context. It may have a direct student-support, teacher-support, administrative, or other purpose. Align use of the application with the SAMR model, and complete the table in the appropriate section of the associated workbook.

Summary

- The skills, competencies, and proficiencies required of 21st century learners.
- The importance of a community of practice and lifelong learning, and why it is important to be able to implement, manage, and work with, and alongside, new technologies.
- The need for practitioners to develop and maintain a range of 21st century teacher skills.
- The place and integration into the teaching and learning sphere of technological, pedagogical and content knowledge.
- How to interpret technologies in light of the substitution, modification, augmentation, and redefinition model.

References

Anderson, M. (2013, May 28). *Technological pedagogical and content knowledge.* ICT Evangelist. https://ictevangelist.com/technological-pedagogical-and-content-knowledge

Crystal, (2006). *Language and the internet.* Cambridge University Press.

Downes, S. (2010). New technology supporting informal learning. *Journal of Emerging Technologies in Web Intelligence, 2*(1), 27-33.

Gee, J. P. (2004). *Situated language and learning: A critique of traditional schooling.* Routledge.

Hao, K. (2019. August 02). *China has started a grand experiment in AI eduction. It could reshape how the world learns.* MIT Technology Review. https://fully-human.org/wp-content/uploads/2019/09/China-AI-experiment-education.pdf

Indriyanti, R., & Prasetyo, X. (2018). Improving the experiment report writing skills of fifth graders thorough the discovery learning method. *Jural Prima Edukasia, 6*(102). https://doi.org/10.21831/jpe.v6i1.17284

Kent, D. (Ed.). (2019). *The fourth industrial revolution and education: Digital language learning.* KOTESOL DCC.

Koehler, M., & Mishra, P. (2009). What is technological pedagogical content knowledge? *Contemporary Issues in Technology and Teacher Educaiton, 9*(1), 60-70.

Kulkarni, A. (2019). *AI in education: Where is it now and what is the future?* Lexalytics. https://www.lexalytics.com/lexablog/ai-in-education-present-future-ethics

Lave, J., & Wagner, E. (1991). *Situated learning: legitimate peripheral participation*. Cambridge University Press.

Levesque, H. (2014). On our best behavior. *Artificial Intelligence, 212*, 27-35. https://doi.org/10.1016/j.artint.2014.03.007

Mandinach, E., & Cline, H. (1993). Classroom Dynamics: Implementing a technology-based learning environment. Routledge.

Marr, D. (1982). *Vision*. MIT Press.

Matthee, D. (2018). *TPACK for the 21st-century educator*. ITSI Holdings. https://itsieducation.com/tpack-for-the-21st-century-educator

Mikolov, Tomas, Ilya Sutskever, Kai Chen, Greg Corrado, and Jeffrey Dean. (2013). Distributed representations of words and phrases and their compositionality. *Advances in Neural Information Processing Systems, 26*, 3111-3119. https://dl.acm.org/doi/10.5555/2999792.2999959

Mishra, P., & Koehler, M. (2006). Technological pedagogical content knowledge (TPCK): A framework for teacher knowledge. Teachers *College Record, 108*(6), 1017-1054.

Mishra, P., & Koehler, M. (2007). Technological pedagogical content knowledge (TPCK): Confronting the wicked problems of teaching with technology. In R. Carlson, K. Mcferrin, J. Price, R. Weber & D. Willis (Eds.), *Proceedings of the Society for Information Technology & Teacher Education International Conference* (2214-2226). Association for the Advancement of Computing in Education (AACE).

Oufela, Y. (2021). 21st century teacher skills. *Teachopians*. https://teachingutopians.com/2019/05/25/a-list-of-the-most-critical-21st-century-skills-teachers-should-have/?fbclid=IwAR22D7aJt31-ZaRDo285poj2S_oI_-OWFhUz9NYC85rLObzhq0MYCNkXx4w

Saubern, R. (2020). Is TPACK a Theory? In D. Schmidt-Crawford (Ed.), *Proceedings of the Society for Information Technology & Teacher Education International Conference,* (1958-1964). Association for the Advancement of Computing in Education (AACE).

Shulman, L. (1886). Those who understand: Knowledge growth in teaching. *Educational Researcher, 14*(2), 4-14. https://doi.org/10.3102/0013189X015002004

Siemens, G. (2005). Connectivism: A learning theory for the digital age. *International Journal of Instructional Technology and Distance Learning,* 2(1).

Slough, S., & Slough, P. (2015). 21st century pedagogical content knowledge. In S. Carliner, C. Fulford, & N Ostashewski (Eds.), *Proceedings of EdMedia 2015 – World Conference on Educational media and Technology,* (1101-1108). Association for the Advancement of Computing in Education (AACE).

Starky, L. (2012). *Teaching and learning in the digital age.* Routledge.

Trilling, B., & Fadel, C. (2009). *21st Century Skills: Learning for life in our times.* Jossey-Bass.

Toffler, A. (1970). *Future Shock.* United States: Random House.

Touretzky, D., & Gardner-McCune, C. (2022, in press). Artificial intelligence thinking in K-12. In S. Kong & H. Abelson (Eds), *Computational thinking in K-12: Artificial intelligence literacy and physical computing* (pp x-x). MIT Press.

Walker, A., & White, G. (2013). *Technology enhanced language learning.* Oxford University Press.

9. Digital Assistants and Voice User Interfaces

Overview

In recent years, disruptive technologies have seen how our students interact with us as teachers change, and transformed how we as teachers prepare and provide learning opportunities. For teachers too, there may also be a change with 'whom' we will teach, and how we might next begin to integrate artificial intelligence (AI) based digital assistants into the classroom as teaching aides or personal learning companions for students. Speaking to machines, and seeing or hearing appropriate responses actioned, provides learners with a reason to speak that is not contrived and one that is inherently motivating and meaningful. To this end, the pedagogical affordances offered by digital assistants are explored in this chapter, along with the means of utilizing them with learners and by teachers. The types of digital assistant, and a number of example activities and use-case scenarios are presented, as well as a means for creating content for digital assistant use.

Learning Outcomes

1. Learn about the different types of digital assistant.
2. Understand the pedagogical affordances offered by digital assistants, and how these might be best implemented with learners.
3. Consider the means of utilizing digital assistants with learners across a range of scenarios.
4. Review and develop example activities and scenarios for use with a digital assistant for both learners and their teachers.
5. Explore content creation for digital assistant use.

Digital Assistants

Digital assistants, AI assistants, or virtual assistants are all names for similar means of supporting a natural way of interacting with machines, each other, and the world around us. They are software-based agents that are able to perform a variety of tasks or services for individuals. They may be run as independent applications or they may be housed in a smart speaker, and although they can work using a variety of interfaces, the most popular is that of a VUI (voice-user interface). In this way, digital assistants are being used to implement a more natural means of interaction between human and machine while also providing increased accessibility options, especially for those with visual impairments. To date, digital assistants are being used for a variety of activities including: the control of home automation (e.g., lights, heating/cooling); the retrieval of real-time data (e.g., news, weather, stocks, commute information, and general information); the reading of audiobooks; the streaming of music or video; the keeping of calendars, shopping lists, reminders, and to-do lists; while also texting, making phone calls, or booking reservations on your behalf; and, the purchasing of products (including food) while tracking and notifying you of delivery.

Types of Digital Assistants

There are several types of digital assistant, and the most well-known of them all might be *Alexa, Bixby, Cortana, the Google Assistant*, and *Siri*. All of these digital assistants are capable of a variety of tasks including voice interaction, music and video playback, creating to-do lists, setting alarms, streaming media, playing audiobooks, telling stories, playing trivia games, and providing real-time information (such as news, weather, traffic conditions, and sports scores), while also controlling a variety of smart devices. Pressing a button, or using a wake-word, activates each assistant.

Alexa

Alexa was developed by Amazon and initially released in November of 2014. It can be found in devices such as the Amazon range of smart speakers. The wake-word can be set by the user, with the default being *Alexa*. The assistant is also available as an application for smartphones and tablets.

Bixby

Bixby was developed by Samsung Electronics and initially released in April of 2017, and it is the voice-powered assistant used on the range of Samsung smartphones and tablets. It is activated with a button press.

Cortana

Cortana was developed by Microsoft and initially released in April of 2014. It is the virtual assistant for Windows 10 and other related

Microsoft products (including smartphones, tablets, Xbox, band fitness tracker, surface headphones, and Windows mixed reality). It also runs on the invoke smart speaker, Android, and iOS. If the always-listening mode has been selected in Windows, then the wake-phrase 'Hey, Cortana' can be used to activate the assistant.

Google Assistant

Google Assistant was developed by Google and initially released in May of 2016. It is primarily accessible on mobile and smart home devices as well as Google smartphones and Android devices including Wear OS. It is also available as a stand-alone application for iOS. The wake-phrases for the assistant include 'Hey, Google', and 'OK, Google'.

Sam

Sam, in development by Samsung electronics in 2021, is a 3D virtual assistant that is capable of natural language processing and being able to carry out a full range of interactions from single tasks to being able to identify what a user's needs may be, even when they do not speak them. It designed to auto-respond to consumer questions and queries (Finn, 2021).

Siri

Siri was developed by Apple Inc. and released in October of 2011. It is the virtual assistant that became part of iOS, watchOS, MacOs, the HomePod, and tvOS. As an application, it was initially released in February of 2010 for iOS. It can also be accessed through the latest version of the MacOS and Apple CarPlay. The wake-phrase for this assistant is 'Hey, Siri'.

Digital Assistants in the Classroom

While paramount for language learning, conversation practice can often prove difficult to obtain and if continually attending classes, expensive to engage in. Digital assistants can serve as a means of providing this practice, especially if integrated into the teaching and learning context both at home and in the classroom (Underwood, 2018). However, the long-term effect of digital assistants and students' perceptions of digital assistants as language learning companions, along with the usefulness of such devices for language learning, remains until now largely unexplored. What we do know is that they can provide a means of interaction that lowers the affective filter (Brown, 2014) of students, which can then lead to the promotion of speaking that is not necessarily contrived. Speaking to machines, and seeing or hearing appropriate responses actioned, provides learners with a reason to speak that is inherently motivating and meaningful (Underwood, 2018).

The significance, then, that this kind of technology affords teachers if integrated into the classroom is that it can be used to provide support for tasks and classroom management while also delivering opportunities for voice-driven learning for students. Also, for learners, both in and outside of the classroom, these devices have the potential to provide one-on-one individualized support for engaging in language learning and language practice (Winkler & Sollner, 2018), as well as for learning in general.

Digital Assistants in the Language Learning Classroom

Working with digital assistants in the language learning classroom is mainly about creating more meaningful speaking opportunities that are integrated in sensible ways to prepare students to use that language in the future (Underwood, 2017). This is particularly important as our students will now be living with AI as part of their daily lives, and they need to know how to engage critically and actively with these intelligences. This is especially relevant now as 70% of children aged 8-17 are using voice-assisted technologies, predominantly for information searches, but also to ask questions, play music, and to get advice or help (UK Safer Internet Centre, 2018). This also illustrates that there is now no need to memorize facts or figures, as these are all available instantly. However, students do need to know how to assess this information and determine how best to apply it for their needs, for solving problems, for completing specific tasks, or for achieving particular outcomes.

Teachers incorporating digital assistants into the classroom or for use with learners need to think about what it is that the AI should be doing, and how this changes the role of language facilitation. For example, establishing an environment where students can work in an atmosphere that supports self, partner, and teacher collaboration with the AI, and one that seeks to provide a means of scaffolding and social interaction as they learn (Vygotsky, 1978). Utilization of AI can also assist teachers in identifying student knowledge gaps particularly when analyzing transcripts of interaction to identify learner needs (e.g., vocabulary improvement, and structure practice), while outside of the classroom, students can use them as language learning companions (e.g., helping them to complete homework, and providing access to additional tutoring or study programs).

Digital assistants for language learners can also provide students with the opportunity to go from the learning of speech to the written word, instead of the other way around. So, it changes the nature of learning. So too, instant access to translations, and with the ability of an AI to make phone calls and have conversations in any language on our behalf (for example, booking a haircut, see Alfa Tech, 2018) clearly illustrates that the reasons humans will have to learn a new language will change.

Digital Assistant Advantages and Disadvantages for Language Learning

Digital assistants offer several affordances, but also come with several shortcomings that you as a teacher will need to consider and aim to circumvent when implementing the technology.

Some of the main advantages that digital assistants present include:
1. Natural interaction, with instant real-time responses that can encourage motivation and learner engagement while lowering their affective filter.
2. Authentic content exposure, particularly when asking factual questions or for further information on a given topic, including spelling and vocabulary. This is effective for learning as it provides students with personalized, and as such, more useful feedback.
3. Active (speaking) and passive (listening) skills development, while also helping students focus upon pronunciation as they communicate their message or intents.
4. Interaction (Chapelle, 2015) that sees students being able to engage in the negotiation of meaning, obtain enhanced input, and direct their attention to linguistic forms.

5. Support for several learning methods and approaches (including game-play).
6. Additional learning pathways for students with various disabilities. This includes those who are visually-impaired, dyslexic, or have dysgraphia, along with those who may have hearing disabilities if screen-based digital assistants are employed.

Shortcomings might arise from:
1. Frustrations, when user commands and questions or responses are continuously misheard, or not understood (especially if students have speech difficulties). This can be alleviated by the instructor guiding students with appropriate models that can be used, helping students understand why the miscommunication occurred, working with the assistant to have it understand what is trying to be communicated, and helping students to work out how to use language to get the answers that they need. This also allows teachers to focus on getting students to think critically, and to help them develop higher-order thinking skills.
2. Fossilization/stabilization might occur as the assistants can understand sentences and utterances that are not always grammatically correct. This does allow students to continuously engage with the device as they are understood and are able to communicate, and it also provides teachers with the opportunity to provide better models for students to practice using with the device.
3. Privacy concerns might need to be considered as the device can record what is being said and asked of it. This does provide an opportunity to raise e-safety concerns and data protection questions with learners. Checking the transcripts of the device after class can also allow instructors to see how students interact with the assistant, and this provides opportunities to analyze student utterances for grammar issues and to see if new vocabulary is being integrated into their language output.
4. Accessibility issues as internet access needs to be stable and reliable for use with these devices. Otherwise, the device may not function at all or it may have trouble retrieving or playing back content.

5. Inappropriateness may arise with particular students asking questions that are rude or distracting. One way to counter this is to discuss responsibilities such as digital citizenship before using the digital assistants in class, and to ensure that learners understand that the device is going to know what they have asked it, and that others will also hear what they say.

6. Voice recognition may be an issue with a rowdy class or many students speaking at the same time. However, this could help develop turn-taking skills in students.

Using Digital Assistants with Learners

As with other technologies, the use of a digital assistant with language learners needs to be guided, with the teacher perhaps preparing content or worksheets that can be utilized with the digital assistant in order to promote the learning outcomes desired. It is a good idea to start small, and keep a list of voice commands or actions and skills handy for teacher and student reference, especially the ones that you would like to try, or find yourself and your pupils using frequently (see Appendix A for some examples). Alternatively, if using actions or skills that involve listening to interactive stories, then activity sheets such as that in Appendix B could be used with learners as an add-on, along with other extension activities (such as those in Appendix C) which focus on word forms for the unknown vocabulary that students have met while listening.

Additionally, when initially starting out, it is important to set guidelines of use for students. You may wish to allow only one student at a time to access the device. In this way, you can then begin to track the kinds of questions or phrases that students are using so that you can record the ones that work (or the ones you would like to provide modeling for). Use of the device in the classroom can also be added to such concepts as the 'ask 3 before me' rule, where students need to talk to three peers in order to learn how to solve an issue or problem before going to the instructor (with the digital assistant counted as one of these peers).

Keep in mind that while *Google Assistant actions* and *Alexa skills* offer a variety of ways to interact with the digital assistants these are developed by the associated companies as well as third-party developers, so build quality and usability prior to use do need to be assessed. Assessing the potential use or modification of the actions or skills that are available through a digital assistant is always important, as it is with any learning material developed by another teacher for use with your own students and teaching style. The *Alexa Skills* section of the Amazon website provides a complete listing of all the Skills that are available to the digital assistant [Link: https://www.amazon.com/alexa-skills/b?ie=UTF8&node=13727921011]. Each listing is available by category and provides information on how to utilize the skill. On the other hand, *Google Assistant Actions* is the website that lists all of the actions available for the Google Assistant [Link: https://assistant.google.com/explore]. Each listing is available by category or search, and provides information about the action as well as what devices and platforms it can be used on.

Essentially, there are three main ways that an instructor may wish to integrate the use of Digital assistants with their learners:
1. for classroom management and teaching purposes,
2. for learning purposes, and
3. as a personal language companion outside of the classroom for students themselves.

These can be broken down into two broad categories: classroom management, and language-learning actions and skills. Both of these categories house content that learners can access when using digital assistants as a personal language companion.

Classroom Management Actions and Skills

From a classroom management perspective, digital assistants provide a gamete of options to employ that include:

Teaching Aide. Digital assistants can take on a number of the activities that a teacher's aide performs. It can be used by students individually to ask questions, including those that can help to develop self-guided learning. It can also be used by teachers to answer any questions that students may pose during a teacher-directed activity, or during homework checks (e.g., spelling words or providing answers to set questions). In this way, students can also hear models of speech to employ with the digital assistant, and see what kinds of answers return. If asking questions of students and they take a little too long to answer, you could request the digital assistant to provide a drum roll before the answer, or a round of applause if the answer is correct.

Timers and Reminders. Timers can be employed to help learners to stay on track, to signify the end of an activity, and when it is time to transition to the next stage of an activity. Timers can also help with students who struggle with organization, serving as reminders to take medications for example. To control timers with a digital assistant phrases such as *'Start [five] minute timer'* can be used. Reminders can be set based on time or location, and are set by saying *'Set a reminder [for Brad to take his medication]'*, or *'Set a reminder for [students to change partners/take an exercise break]'*.

Choosing Volunteers and Team Leaders. Random number generation can be used to select students based on their roll sheet order by saying *'Pick a number between [x] and [y]'*. Heads or tails (available by saying *'Heads or tails'*) or rock, paper, scissors (available by saying *'Play rock, paper, scissors'*) can also be used to select those who will be a team captain, those who might lead a presentation or take the first turn in an activity, and so on.

Streaming Content. A variety of audio and video is available for streaming in the classroom through digital assistants. They are able to play white noise by saying *'Play [white noise/rain forest sounds/beach noises]'*. Music can also be streamed by saying *'Play [artist name/genre of music/song name]'*, with video displayed on TVs and controlled from the device if using Chromecast or a Fire TV Stick by saying *'Play [artist name/genre of music/song name/movie name/TV episode name and number] on [Chromecast/Fire TV Stick]'*. Saying *'Play [podcast/podcast number]'* can also be used to playback podcasts for class listening, with other content like news also available by saying *'What's the latest news?'* Streaming of audiobooks and the reading of a Kindle book is also possible using Alexa.

Language-Learning Actions and Skills

From a language-learning perspective, a number of options are available that both learners and teachers will find useful. Of note, when asking for information, the devices may also forward additional links to the device application on a smartphone, or these may appear on the devices display if it has one.

Answering Inquiries. Specific fact-based questions can be asked of digital assistants, and these can be used to obtain general information or to help conduct specific tasks. For example: conducting research for a writing assignment; listening to information before performing a retelling task; completing questions assigned by the teacher on a specific topic; or for getting information on the vocabulary or themes under study in any given unit. Digital assistants can also be used to assist students in completing WebQuests, which are activities that require students to take on a role and perform certain tasks that involve both data collection and fact-checking guided by an inquiry-based process (Levin-Goldberg, 2014). Any factual-based question can be asked and answered on any topic or unit that students are studying, from hobbies through to travel and entertainment, along with statistical and historical information, recipes, conversions, jokes, and real-time information such as temperature, weather, store hours, and news. Unique Actions such as *Safari Mixer* which uses voice prompts to ask what kind of body parts an animal has in order to create a new animal, can see the Google Assistant asking questions of students [Link: https://safarimixer.beta.rehab]. Once the questions are answered, an image of the animal that was created is then sent to the user's phone. The noise that new animal makes is played along with a fun 'fact' about the animal, leading to reading practice and vocabulary-development opportunities.

Vocabulary, Pronunciation, and Writing. A variety of simple questions can be used with digital assistants that can help with the acquisition of vocabulary, its pronunciation, and in the writing of these terms. These include:
- *'How do you spell [word/phrase]?'*
- *'What is the definition/meaning/synonym/antonym of [word/phrase]?'* *'Define [word/phrase].'* *'What is a [word/phrase]?'*
- *'How do you pronounce [word/spelled out word by letter]?'*

- *'What is the plural of [word]?'*
- *'Translate [word/phrase] to [language].' 'How do I/you say [word/phrase] in [language]?'*
- *'Repeat [word/phrase].'*

The teacher can also provide controlled practice tasks such as using the spelling ability of the assistant and having students ask it to spell hard-to-distinguish sounds (e.g., minimal pairs, such as *ship/sheep*). Just saying *'Tell me a new word'* to Google Assistant, or activating skills such as *Daily Word* on Alexa, can also be used to expand vocabulary [Link: https://www.amazon.com/Matchbox-mobile-Daily-Word/dp/B017VAOYN0]. Consider also perhaps preparing a pronunciation activity focusing on tongue twisters with a digital assistant add-on component (see Appendix D for an example).

Listening and Speaking. Games like Simon Says, can also be played using the assistant to actively practice listening skills. Student directed free talk can also be conducted, where students brainstorm their own questions (based on the unit theme), try asking them of the digital assistant in a kind of trial and error language use, and making note of and, depending on the level, discussing the answers that result. For lower level learners, challenges such as, *'Which group can get all the answers from the digital assistant first?'* might inspire increased language output and input. An example activity might involve students practicing wh-type questions (see Appendix E, which provides an example sheet of wh-type questions with a grammar and speaking focus, and one that also sees students seeking answers from their partner as well as the digital assistant in practice).

Reading and Writing. As a reading assistant, Alexa has access to audio books and can read Kindle content. Google through *Story Speaker* [Link: https://workspace.google.com/u/1/marketplace/app/story_speaker/888339379807], and Alexa through *Invocable* [Link: https://invocable.com], allows for the development of actions and skills that can read back blocks of text that students have previously met during study, with the instructor developing questions for review and those that move students on to more text and practice with content.

Creating Content. Creating a voice-driven application cannot only help students in the reading and writing process, but it also gets students started with developing the kinds of digital skills that they will need in the future. During such a process, they will also need to think critically and creatively about language and communication in terms of how they use language, the questions that they need to ask, questions that they expect someone might ask a digital assistant, and all of the ways that those questions then need answering. *Alexa Blueprints* [Link: https://blueprints.amazon.com], and Google Voice Experiments such as *Story Speaker* [Link: https://workspace.google.com/u/1/marketplace/app/story_speaker/888339379807] might be used to assist learners (and even teachers) in developing skills without coding, while developing actions with voiceflow can be achieved from within the *Google Actions Console* [Link: https://developers.google.com/assistant/console].

Games. A variety of games exist that are worthwhile for language learning via a digital assistant. These include flash-card and trivia-based games that can be used for review, speaking, listening, vocabulary, or pronunciation practice. If a teacher is time poor, then they may rely on ready-made games that are available and include those that have a Jeopardy! style format or those that are similar to Twenty Questions. These might include *Mystery Animal*, where the assistant pretends to be an animal and users need to guess what animal it is by asking relevant questions [Link: https://mysteryanimal.withgoogle.com]. Questions need to be those that draw a yes or no answer, such as *'Do you have feathers?', 'Do you sleep at night?'*. It can be played on Google Assistant or on the website [Link: https://mysteryanimal.withgoogle.com]. An alternative for Alexa is *Twenty Questions* [Link: https://www.amazon.com/Amazon-Twenty-Questions/dp/B01C3CO48G], where the digital assistant will attempt to guess the animal, vegetable, mineral, or music-related item that you or a student has chosen.

Stories. The educational value of storytelling and using stories for teaching is undisputed (Kalantari & Hashemian, 2015). The stories presented by digital assistants include short stories such as fairy tales as well as those stories that are quite interactive, and these are the choose-your-own adventure type stories. In either case, there are a number of ways to extend the potential that such stories provide. Students can listen to the stories, or work their way through them, and then complete a retelling task by paraphrasing the story in spoken or written form. They can also be asked to write a dialogue between two of the main characters (which in the choose-your-own adventure would include the student). They could also be provided with a handout from which they could be asked to summarize the story in three sentences, including the main character(s), the setting, conflict, climax, and resolution, or simply write one sentence on the theme of the story (see Appendix B).

Teachers can also ask various follow-up questions and have students complete word-form charts for terms that learners had to use in order to progress through interactive stories. For example, completing the participle, adjective, noun, verb, and adverb forms for their choices using a pre-fabricated handout (see Appendix C). Learners can also compile a list of terms that they do not understand as they progress through the story, and later ask the digital assistant how to spell these words, the definition for them, a synonym, an antonym, and the translation. Students might also engage in writing their own choose-your-own adventure type stories using applications like *Story Speaker* [Link: https://workspace.google.com/u/1/marketplace/app/story_speaker/888339379807] to create Actions for the Google Assistant or *Invocable* to create skills for Alexa [Link: https://invocable.com]. In these cases, they could be given a scenario such as being tech support where they need to think through a story process where various clients might telephone them with computer problems, and they need to offer solutions. They could also be given a scenario where they take a short holiday and have to choose between a cheap or expensive hotel, and go on to provide interactions and (mis)adventures that can be experienced while on holiday (see Appendix F). If students are not up to the challenge of developing an action or using a template to create a skill for their own interactive stories, there are many other types of templates available to create skills, and a walkthrough of using one will be provided a little later.

An existing interactive story, provided through Alexa, is that of *My African Safari* [Link: https://www.amazon.com/Zengrant-My-African-Safari/dp/B07BJLSV9M]. It takes users to Kruger National Park in South Africa, and provides a variety of experiences over two chapters, eight stories, and 26 possible endings.

Another interactive story is that of *Magic Door* [Link: https://www.amazon.com/The-Magic-Door-LLC/dp/B01BMUU6JQ]. It spans various regions, such as a castle, garden, forest, and the sea. The intent of the story is to have listeners solve riddles, collect hidden items, and help magical creatures as they progress through the story. In order to explore the entire land, the skill description states the following as the order to use:

1. Take the garden path in the mountains to help the Princess find her crown.
2. Talk to the rabbit in the garden and find his eggs hidden beyond the gate.
3. Take the forest path in the mountains to help the gnome find the key to his home.
4. Take the boat across the sea to the tropical island to help a family of monkeys.
5. Follow the fiddle along the sea to a fortune teller who will direct you to a haunted lighthouse.
6. Travel up the bluff along the sea to gather items for the gnome with the flute.
7. Explore various lands to gather potion ingredients to grow a fern to the clouds.
8. Travel to the dark forest and search the witch's mansion for the wise wizard.
9. Journey past the garden gate to the holiday party in the princess' castle.
10. Search for the wizard in his tower, repair his broken mirror, and collect his wand.
11. Finally, meet the wise wizard in the ancient temple and help him turn back time.

Songs, and Streaming Content. Songs are a staple of many language teachers' classrooms, and for good reason. They offer a variety of new vocabulary and can be chosen to suit the needs and interests of students. They can also be used to introduce slang and cultural aspects of a language. So too, the common repetitive pattern found in songs can assist learners in the practice of syntax and semantics while they internalize language from a meaningful learning context (Romero, 2017). A number of sing-along skills are available for Alexa, while Google

Assistant can play back karaoke versions of songs. Further, skills might be used by learners to turn any spoken phrase or simple message into a musical ditty by matching it to popular music (which can then be shared via Twitter). Example sentences from the text or what students create can be used for this purpose. If students are interested in creating music, then the *Google Assistant Mixlab* [Link: https://mixlab.withgoogle.com] might be a more preferred Action, with users creating music by using voice-commands such as *'Play me a funky bass'* or *'Add some jazz drums'*. It can be played on Google Home or on the website. Also, for those students who might require white noise to concentrate, a variety of options are available by saying *'Play [white noise/rain forest sounds/beach noises].'* Music can also be streamed by saying *'Play [artist name/genre of music/song name]'* with video displayed on TVs and controlled from the device if using Chromecast or a Fire TV Stick by saying *'Play [artist name/genre of music/song name/movie name/TV episode name and number] on [Chromecast/Fire TV Stick].'* Streaming potential for podcasts and other content is also available by saying *'Play [podcast/podcast number]'*; *'What's the latest news?'*; or *'Read'*, *'Get audible'*, *'Read Kindle'* if using Alexa to read audio books.

Formative Assessment. Opportunities exist for the teacher to access the transcripts of what students have said to the digital assistant, and to utilize this data to undertake continuous formative assessment. For example, if you have set an activity that requires students to use set phrases, vocabulary, and structures with the digital assistant you would be able to review the transcript of the session parsing it through such websites as the *Compleat Lexical Tutor* in order to profile the vocabulary and grammar used [Link: https://www.lextutor.ca].This would then allow teachers to identify which aspects of language use students may need to work on further, and what could be covered more extensively in other classes and for review.

Additional Voice-Based Content

Teachers and students should keep in mind that digital assistants are not the only voice user interface that they have access to, and that there are a number of websites that also provide such opportunities as working with speech as part of activities and in order to gain information. These include:

- *Dictation.io* is a website that uses Chrome to provide speech recognition for dictation. It helps to write emails, documents, and essays using only voice [Link: https://dictation.io].
- *Dumpling the Pug* provides a voice-user interface to control the actions of a virtual pug. Commands can be given in English or in Mandarin Chinese [Link: https://www.dumplingthe pug.com/pug-vr].
- *Forvo* is the largest pronunciation dictionary in the world. The aim of the website is to have a database consisting of all the vocabulary from every language in the world pronounced by native speakers. You can type in a word to hear its pronunciation [Link: https://forvo.com].
- *The Peanut Gallery* is a Google Chrome extension that allows users to select short movies to subtitle with text produced from their speech [Link: https://chrome.google.com/webstore/ detail/peanut-gallery/lhbgfmofpkinopfbafkklckgbkojgknp?hl= et].

Workbook Activity 9.1

Consider the following, and then respond in the associated workbook.

9.1a Have you ever used a digital assistant in the language learning classroom before? If so, in what ways?

9.1b What do you consider might be the possibilities and the difficulties involved with the use of such devices for language learning in the classroom and at home?

9.1c How might you use a digital assistant with your learners? Outline an example activity and provide an accompanying worksheet(s) to go along with it. Provide enough detail so that another instructor would be able to teach the activity or lesson with the outline and worksheet(s) that you have provided if they had to substitute for. You might like to consider some of the activities in the Appendices of this chapter to serve as inspiration to help you answer this question.

Creating Content for Use with a Digital Assistant

Digital assistant content can be created by coding, but there is an increasing number of templates and walkthroughs available for content creation of an action or skill. All of these can contain multimedia elements alongside voice components. For the Google Assistant, these are available from the *Actions on Google* website, and for Alexa, from the *Alexa Blueprints* website. Google also offers several voice experiments, of which *Story Speaker* is one.

Alexa Blueprints

Alexa Blueprints allows you to create personal Alexa skills, using a variety of templates, which include flash cards, trivia-based games, and stories through to customizations that can help extend the functionality of Alexa across devices such as the Echo smart speaker. Guided completion of templates is conducted while working online through the web page [Link: https://blueprints.amazon.com].

Actions on Google

Actions on Google allows you to create personal Google Assistant Actions ranging from those dealing with smart homes, food ordering, game, storytelling, and education. All of these can be used on Google assistant devices, such as the Google Nest, through to the Google Assistant application on smartphones. These are accessible through the Google actions console [Link: https://developers.google.com/assistant/console].

Story Speaker

Story Speaker is one of the many existing Google Assistant voice experiments, but do be aware that you may need to make use of a VPN or virtual private network in order to access it). It is a Chrome extension that allows you to use a Google Document to write a choose-your-own adventure type story that plays as an interactive talking story. The story can also be played through the Google digital assistant. [Link: https://experiments.withgoogle.com/story-speaker].

Developing Content for Digital Assistant Use

If you wish to go a little further with the use of digital assistants in the classroom you might like to start developing Actions and Skills. As such, the following section covers the development of a flash card based activity as an Alexa Skill, so that you can determine if this might be something that is best suited for you to do in your teaching and learning context.

Alexa Blueprints – Flashcards

In this example we will look at building a simple flashcard style voice user interface for language learners to help them in memorizing and practicing vocabulary recall. A walkthrough of the development process is listed below. You might also like to watch a short clip detailing a similar process, that of developing a geometry-based flashcard quiz (see *create Flashcard Skill for Alexa* [Video: https://www.youtube.com/watch?v=j9-RZw51Cbo].

Step One – Preparation

1. Go to *skill blueprints* [Link: https://blueprints.amazon.com]. Once you are at that page, on your home screen you will see a variety of skills listed by categories.
2. Under *Learning & Knowledge* you will find the skill *Flashcards* (see Figure 9.1). Click on 'Flashcards', and you will be taken to a page with an overview of the skill.

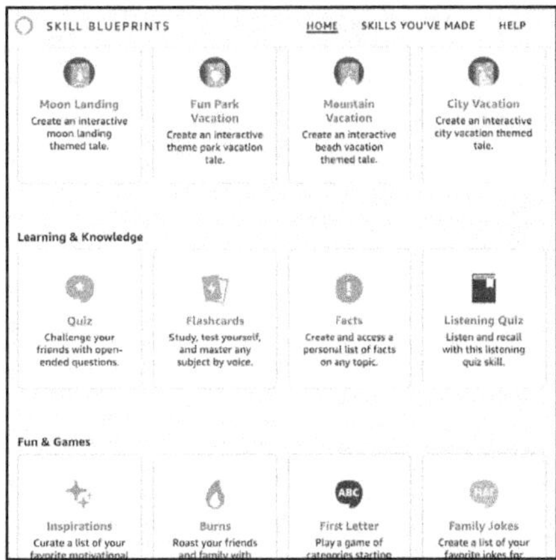

Figure 9.1 Skill blueprints

3.   After clicking on 'Flashcards' you will be taken to a page where you can see the invocation required to start the skill, and be on a page where you have the ability to play an audio sample of typical voice user interface interaction between a person and *Alexa* when using *My Flashcards*. You will also be able to see a list of the basic steps required to develop the skill under *How to create*, with the manner in which to start the skill and its two modes also depicted (under *How to use*), after which a number of other *Learning & Knowledge Blueprints* are available for selection. On this page, the blueprints *Flashcards* screen, start by clicking on 'MAKE YOUR OWN' (see Figure 9.2).

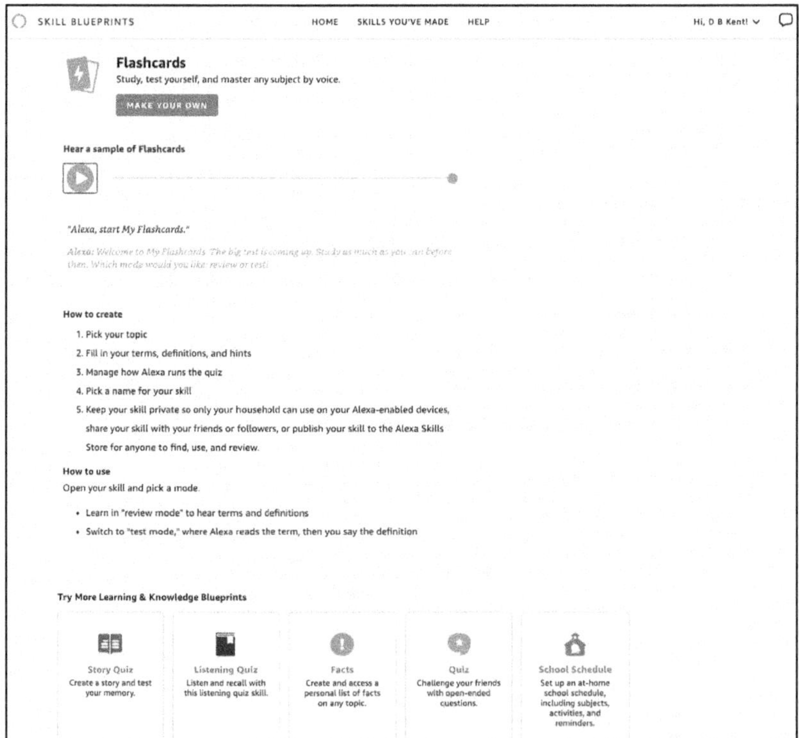

Figure 9.2 Flashcards Blueprint overview

Step Two – Building the Action

1. On the *Customize the cards* screen, you will be able to start setting up your Alexa Skill (see Figure 9.3).

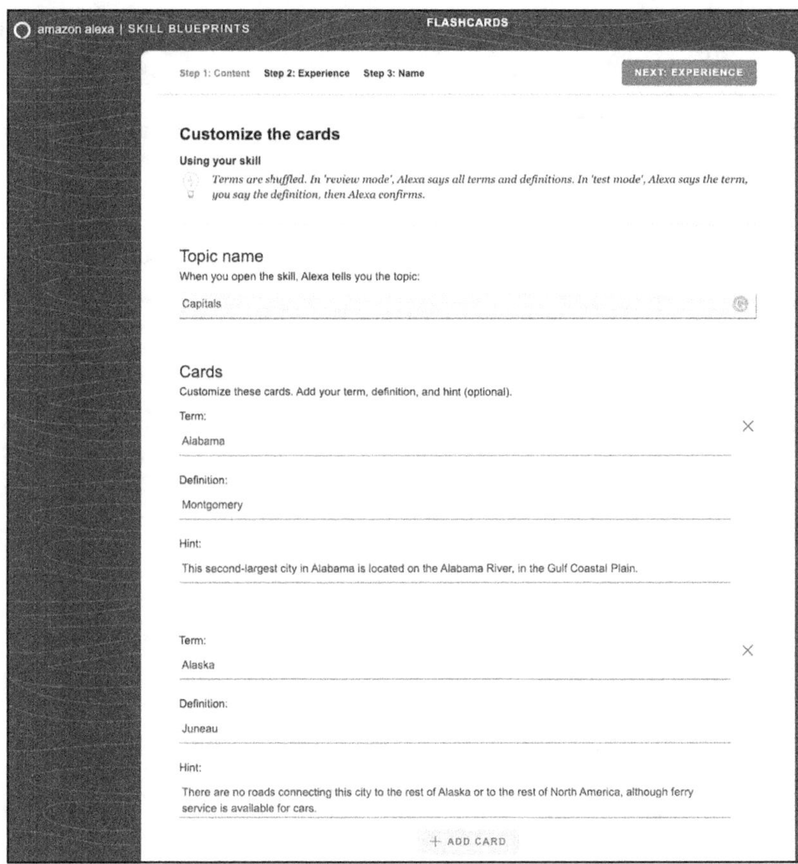

Figure 9.3 Customize the cards page

2. On the *Customize the cards* screen you will also see some sample cards, and you can feel free to look them over before deleting them (by clicking on the 'x' to the left of each). You will need to delete them as you will want to create your own.
3. Under *Topic name* type the topic of your flash card quiz (e.g., *British versus American English*).
4. Click 'add a card' at the bottom of the screen.
5. In the *Cards* section add a *Term* (e.g., *flashlight*).

6. In the *Cards* section provide a *Definition* (e.g., *torch*).
7. In the *Cards* section type in a *Hint* (e.g., *This term starts with a 'T'*).
8. To add another card click on 'add a card' at the bottom of the screen, following steps 5 through 7 using the appropriate term, definition, and hint for each card that you would now like to add (see Figure 9.4).

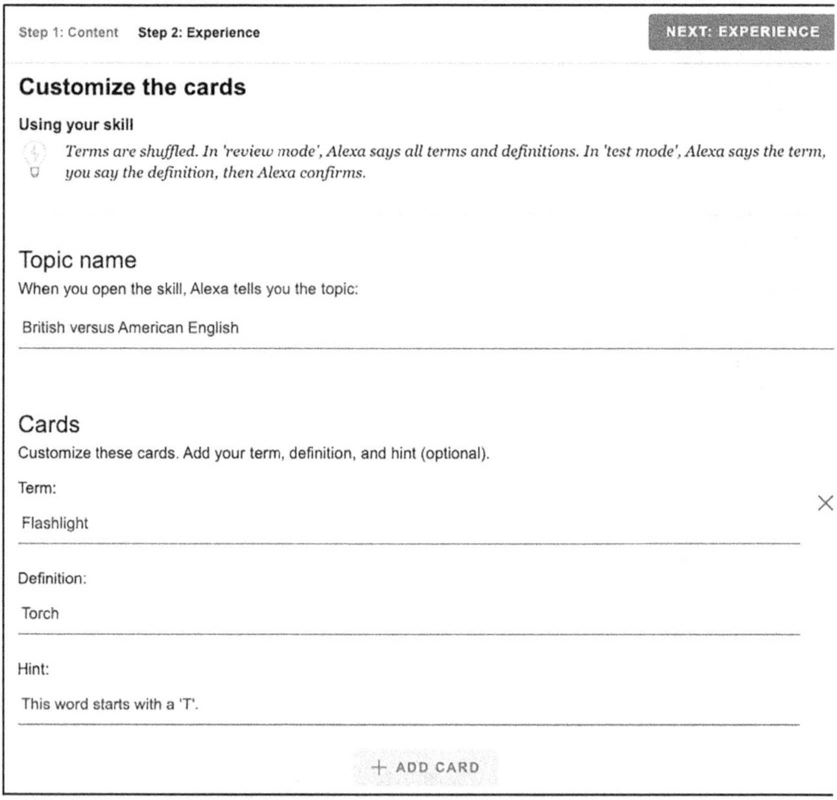

Step 1: Content   **Step 2: Experience**   **NEXT: EXPERIENCE**

Customize the cards

Using your skill

Terms are shuffled. In 'review mode', Alexa says all terms and definitions. In 'test mode', Alexa says the term, you say the definition, then Alexa confirms.

Topic name

When you open the skill, Alexa tells you the topic:

British versus American English

Cards

Customize these cards. Add your term, definition, and hint (optional).

Term:

Flashlight

Definition:

Torch

Hint:

This word starts with a 'T'.

+ ADD CARD

Figure 9.4 Add data to customize the cards

9. After clicking 'NEXT: EXPERIENCE' you will then be taken to the *Customize the experience* screen (see Figure 9.5), and it is here where you will then have the ability to customize the skill welcome message, card options, the exit message from Alexa, as well as some other options.

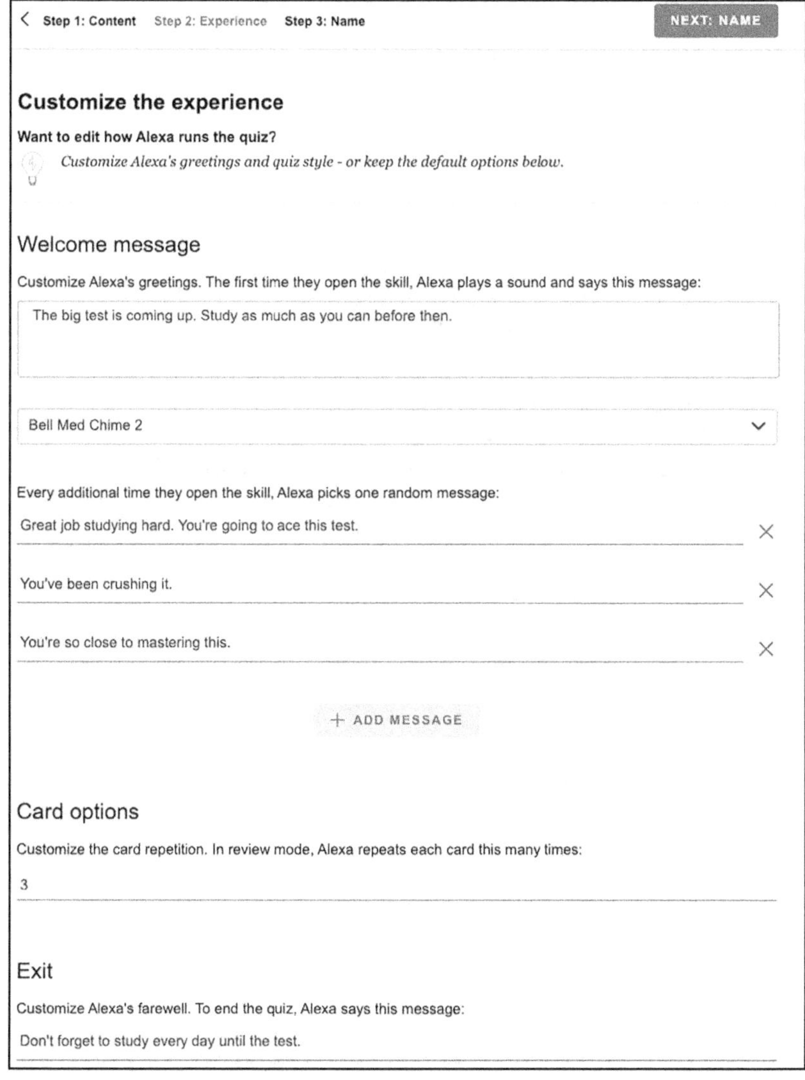

Figure 9.5 Customize the experience page

10. After customizing the experience click 'NEXT: NAME' at the top right of that page.

11. On the name page for your skill, type in the name that you will use to invoke the quiz to start. For example, *My traumatizing test* (see Figure 9.6). Then, click on 'NEXT: CREATE SKILL' at the top right of that page.

Figure 9.6 Customize the experience page

12. On the *Skills* page you will then see the details for the flashcard quiz that you just created (see Figure 9.7). You can then edit it further, delete it, change the invocation, or share it. You are also presented with a number of other skills that you might consider developing, such as those to deliver a listening quiz to students.

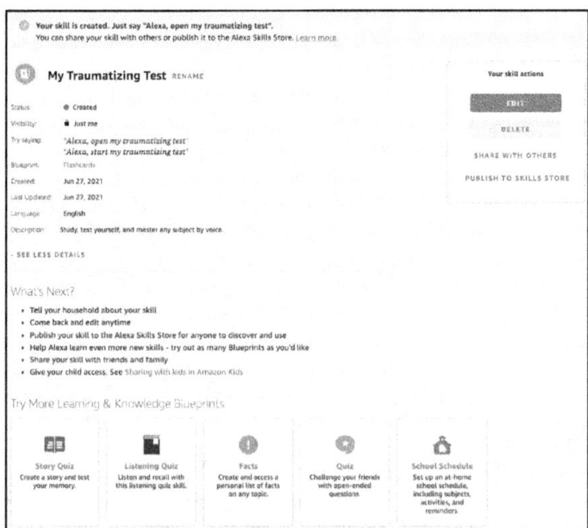

Figure 9.7 Skills page

13. You can also view all of the skills you have created and their status by visiting the *Skills you've made page* (see Figure 9.8).

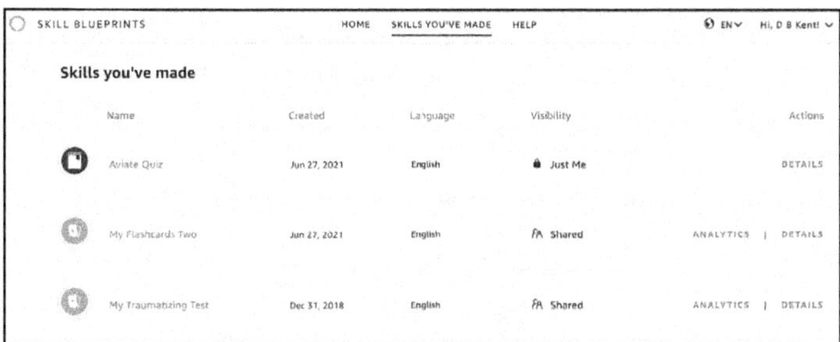

Figure 9.8 Skills you've made page

Story Speaker Google Chrome Extension – Choose-Your-Own-Adventure Story

Story Speaker is one of the many existing Google Assistant voice experiments. It is a Chrome extension that allows you to use a Google Document to write a choose-your-own adventure story that plays as an interactive talking story. It can also be modified and used to read blocks of text that students have previously met during study, with the instructor developing questions for review [Link: https://workspace.google.com/u/1/marketplace/app/story_speaker/888 339379807]. Do note that in recent months the ability to utilize the extension requires geolocating to the United States of America, but if you make use of a virtual private network (VPN) you may choose to explore development with it. As such, you might like to review the below walkthrough regarding its use. So that you can further understand the concept of the action, and follow the use of decision trees in development of an interactive story, an example short story developed for use with the extension is available to look over in Appendix F).

Preparation

You will need to have already prepared a choose-your-own-adventure story, or have permission to use one that someone else has developed, and one that you want to convert to a Google Action. The story does not have to be very long but it needs to have a decision tree that drives the forks provided as selections to the user. A mind-map program could be used to create the decision tree.

Begin by sketching out your story and writing it in blocks, with each block having a series of questions (forks) that will take the reader/listener to another story block. Story block questions might include:
1. People/creatures/things that the protagonist has met (e.g., friends, travelling companions, mythical creatures, peripheral characters).
2. Inventory that the protagonist carries/loses/requires (artifacts, clothing, food, money, weapons).
3. Possessing special abilities or knowledge (e.g., actions undertaken, meeting location objectives).
4. Achieving a goal (e.g., reaching a destination, slaying an enemy, finding love, finding a treasure, rescuing a prisoner or a princess).

Each story block then links to others, depending on the fork chosen by the reader/listener, until they reach a story ending. Here are five possible story endings.
1. The protagonist dies.
2. The protagonist is captured.
3. The protagonist fails in the quest.
4. The protagonist finds love.
5. The protagonist finds a treasure.

Once your story is complete, you will be able to use it to create an Action using the Google Voice Experiment Story Speaker.

Step One – Getting Started

To use Story Speaker, you need to install the Chrome extension.

1. Download and install the Chrome browser, then open it (if not already installed on your device).
2. Add the Story Speaker extension to the Chrome browser [Link: https://workspace.google.com/u/1/marketplace/app/story_spea ker/888339379807]. (As mentioned, the extension is now only available to those in the United States of America geolocation. So, you may need to use an appropriate VPN (virtual private network) if choosing to develop a story with the extension.
3. Open a new Google Document.
4. Click on the 'Add-ons' menu item, and select 'Story Speaker'.
5. Choose either the 'Basic Template' or the 'Advanced Template'. This guide will use the 'Basic Template'.
6. Click 'Yes' to clear the document and have Story Speaker load the Basic Template.

Using the Basic Template

Open a new Google Document, and open the template by clicking on new template, then:

1. From within the template, you will see links to a video, and Story Speaker 'docs'. It is advisable to both watch the video and read the document before moving on.
2. You can then begin to cut and paste your previously created choose-your-own adventure story into the Google Document.
3. Normal text represents Text-to-Speech (TTS), and this will be read aloud by the Google Assistant. Text that is in bold defines how the story will work, for example: it might represent choices that the listener can select to go to another story block. Story blocks need to have the same level of choice, and need to be indented to the same level across the page (see Figure 9.9).

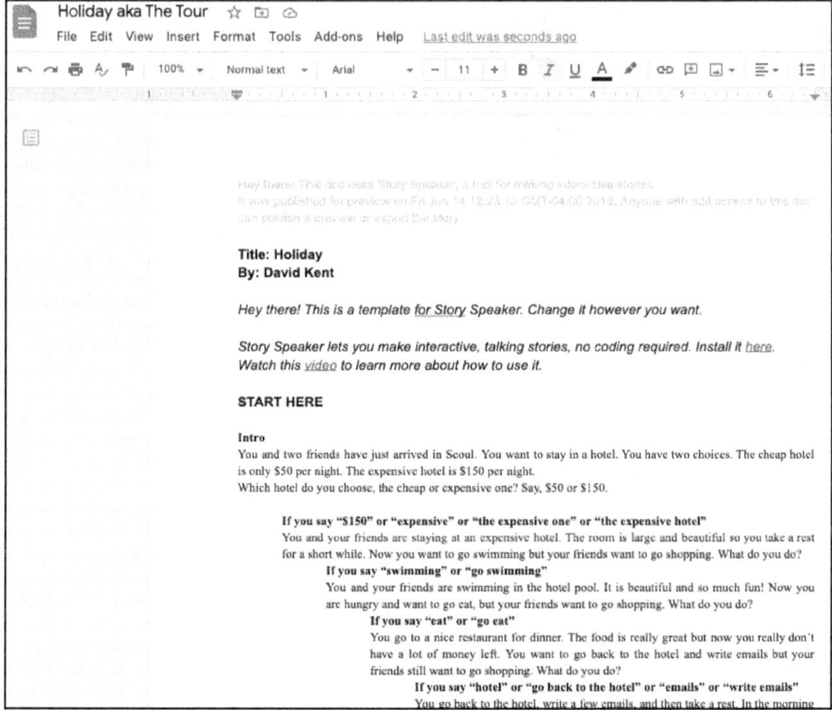

Figure 9.9 Story Speaker block choice levels and action workings

4. Each story should have a 'title' and an 'intro', but an author is not required.

5. Paths are the smallest section of a story. They have a bold line for a choice that a user can make (e.g., **If you say "right"**), and an unbold line for what the user will then hear (e.g., You walk down the path to the right).

6. Forks are moments when the listener can make a choice. To create a fork, indent a path below another path. For example, **Intro** is used to provide an introduction that presents a choice. The path then needs to be indented one level and the choices provided.

7. Choices can be provided with **If you say " "**.

8. 'Otherwises' can be used to respond to listeners when they do not choose one of the choices provided. They are created in the same way as a path with a bold line (e.g., **Otherwise**) and an unbold line for what the user will then hear (e.g., Sorry, I didn't catch that. Try saying 'right' or 'left'.

9. Story endings should use [[END]]. When the listener reaches an end, they will be given a choice to go back and restart the story. There can be multiple endings.

10. There are a number of other features and an advanced template to explore. However, the above should get you started with the process, and a complete story is included in Appendix F that illustrates how the choice levels, paths, forks, otherwises, and so on can be utilized in practice.

11. When you are ready to see how your story plays, select 'Play Your Story" from the sidebar on the right of the Google Document.

12. You can choose to play the story in a chat preview box or on your Google Home device.

Workbook Activity 9.2

Consider the following, and complete the appropriate section in the associated workbook.

> **9.2** Work with one of the templates available to create an Amazon Alexa skill.
>
> **a)** Detail the skill template that you have chosen,
>
> **b)** including the invocation,
>
> **c)** providing the particulars for your activity regarding the template chosen (e.g., how the activity works, along with the questions presented, such as the card terms, definitions, and hints if using the flashcard template), then
>
> **d)** note how you foresee yourself or your learners using the skill, considering also the benefits and disadvantages that you think that it might bring to your language learning and teaching process if you were to apply it in your educational context.

Summary

In this chapter you learned about:

- The different types of digital assistants.
- The pedagogical affordances offered by digital assistants, and how these might be best implemented with learners.
- The means of utilizing digital assistants with learners across a range of scenarios.
- Preparation of activities and scenarios for use with a digital assistant for both learners and their teachers.
- Content creation for digital assistant use.

Resources

Amazon. (2021). *Alexa Skills*. Alexa Features. https://www.amazon.com/alexa-skills/b?ie=UTF8&node=13727921011

Amazon. (2021). *Twenty Questions*. Alexa Skill. https://www.amazon.com/Amazon-Twenty-Questions/dp/B01C3CO48G

Amazon. (2021). *Skill Blueprints.* https://blueprints.amazon.com

Assistive Technology Blog. (2018, October 10). *Flashcard Skill for Alexa.* [Video]. YouTube. https://www.youtube.com/watch?v=j9-RZw51Cbo

Forvo Media S.L. (2021). *Forvo.* The pronunciation dictionary. https://forvo.com

Google. (2021). *Actions Console.* https://developers.google.com/assistant/console

Google. (2021). *Google assistant actions.* Hey Google. https://assistant.google.com/explore

Google. (2021). *Mixlab.* Voice experiment. https://mixlab.withgoogle.com

Google. (2021). *Mystery animal.* Voice Experiment. https://mysteryanimal.withgoogle.com

Google. (2021). *Peanut gallery.* Chrome extension. https://chrome.google.com/webstore/detail/peanut-gallery/lhbgfmofpkinopfbafkklckgbkojgknp?hl=et

Google. (2021). *Story speaker.* Voice experiment. https://workspace.google.com/u/1/marketplace/app/story_speaker/888339379807

Invocable. 2021. *Invocable.* Alexa skill creator. https://invocable.com

Matchbox Mobile (2021). *Daily word.* Alexa skill. https://www.amazon.com/Matchbox-mobile-Daily-Word/dp/B017VAOYN0

Rehab. (2021). *Safari mixer.* Voice experiment. https://safarimixer.beta.rehab

The Magic Door LLC. (2021). *The magic door.* Alexa skill. https://www.amazon.com/The-Magic-Door-LLC/dp/B01BMUU6JQ

Zengrant (2021). *My African safari.* Alexa skill. https://www.amazon.com/Zengrant-My-African-Safari/dp/B07BJLSV9M

References

Alfa Tech. (2018, May 09). *Google Assistant making a haircut appointment | Google IO 2018.* [Video]. YouTube. https://www.youtube.com/watch?v=YCWJ0z6_z34

Brown, D. (2014). *Principles of English language teaching,* 6th Ed. USA: Pearson Education.

Chapelle, (2005). Interactionist SLA theory in CALL research. In J. L. Egbert & G. N. Petrie (Eds.), *CALL research perspectives* (pp. 53-64). Lawrence Erlbaum.

David, G. (2021, June 05). Samsung's Sam virtual assistant a hoax? Here's why Lightfarm creates her 3D appearance. Tech Times. https://www.techtimes.com/articles/261112/20210605/attn-samsungs-sam-virtual-assistant-hoax-heres-why-lightfarm-creates.htm

Kalantra, F., & Hashemian, M. (2018). A story-telling approach to teaching English to young EFL Iranian learners. *English Language Teaching, 9*(1), 221-234, https://doi.org/10.5539/elt.v9n1p 221

Levin-Goldberg, J. (2014). WebQuest 2.0: Best Practices for the 21st Century. *Journal of Instructional Research, 3,* 73-82.

UK Safer Internet Center. (2018). *7 in 10 children are using voice assisted technology finds new research from UKSIC partner childnet.* Retrieved from https://www.saferinternet.org.uk/blog/7-10-children-are-using-voice-assisted-technology-finds-new-research-uksic-partner-childnet

Underwood, J. (2017). Exploring AI language assistants with primary EFL students. In K. Borthwick, L. Bradley & S. Thouesny (Eds), *CALL in a climate of change: adapting to turbulent global conditions – short papers from EUROCALL 2017* (pp. 317-321).

Underwood, J. (2018). *Using voice and AI assistants for language learning.* British Council Teaching English Webinar. https://www.teachingenglish.org.uk/article/using-voice-ai-assistants-language-learning

Vygotsky, L. S. (1978). Tool and symbol in child development. In M. Cole, V. John-Steiner, S. Scribner, & E. Souberman (Eds.). Mind in Society: The development of higher psychological processes. Harvard University Press.

Winkler, R., & Sollner, M. (2018). Unleashing the potential of chatbots in education: A state-of-the-art analysis. In: *Academy of Management Annual Meeting (AOM)*. Chicago, USA.

Appendix A

Digital Assistant Classroom and Language Learning Use-Case Examples

Classroom Management	**Command**
Timers	*'Set a timer for [x] minutes/hours/days', 'Set [x] minute/hour/day timer'*
Reminders	*'Set a reminder [for Brad to take his medication]', 'Set a reminder for [students to change partners/take and exercise break/etc]'*
Choosing volunteers	*'Pick a number between [x] and [y]', 'Heads or tails', 'Play rock, paper, scissors'*

Language Learning	**Command**
Vocabulary/Phrases	
Definitions	*'Define [word/phrase'], 'What is a [word/phrase]?', 'What is the definition/meaning of [word/phrase]?'*
Synonyms/Antonyms	*'What is the synonym/antonym of [word/phrase]?'*
Spelling	*'How do you spell [word/phrase]?'*
Grammar	*'What is the plural of [x]', 'What is a [word or phrase form/grammar]?', 'What is the use of [word or phrase form/grammar] in English?'*
Translation	*'Translate [word/phrase] to [language]', 'How do I/you say [word/phrase] in [language]?'*
Speaking	
Pronunciation	*'How do you pronounce [word/spell out word by letter]?'*

Listening

Books	'Read', 'Get audible [book name]', 'Read Kindle [book name]'
News	'What's the latest news?'
Wikipedia	'Wikipedia [topic]'
White Noise	'Play [white noise/rain forest sounds/beach noises/etc]'
Streaming music	'Play [artist name/genre of music/song name]'
Streaming video	'Play [artist name/genre of music/song name/movie name/TV episode name and number] on [Chromecast/Fire TV Stick]'
Streaming podcasts	'Play [podcast/podcast number]'
Stories	'Tell me [a story/a fairy tale]'
Facts	'Tell me [something interesting]'

Fun	**Assistant**	**Action/Skill**
Interactive Stories	Alexa	*Magic Door, My African Safari*
	Google	*Magic Door, 'Let's read along with Disney'*
Music	Alexa	*Ditty, 'Sing a song'*
	Google	*Mixlab, 'Sing a song'*
Games	Alexa	*20-Questions, Simon Says, Spelling Bee, Spelling Master*
	Google	*Akinator , Freeze Dance, Mystery animal, Mystery Sounds, Simon says*
Jokes	Alexa/Google	*'Tell me a joke'*

Miscellaneous	**Command**
Weather	*What is the temperature?*
	What is the weather [today/for tomorrow/ in X]?
	When is the [next full moon]?
	When/what time is [sunrise/sunset]?
Astronomy	*How many planets are there?*
	What is the closest planet to the sun right now?
Animal/vehicle noises	*What noise does an [animal/vehicle] make?*
Math	*What is the [sum/product/difference/quotient] of [x] and [y]?*
Statistics	*What's the population of [place]?*
Capitals	*What is the capital of [state/country]?*
Celebrities	*Who is [famous person/celebrity name]?*
Inventors	*Who invented [item]?*
	Who was the inventor of the [item]?
Health/Anatomy	*How many [bones does the human body have]?*
	What does the [body part] do?
Hobbies	*What books did [author] write?*
	What is [book title/movie] about?
	What books would you recommend for [me/a x year old]?
	What is a good movie to see right now?
Cooking	*Find me a recipe for [food].*
	How do I make [food]?
	Convert [imperial] to [metric]
Finance	*How much is [x currency] in [y currency]?*
	What is the exchange rate from [x currency] to [y currency]?
Occupations	*What does a/an [x] do?*
	What is it like to be a/an [occupation]?
Shopping	*What time is [x] open until?*
	Where can I buy a/an [item]?

Development	**Tools**
Alexa	Alexa Blueprints (https://blueprints.amazon.com).
	Invocable (https://invocable.com).
Google Assistant	Actions on Google (https://console.actions.google.com/u/0/?pli=1) .
	Story Speaker (https://workspace.google.com/u/1/marketplace/app/story_speaker/888339379807).

Actions/Skills	**Lists**
Alexa	Alexa Skills
Google Assistant	Google Assistant Actions

Appendix B

Interactive Stories – Activity Sheet

Digital Assistant: Action/Skill:

THEME	VOCABULARY
What was the theme of the story? (Write one sentence).	*Words*
OVERVIEW	*Spellings*
Paraphrase the entire story.	

CONVERSATION	Definitions
Write a short dialog between two of the main characters.	

SUMMARY	Synonyms
Summarize the story in three sentences. Include the main character, the setting, the conflict, the climax, and the resolution.	
	Antonyms
	Translations

Appendix C

Vocabulary Word Forms Activity Sheet

WORD FORMS				
Verb	*Adverb*	*Participle*	*Adjective*	*Noun*

Appendix D

Tongue Twister Activity Sheet

Tongue Twisters!

Warm-up

Tongue twisters are tricky, but they can help us practice pronunciation.

What is a tongue twister from your language?

____

____

____

____

Activity

Let's ask our digital assistant for a tongue twister.
Listen carefully! Practice speaking the tongue twister you heard by saying it aloud. Then, write it out here:

____

____

____

Here are some more tongue twisters.
Try speaking them aloud now with a partner.

- *Fuzzy Wuzzy was a bear. Fuzzy Wuzzy had no hair. Fuzzy Wuzzy wasn't fuzzy, was he?*
- *How many cookies could a good cook cook, if a good cook could cook cookies?*
- *I saw a kitten eating chicken in the kitchen.*
- *I scream, you scream, we all scream for ice cream.*
- *If a dog chews shoes, whose shoes does he choose?*
- *Four fine fresh fish for free.*
- *Fred fed Ted bread, and Ted fed Fred bread.*
- *She sells seashells by the seashore.*

Practice

Get into teams of five, and make your own tongue-twisters.
For each person:

1. On a piece of paper, write your first name. (Pass the paper to the person on your right).
2. Write down something that he/she did. (Pass the paper to the person on your right).
3. Write down where he/she did it. (Pass the paper to the person on your right).
4. Write down when he/she did it. (Pass the paper to the person on your right).
5. Write down the reason why he/she did it. (Pass the paper to the person on your right).

This will give your group five tongue twisters.
For example,

- *David drank a drink in downtown Denpasar at daylight to destress.*
- *Noddy needed noodles in Neverland at noon to 'nom nom nom'.*

You might need to ask the digital assistant to help you create your tongue twister.
Ask questions like:

- *What are some actions that begin with the letter [...]?*
- *What are place names that begin with the letter [...]?*
- *What are emotions that begin with the letter [...]?*

Further practice

1. Ask the digital assistant to repeat your tongue twister after you. See if it can repeat it the same way, or if you can trick it. *Did you trick it? Yes or No.*

2. Hear some more tongue twisters. Ask the digital assistant to tell you some more tongue twisters. Write down the tongue twisters that you hear.

    a) ____

    ____

    ____

    ____

    b) ____

    ____

    ____

    ____

    c) ____

    ____

    ____

    ____

    d) ____

    ____

    ____

    ____

    e) ____

    ____

    ____

    ____

Appendix E

Wh-type Question Words Activity

WH-Type Question Words Example Sheet

TO ASK

Question Words	Meaning	Examples
Who	Person	Who is he/she/that? He/she/that is MinSu.
Where	Place	Where do you live? In Seoul.
Why	Reason	Why do you go to bed early? Because I have to be at work early.
When	Time	When do you go to work? At 6am.
How	Manner	How do you go to work? I go by public transport.
What	Object	What is it? It's a frog.
	Idea	What are you thinking about?
	Action	I'm just day dreaming. What do you do? I am a teacher.
Which	Choice	Which one do you want? I want the cheap one.
Whose	Possession	Whose book is this? It's hers/his/theirs.
Whom	Object of the verb	Whom did you meet? I met the director.
What kind	Description	What kind of music do you like? I like all kinds of music.
What time	Time	What time did you get home? I got home at 9pm.
How many	Quantity (count)	How many students are there? There are five.

How much	Amount Price (non-count)	How much time do we have before class ends? Five minutes. How much is the fish? Five dollars.
How long	Length Duration	How long is a mile in kilometers? It's almost 1.61 kilometers. How long did you stay in Japan? I stayed overnight.
How often	Frequency	How often do you exercise? I exercise every day.
How far	Distance	How far away is your school? It's 5 minutes away by car.
How old	Age	How old are you? I'm 18.
How come	Reason	How come I didn't see you in class yesterday? I was sick

TO ANSWER

To ask about the subject of the sentence add the question word at the beginning. For example,

> *Sharon* writes great poetry.
> *Who* writes great poetry?

To ask about any other part of the sentence and there is an auxiliary (helping) verb, put the question word and the auxiliary verb in front of the subject. For example,

> <u>She can</u> speak *Korean*. – *What* <u>can she</u> speak?
> <u>They are</u> leaving *tomorrow*. – *When* <u>are they</u> leaving?

If there is no auxiliary verb and main verb is a form of be (am, is, are, was, were), put the question word and the form of *be* in front of the subject. For example,

> <u>The movie was</u> *interesting*. – *How* <u>was the movie</u>?

If there is no auxiliary verb and the main verb is not a form of *be*, put the question word and a form of *do* (do, does, did) in front of the subject. For example,

> They go to *the park* every Sunday.
> *Where* <u>do</u> they go every Sunday

> She wakes up **early**.
> *When* <u>does</u> she wake up?

> He ate **a hamburger**.
> **What** <u>did</u> he eat?

WORD ORDER

a)   General: Question word + auxiliary + subject + verb
  Where were you born?
  I was born in ________.

b)   Subject questions (with no auxiliary)
  Who sang the song Gangnam style?
  ______ sang the song Gangnam Style.
  Which team won the 2018 World Cup?
  ______ won the 2018 World Cup.

c)   Object questions (with answers to the question the object)
  Who is your favorite singer?
  My favorite singer is ______.

PRACTICE

The kinds of questions to ask our digital assistant
- *What is the largest city in the world?*
- *What is the smallest country in the world?*
- *What is the tallest building in the world?*
- *Where is the <u>Burj Kalifa</u>?*
- *Which football team won the 2014 World Cup?*
- *How do you spell <u>context</u>?*

ASK THE DIGITIAL ASSISTANT

1. Think of five questions to ask our digital assistant.
2. Write down the questions, and then the answers that you hear?
3. While waiting to speak to the digital assistant you can ask your partner your question.
4. Check to see if the answers they give are the same!

Who?

Assistant:

Partner:

What?

Assistant:

Partner:

Where?

Assistant:

Partner:

When?

Assistant:

Partner:

How?

Assistant:

Partner:

Appendix F

A Story Speaker Choose Your Own Adventure Example

Title: Tale of the Travelers
By: David Kent

START HERE

Intro
You and two friends have just arrived in Seoul. You want to stay in a hotel. You have two choices. The cheap hotel is only $50 per night. The expensive hotel is $150 per night.
Which hotel do you choose?

> **If you say "expensive" or "the expensive one" or "the expensive hotel"**
> You and your friends are staying at the expensive hotel. The room is large and beautiful so you relax and unpack. Now you want to go swimming but your friends want to go shopping. What do you do?
>
> > **If you say "swimming" or "go swimming"**
> > You and your friends are swimming in the hotel pool. It is beautiful and so much fun! Now you are hungry and want to go eat, but your friends want to go shopping. What do you do?
> >
> > > **If you say "eat" or "go eat"**
> > > You go to a nice restaurant for dinner. The food is really delicious but now you really don't have a lot of money left. You want to go back to the hotel and write emails but your friends still want to go shopping. What do you do?
> > >
> > > > **If you say "hotel" or "go back to the hotel" or "emails" or "write emails"**
> > > > You go back to the hotel, write a few emails, and then relax for the rest of the day. In the morning you take the

train back to Daejeon. You don't have a lot of money left but you had a lot of fun. You can't wait to go back to Seoul! [[END]]

If you say "shopping" or "go shopping"

You and your friends enjoy shopping but spend too much money. Now you can't pay for your hotel. You had to call home and get your parents to send you money. This is the end of your trip! [[END]]

Otherwise

Now that you're full, what will you do? Say "go back to the hotel", or "go shopping". The waiter is ready to kick you out of the restaurant.

If you say "shopping" or "go shopping"

You and your friends enjoy shopping but spend too much money. Now you can't pay for your hotel. You had to call home and get your parents to send you money. This is the end of your trip! [[END]]

Otherwise

The lifeguard is no longer on duty, so the pool is closed. Say "go eat" if you want to go to a restaurant, or say "shopping" if you want to go to a department store.

If you say "shopping" or "go shopping"?

You and your friends enjoy shopping but spend too much money. Now you can't pay for your hotel. You had to call home and get your parents to send you money. This is the end of your trip! [[END]]

Otherwise

It really is a lovely room, but it is starting to look like a nice day outside. Say "aquarium" or "department store." Get out and do something!

If you say "cheap" or "the cheap one" or "the cheap hotel"
You are staying in the cheap hotel. The room is very dirty so you don't want to stay in the room. You decide to go sightseeing. You can go to the aquarium or you can go shopping at Lotte Department Store.

If you say "aquarium" or "the aquarium"
The aquarium is great. There is a lot of fish, and you take a lot of pictures. But, now you're tired and hungry. You want to go back to the hotel to rest, but your friends want to get something to eat. What do you do?

If you say "hotel" or "go back to   the hotel" or "rest" or "go to   rest"
You go back to your hotel. Someone has broken into your room and stolen all of your belongings! Now you are stuck in Seoul with no way home. What a terrible trip! [[END]]

If you say "eat" or "go eat"
You and your friends get something to eat at a street vendor. You didn't have a lot of money to spend but the food was tasty. You go back to the hotel, and in the morning take the train back to Daejeon. You may not have had the best hotel, but you had a great time with your friends. You can't wait to go back to Seoul! [[END]]

Otherwise
The aquarium is a nice place to visit but you've spent too long here. Say "eat" or "hotel". Time to move on.

If you say "Lotte Department store" or "Lotte" or "department store" or the "department store"
You and your friends are shopping for souvenirs at Lotte Department Store. It's amazing! (And, they're expensive!) You are exhausted, and now you want to go back to the hotel, but your friends want to eat something. What do you do?

If you say "hotel" or "go back to the hotel"

You go back to the hotel and have a wonderful night's sleep. In the morning, you catch the train back to Daejeon. You give your souvenirs to your friends and tell them that Seoul is a very expensive place to visit. You think to yourself, "Next time I will stay with relatives!" [[END]]

If you say "eat" or "go eat"

You don't have much money so you decide to eat at a fast food restaurant. The food makes you feel sick and you have a stomachache for the rest of the trip! Your trip of a lifetime is over. [[END]]

Otherwise

The department store is closing, and you've spent all day shopping. Say "hotel" to go back to the hotel, or "eat" to curb your hunger.

Otherwise

Do you really want to stay in this dirty room? Say "aquarium" or "department store." It's really dirty here.

Otherwise

Do you really want to sleep on the streets? Say "expensive" or "cheap." Brrr, it's getting cold out here.

If you say "It's a mystery"

No, it's a choose-your-own adventure story!

Anytime you say "What is this?"

This is the story Tale of the Traveler by David Kent.

Fallback

Sorry, I didn't get that. Try asking once more.

10. Chatbots and Robots in the Classroom

Overview

This chapter considers the role of chatbots and robots in the learning process. Two chatbot examples are presented in detail, and the means of chatbot development is presented. The concept of robot-assisted language learning (RALL) is also introduced, along with a brief consideration into how robots can be applied in the classroom with students. This is then coupled with a synopsis of the benefits that such systems provide learners engaged in the language learning process.

Learning Outcomes

1. Explore the concept of robot-assisted language learning.
2. Appreciate how robot-assisted language learning is being used in the classroom for the benefit of learners today.
3. Increase understanding regarding the use of chatbots, particularly in education.
4. Understand how chatbots work, and are developed.
5. Create a working chatbot for use with language learners.

Robots

It can be difficult to classify robots, as they can be used in a wide range of scenarios including those from aerospace, through to disaster response as well as in industrial settings and others like medical ones. Is an autonomous vehicle a robot? What about drones? We can see robots in our house (automated vacuums), and as toys for children. We also see social robots in public spaces, assisting us with information on demand (see Figure 10.1).

Robots can be autonomous or teleoperated, and based on appearance can be classified either singularly or as possessing a mixture of qualities that include:
- anthropomorphic (human-like),
- cartoon-like,
- zoomorphic (animal-like), or
- mechanomorphic (machine-like).

Robot size and behavior also determines how we perceive them, either being more toy-like or as a social robot, one that we can interact with in order to gain some benefit over simple play.

Figure 10.1 Information Robot InCheon Airport, Korea
(Image by Kent, 2019)

Robot Assisted language Learning

As a subdomain of robot-assisted learning, a niche area of social robotics and human-robot interaction, robot-assisted language learning refers to teaching language expression or comprehension skills in either the native or non-native language, or an artificial language, along with non-verbal languages such as sign via a robot.

Although research on RALL has been undertaken globally, 40% of the literature is primarily based on that emerging from Japan, South Korea, and Taiwan (Randall, 2019), and it is largely undertaken in school settings (i.e., the classroom). This has seen a lot written in the literature regarding robot assisted language learning, and while research illustrates that robots can support native and foreign language acquisition, it is unclear as to what benefits robots over other aspects of computer-assisted language learning (CALL) actually provide. However, results do indicate that robots are uniquely suited to assist in language production, they also provide increased motivation and in-task engagement, and can help to decrease anxiety and lower the affective filter of learners. They can provide support and engagement across a wide range of language learning aspects from acting as conversational partner and as a proxy or avatar for the learner/teacher to assisting with vocabulary or the learning of grammar. They can also guide pronunciation, help to clarify writing and improve upon listening and reading comprehension skills, in addition to assessing learner language ability. Generally then, robots employed in language learning endeavors tend to exhibit one of four social roles, that of:
- teacher,
- teacher's aide,
- peer/tutor, or
- learner.

Of note, the teacher role (unless through telepresence) is used infrequently with that of teacher's aide more common, and the role of peer more regular. It is the latter role that can see robots serve as guides for students, challenging them from within their zone of proximal development (ZPD) to provide scaffolding and promote learning.

Robots in the Classroom

In the classroom robots include those that we can use code to program, and for learners of languages these might be practically employed while teaching directions or other skills, for example. A robot that might be useful for this purpose is *TrueTrue,* and you can learn more about it by watching *TrueTrue | All-in-one coding robot* [Video: https://www.youtube.com/watch?v=hyj1mA9Yyco&feature=youtu.be].

For now, we will explore a simple virtual robot, *TJBot*. It is also accessible as a physical robot that you can buy, and then use in the classroom, with the virtual one used as a simulator to see how code will make the physical robot function.

You can see tabs on the top right above *TJBot* (in Figure 10.2), and clicking on 'docs 'there will provide you with snippets of code that you can place into the box on the left, and then by pressing the play icon see this code acted out.

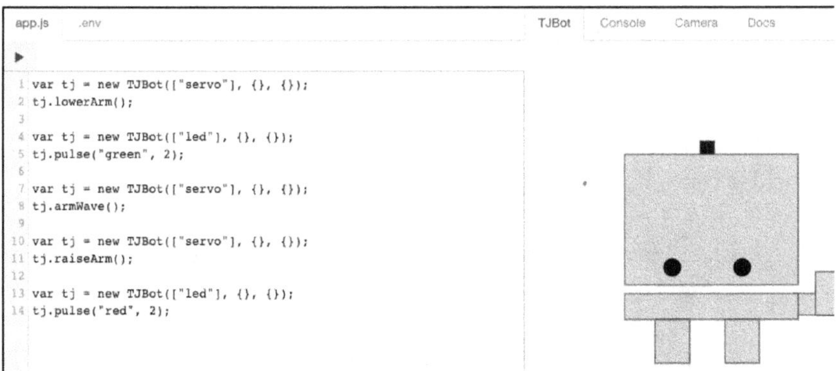

Figure 10.2 TJBot simulator

For example, the following code will make the robot lower its arm:

```
var tj = new TJBot(["servo"], {}, {});

tj.lowerArm();
```

Whereas, this code will make the LED beacon on its head shine red:

```
var tj = new TJBot(["led"], {}, {});

tj.shine("red");
```

Try out the *TJBot simulator* for five minutes [Link: https://my-tjbot.mybluemix.net].

Adding AI to Robots

Not all robots rely on artificial intelligence, some just follow commands. However, we can link artificial intelligence algorithms to such robots so that they can then follow physical commands based on these algorithms. For example, to add an AI element to *TJBot* you could have it monitor a Twitter account for sentiment using keywords, and when people are happy the LED light could shine yellow, blue for when they are sad, red for when they are angry, purple when they are fearful, and so on. You can see this concept in the video *make your robot respond to emotions* [Video: https://www.youtube.com/watch?v=KU8DNzZNdBY].

Workbook Activity 10.1

Consider the following and respond in the companion workbook.

10.1a Have you used RALL before with learners? If so, in what context?

10.1b How do you think such technology could be applied from within your teaching and learning context?

Chatbots

Chatbots are computer programs that can carry on a conversation with a human via text and/or speech. Today, chatbots are typically used as a means to respond to user queries about a specific set of subjects. They can be seen on websites in the form of a text chat where users type in questions and receive an immediate response, providing the sense that a human is answering. They can be designed to carry on general conversations—although most focus on providing a specific service. Keep in mind that chatbots only work well for very stereotyped tasks, like ordering pizza or asking about the price of a product, particularly if designed utilizing decision tree type algorithms.

In 1966, the chatbot *Eliza* was created at the MIT AI Laboratories to simulate human conversation. It presented the illusion of understanding by matching user prompts to scripted responses (pattern matching), but it had no built-in framework for the contextualization of events.

Since then, there have been many chatbots created for many different purposes, two of interest are *ALICE* and *Watson*. ALICE (artificial linguistic internet computer entity) is a natural language processing chatbot which relies upon heuristic pattern matching rules when receiving human input (AbuShawar & Atwell, 2015). Watson, developed by IBM, was originally designed to compete on the television show Jeopardy! in which it went on to beat two of the show's former champions (IBM Research, 2013), and has since gone on to be used to help analyze Big Data. More recently, messenger bots have been used to engage people using text-based messenger applications, such as *Facebook Messenger*, for a variety of purposes including that of education (Smutny & Schreiberova, 2020) or for customer service inquiries. Evidence also suggests that an increasing amount of social media content is being generated by autonomous entities like social bots that interact both with each other and with humans (Varol et al., 2017). If interested, you can read more about the history of chatbots in the article *Chatbots: History, technology, and applications* [Article: https://doi.org/10.1016/j.mlwa.2020.100006]. See also the History of chatbots: A timeline (Ramos, 2018) in Figure 10.3.

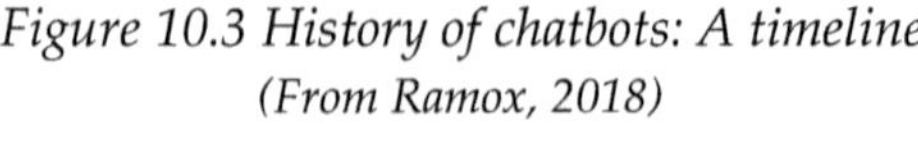

Figure 10.3 History of chatbots: A timeline
(From Ramox, 2018)

Chatbots and the Turing Test

It will only be a matter of time before chatbots, social bots, and digital assistants come to consistently pass the Turing test, or the imitation game (Turing, 1950) where an intelligent machine is indistinguishable from a human during a text-only conversation. The conversation in this test is limited to text-only, so there is no reliance on a verbal rendering component.

One chatbot, *Kuki* (previously *Mitsuki*) is a multi-award winner of the Loebner Prize. The Loebner prize is an annual competition in artificial intelligence that awards prizes to the computer programs considered by judges to be the most human-like, with the format of the competition that of the standard Turing test. Of note also, the *Google Assistant* has been seen to verbally pass the Turing test on at least one occasion when it was asked to make a phone call and to book a hair appointment [Video: https://www.theverge.com/2018/5/8/17332070/google-assistant-makes-phone-call-demo-duplex-io-2018]

Chatbots in Education

Chatbots can be incorporated into the classroom in a number of ways, and in ways that can enhance the educational experience for learners. Yet, their use does not need to be limited to that of the classroom, or to students and teachers. Chatbots can prove useful for interacting with parents and other stakeholders as well, and are available to interact with 24 hours a day. They can be employed from the school website, and through messaging apps, and in this way specific and accurate information can be provided to all stakeholders able to interact with them. For example, students can find out information about their class schedule, parents can gain access to term dates and other important information regarding excursions, and gain answers to any common school related questions that they might need to ask. As people are familiar with using messaging services, chatbot use is essentially a relatively easy way to gain access to just-in-time information on demand in a similar fashion. *Oli* is one such chatbot that is being utilized to assist college students in the enrollment process, and in gaining access to scholarship information (Hobbs, 2021) [Article: https://www.upworthy.com/this-ai-chatbot-named-oli-guides-students-through-complicated-college-enrollment-process].

A few examples of the global benefits of chatbot use in education might include those of student access, administrative purposes, engaging and enabling students, and providing teacher assistance.

Student Access
Chatbots can provide teachers and students with information relating to schedules, such as who is teaching what class, and at what times those classes start. Reminders can be sent to students about when assignments are due, with the chatbot also answering questions like what the passing grade might be, and perhaps also allowing students to sign up and register for activities that may be of interest to them. New students may also be able to rely on a chatbot to navigate their way around a school, by asking in what rooms particular classes are being provided.

Administrative Purposes
Chatbots serve a very useful purpose in dealing with very common questions that stakeholders may need to ask at any given time. These might include those such as admissions and enrolment (e.g., When is the deadline to pay tuition?); campus tours and events (e.g., When is the next university tour?, When will the university festival be held?); scholarships (e.g., What tuition fee waivers are available?); information about school operations (e.g., What time does the library close?). Chatbots are also useful for sending proactive reminders to stakeholders (e.g., history test on Wednesday at 10am, building W7 is closed for maintenance from 9 am – 11 am tomorrow).

Engaging and Enabling Students
Chatbots can engage students by providing instant answers, using decision trees to guide students with a series of questions to help them understand a topic better or to help them practice working with content that they have learned in class. Artificial intelligence can also be incorporated into chatbots to extend their capabilities, and an example of this is *Frosty* the QuizBot, who is able to help students learn more effectively over reliance on flashcards. See the video on *QuizBot* https://www.youtube.com/watch?v=xL6_CTiD2DU&feature=emb_title

Teacher Assistance

Chatbots might be used by teachers to provide details about lessons or assignments, based on the common questions that students ask. They might be used to provide short practice tests for formative assessment. Chatbots can also be used to provide feedback on aspects of the course, or particular lessons.

Overall, in the TESOL context, it has long been known that those students who possess low self-confidence in their foreign language abilities do prefer to interact with a chatbot over a human (Fryer, 2006). However, there have also been instances where benefit has been determined to derive from a novelty effect (Fryer et al., 2017), or where chatbot interactions have come to confound communication (chatbot-student) by veering off topic, or where instances of miscommunication (student-chatbot) have occurred (Fryer & Nakao, 2009). So too, teacher attitude to chatbot use, as with many activities, has been seen to impact upon the classroom success of these technologies (Bii, Too, & Mukwa, 2018) or lack thereof.

Workbook Activity 10.2

Spend three minutes engaging with a chatbot, try chatting with *Kuki* [Link: https://chat.kuki.ai]. Then, respond to the following questions in the associated workbook.

10.2a What did it feel like when chatting with *Kuki*?

10.2b What type of language do you think this chatbot was trained on?

10.2c What age group do you think was used to inform how this chatbot should respond?

10.2d Where do you feel the data used to train this chatbot came from?

Keep in mind that chatbots are trained on human language. Consider what training a chatbot with the wrong language can do. Spend a few minutes reading about the following cases from Korea and the United States of America.

Korea:
In 2020, *Chatbot Luda controversy leave questions over AI ethics, data collection* https://en.yna.co.kr/view/AEN20210113004100320.

United States of America:
In 2016, *Microsoft's racist chatbot revealed the dangers of online conversations*
https://spectrum.ieee.org/tech-talk/artificial-intelligence/machine-learning/in-2016-microsofts-racist-chatbot-revealed-the-dangers-of-online-conversation.

Further reading:
Before moving on to looking at how chatbots are built, another interesting article to read is that of *the ethical implications of the chatbot user experience,* where some users have mistaken humans for chatbots, you can look that over here https://www.bentley.edu/centers/user-experience-center/ethical-implications-chatbot-user-experience.

Constructing a Chatbot

In the following exercise you will look at two chatbots based on existing content, the first is *Make Me Happy,* and the second the *Sphinx Riddle Bot.* After completing this section you will have a chance to develop a chatbot of your own.

Chatbot 1 – Make Me Happy

For this exercise we will create a simple chatbot using *Machine Learning for Kids.* This is a great website to explore regarding machine learning and the various projects that can be created with it. You can learn more about it, and the projects that can be developed using machine learning models by watching the video *machine learning for kids* https://youtu.be/EjbHXMzeX4c.

The following exercise is based on an existing project that you can download from the site, called 'Make me happy' https://machinelearningforkids.co.uk/#!/worksheets.

The objective is to teach a computer to recognize compliments and insults. So, this can help you to understand how computers can be trained to recognize tone, and how supervised learning builds systems that can deal with unexpected input. Such a system can also be used with language learners to work with and improve their vocabulary, and writing skills.

Development Steps

The following instructions are those that can be found in the 'make me happy – easy worksheet (licensed under a Creative Commons Attribution Non-Commercial Share-Alike License http://creativecommons.org/licenses/by-nc-sa/4.0).

1. To start building the 'make me happy' project go to https://machinelearningforkids.co.uk.
2. Click 'get started'.
3. Click 'try it now'.
4. Click '+ add a new project'.
5. Call your new project 'make me happy' and set it to learn how to recognize 'text'. Then, click the 'create' button. (See Figure 10.4.)

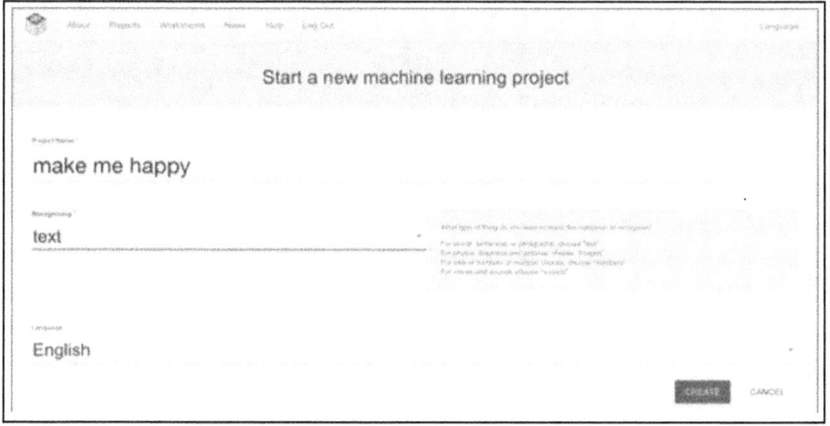

Figure 10.4 Make me happy project

6. You should now see 'make me happy' in the list of your projects. Click on it.

7. Now, click the 'train' button (see Figure 10.5).

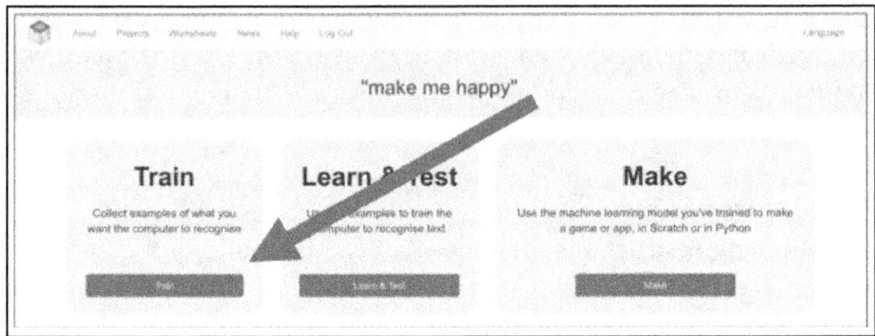

Figure 10.5 Train button

8. Click on '+add new label' and call it 'kind things'. Do that again and create a second label called 'mean things'. (See Figure 10.6.)

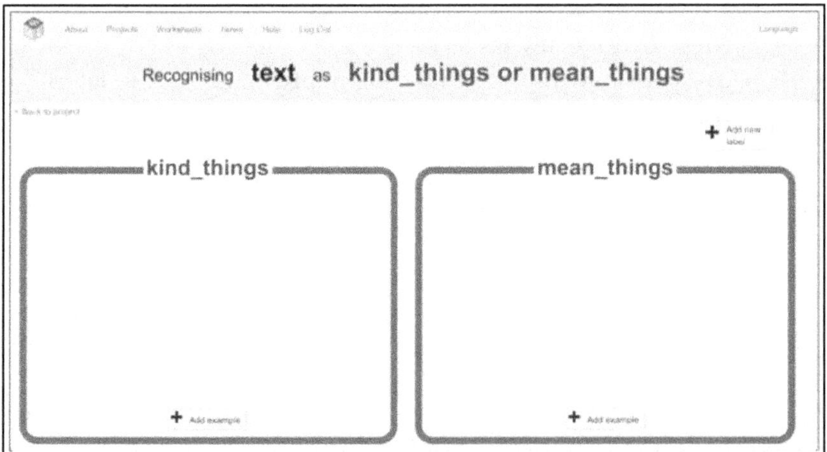

Figure 10.6 'Mean things'

9. Click the 'add example' button in 'kind things' and type in the nicest, kindest compliment that you can think of.
10. Click on the 'add example' button in the 'mean things' bucket, and type in the meanest, cruelest insult that you can think of.
11. Repeat the above two steps until you have at least six items under each label (see Figure 10.7).

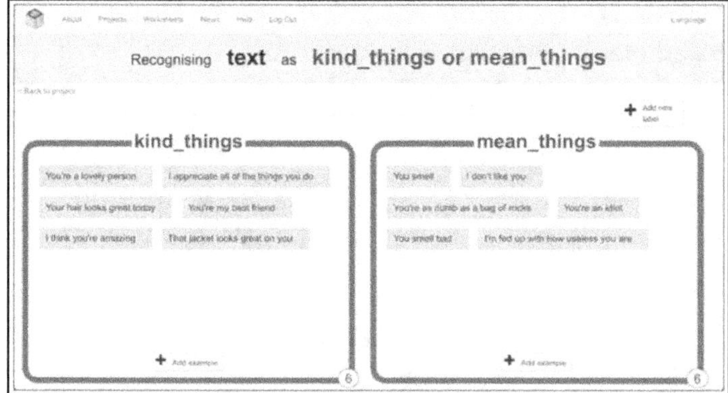

Figure 10.7 Training data

12. Click on '< back to project'.
13. Click on the 'learn & test' button.
14. Click on the 'train new machine learning model' button (see Figure 10.8).

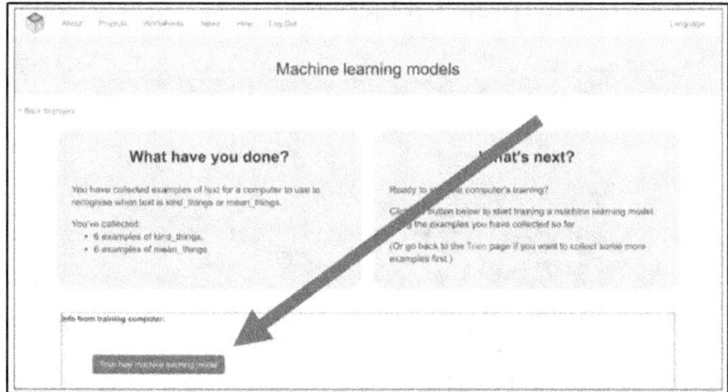

Figure 10.8 Train new machine learning model button

15. Wait for the training to complete.
16. Once the training is complete a text box will be displayed. Try testing the machine learning model to see what the computer has learned. Type something kind, and press enter. It should be recognized as kind. Type something mean, and press enter. It should be recognized as mean. You can also test it with

examples that you have not shown it before to see how it responds (see Figure 10.9.) You can go back and add more examples if you wish, or continue on.

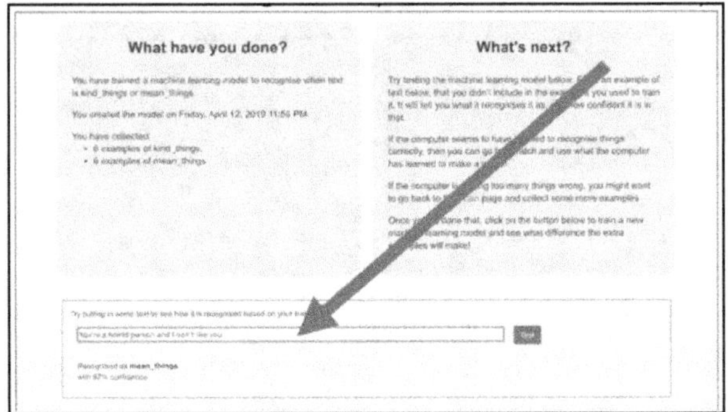

Figure 10.9 Add more examples

17. Click the '< back to project' link.
18. Click the 'make' button.
19. Click the 'Scratch 3' button.
20. Click the 'open in Scratch' button, and you should see new blocks from the project at the bottom of the list (see Figure 10.10).

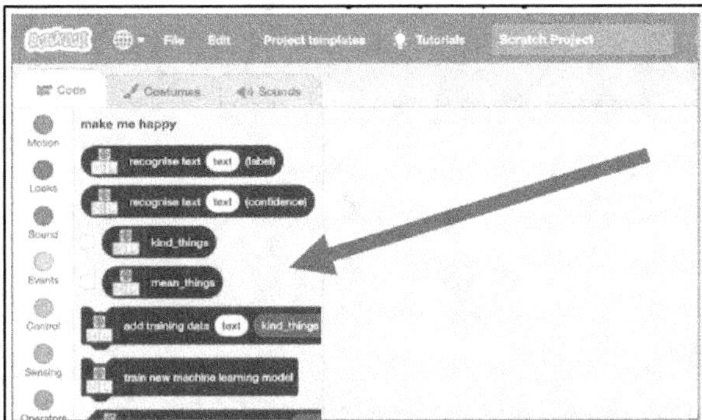

Figure 10.10 Open in Scratch button

21. Delete the cat sprite (see Figure 10.11).

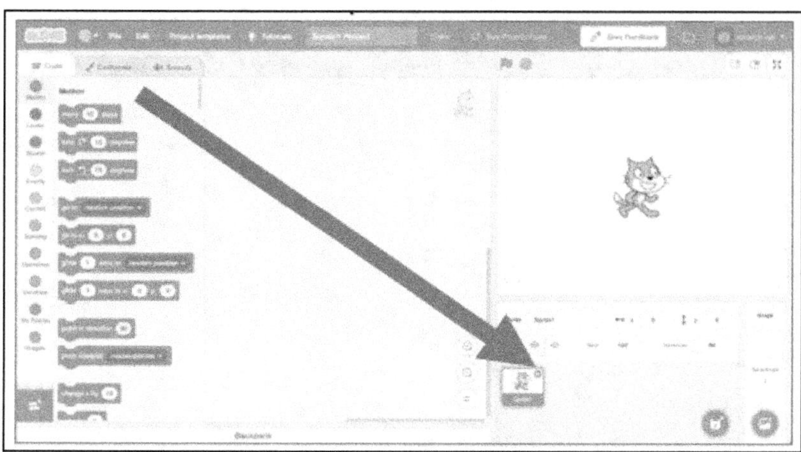

Figure 10.11 Delete the cat sprite

22. Create a new sprite by clicking on the 'paint' icon (see Figure 10.12).

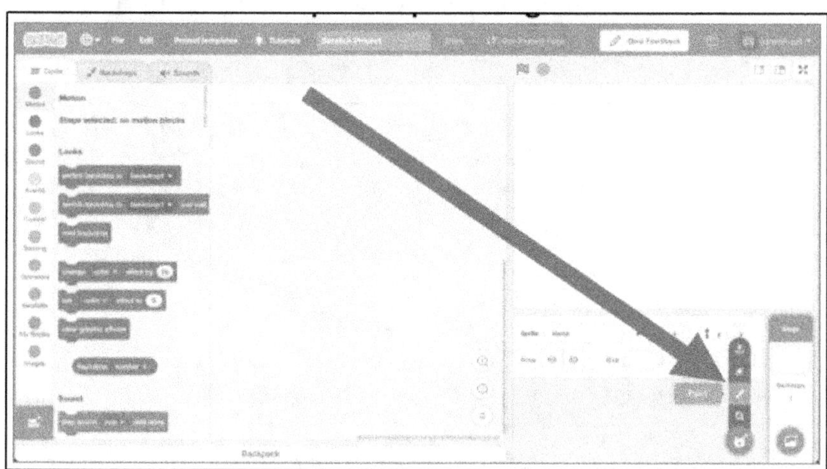

Figure 10.12 Paint icon

23. Draw a face without a mouth in the 'costumes' tab (see Figure 10.13).

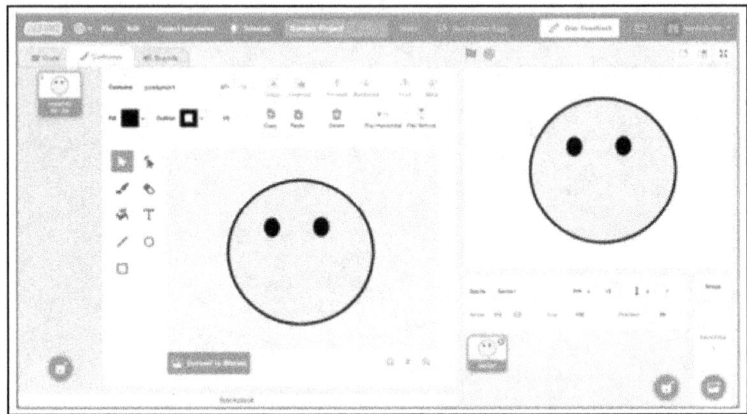

Figure 10.13 Draw a face

24. Right-click on the costume and click 'duplicate'. Do that once more, so that you have three copies of the costume. Make sure that you are duplicating the costume (not the sprite). (See Figure 10.14.)

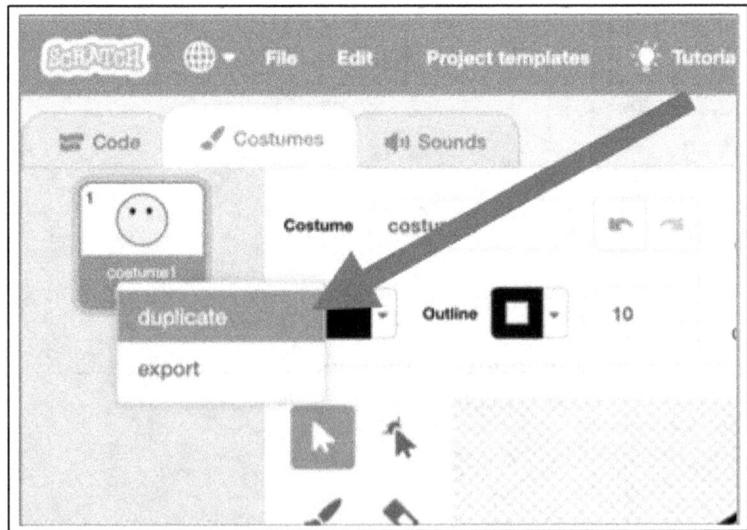

Figure 10.14 Duplicate the costume

25. Name the three costumes 'not sure', 'happy', and 'sad'. Type the names into the white box for the costume name. (See Figure 10.15.)

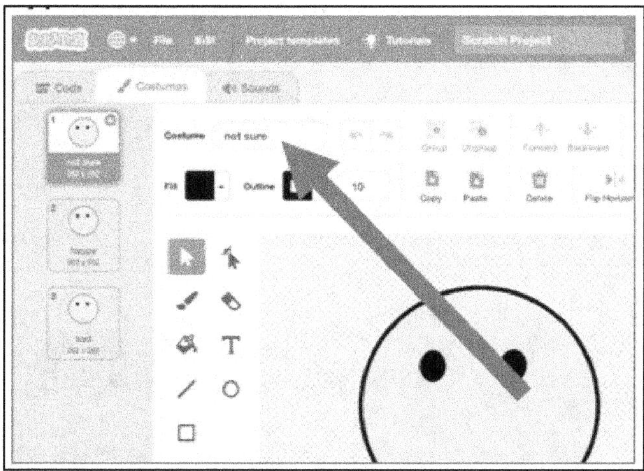

Figure 10.15 Name costumes

26. Draw a mouth on each of the costumes. The 'not sure' face should have a straight line. The 'happy' face should have a smile. The 'unhappy' face should look sad. (See Figure 10.16.)

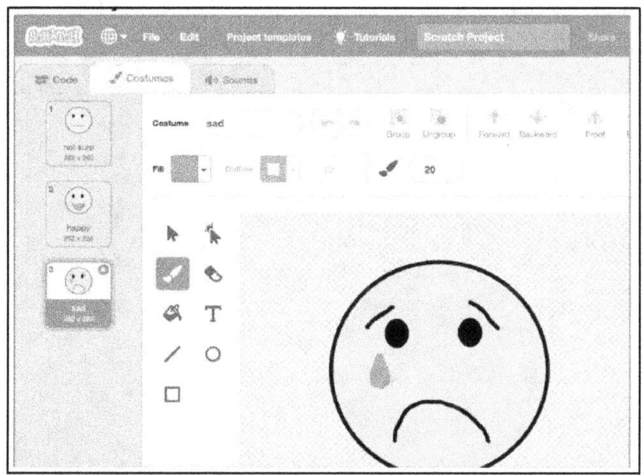

Figure 10.16 Draw expressions

27. Click the 'code' tab and enter the following script. The "recognize text … (label)" block is a new block added by your project. If you give it text, it will recognize it as 'kind things' or 'mean things' based on the training that you provided to the computer earlier. (See Figure 10.17.)

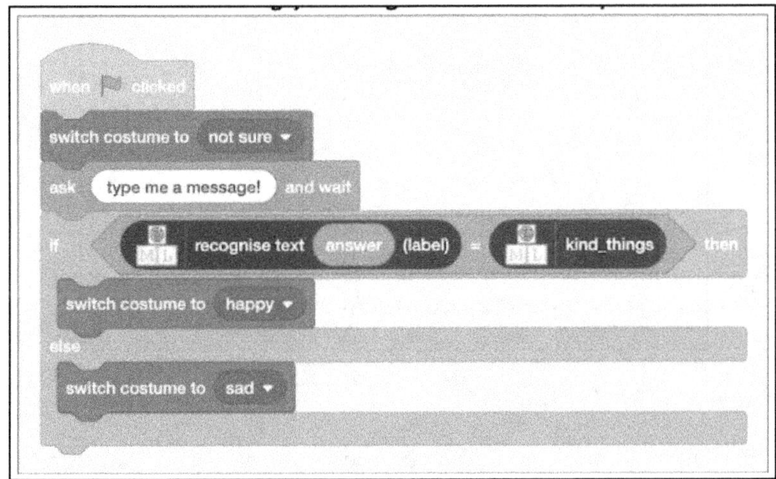

Figure 10.17 Enter code script

28. Click the green flag to test the system (see Figure 10.18).

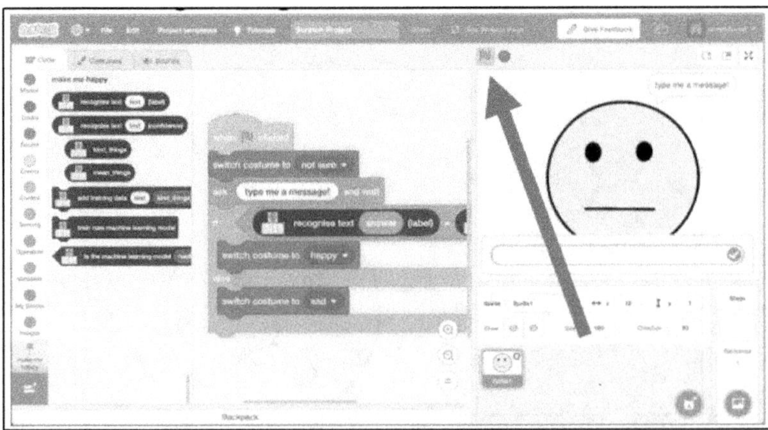

Figure 10.18 Click the green flag

29. Type in a message and watch it react. Type a kind message and press enter. The character should smile. Click the green flag again. Type a mean and unkind message and press enter. The character should look sad. This should also work for messages that you did not include in your training. Congratulations, the chatbot is complete!

In this example exercise you have started to train a simple chatbot to recognize text as being kind or mean. Instead of writing rules to be able to do this, such as using a decision tree, examples have been provided to train the system using a machine learning model. This model uses supervised learning constructs with the computer learning from the examples provided to it, which then allows it to recognize new messages.

Chatbot 2 – Sphinx, The Riddle Bot

In the next example, the *Sphinx Riddle Bot* was developed from an existing template found on the *Snatchbot* website called Quiz Education Bot [Link: https://snatchbot.me].

The *Sphinx Riddle Bot* contains 17 interactions. These include a welcome message ('welcome'), 5 questions ('1st through 5th question'), 10 responses to those questions as 'correct answer', 'incorrect answer', 'correct answer 2', 'incorrect answer 2', and so on, as well as a closing message ('total'). The closing message provides a goodbye and totals the number of correct and incorrect answers in order to respond appropriately to the user.

The welcome bot message is as follows:

> Hello there! 👏👏👏😊
> My name is Sphinx, the Riddle Bot, and I love riddles.
> Do you like riddles? I have 5 riddles for you to answer.
> Get ready, and click the "Let's go!" button to begin.
> [customVar Result=0]

Users do not see what is in the square brackets, but this helps us to track their score and provide this in the total or closing bot message. (See Figure 10.19.)

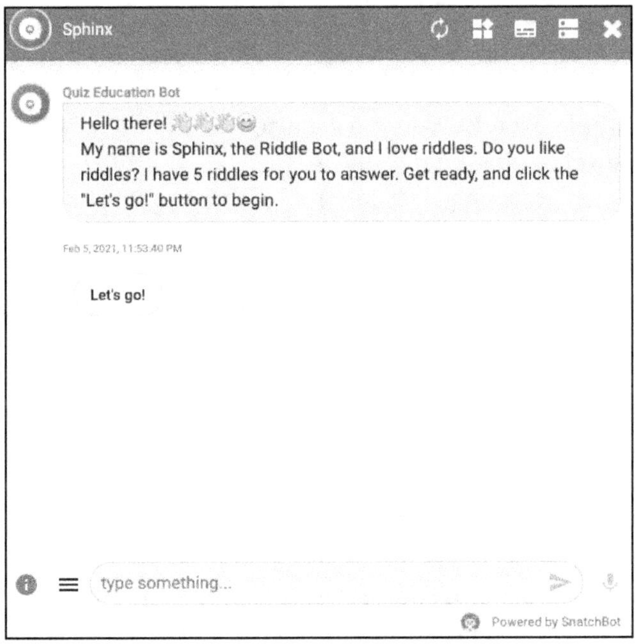

Figure 10.19 Bot message

Once the user clicks on 'Let's go!', they will be taken to the first question with the bot message:

> I help you from your head to your toe.
> The more I work, the smaller I grow.
> What am I?

The connections for the bot message associated with the first question are the following (see Figure 10.20):

If response to this action contains all of soap then go to correct answer

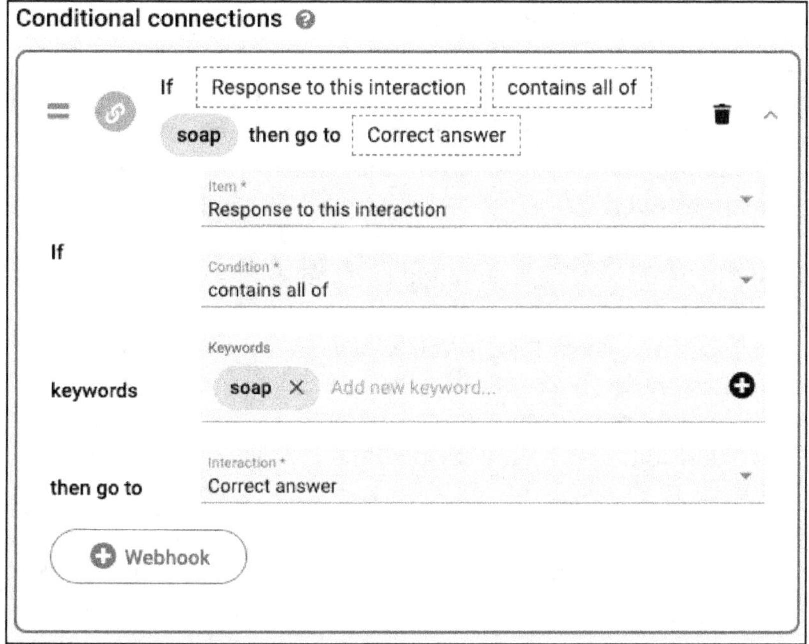

Figure 10.20 Bot message

Using 'contains all of' instead of 'exactly matches' as a condition allows for accepting those answers that may be written in a wider scope, such as: 'A bar of soap'.

If the user answers correctly they will be taken to 'correct answer' with the bot message:

> 😁 😁 😁 Congratulations, that is the right answer!
> Click on next riddle to continue.
> [customVar Result1=[ADD [[showVar=Result], 1]]]

If the user answers incorrectly they will be taken to 'incorrect answer' with the bot message:

> 😬 Too bad, that isn't right. The answer is soap.
> Click on next riddle to continue.
> [customVar Result1=[SUB [[showVar=Result], 0]]]

The closing message 'total', shows the bot message:

> You got [showVar=Result5] riddles correct out of 5.
> [IF([showVar=Result5]=5){You really aced it, congratulations!}]
> [IF([showVar=Result5]=4){Congratulations, you missed only one question.}]
> [IF([showVar=Result5]=3){Not bad, you only missed two questions. Next time, you might best me!}]
> [IF([showVar=Result5]=2){Ok, that is not bad.}]
> [IF([showVar=Result5]=1){Well, you are not the worst, try again and best me.}]
> [IF([showVar=Result5]=0){Unfortunately, all your answers are wrong. I told you I am a Riddle Bot! Try again, if you dare to best me.}]

Now that you have a general understanding of how the Sphinx Riddle Bot works, spend 10 minutes interacting with it on Telegram [Link: https://web.telegram.org/#/im?p=@SphinxRiddleBot], and you will notice that this kind of chatbot is clearly using a decision tree style.

Workbook Activity 10.3
Consider the following, and then respond in the associated workbook.

> **10.3** How would you apply use of one of the chatbots from the exercise (*Make me happy/Sphinx Riddle Bot*) with a class of language learners that you teach (or intend to teach)?

Chatbot Development

Now it is your turn to experiment with the creation of a chatbot. You can use any chatbot development tools/sites that you prefer to complete this exercise. For this exercise planning is key, and so is the selection of a target platform that you can comfortably work with to develop your chatbot. You might consider one of the following:

> *Chatbot Development Tools:*
> - *Snatchbot* [Link: https://snatchbot.me] (This development tool might be the easiest to use).
> - *IBM Watson Assistant.* [Link: https://www.ibm.com/cloud/garage/dte/producttour/create-chatbot-plan-trip]. (Keep in mind that when using this tool you might need to also access the facilitator guide for building a chatbot with it. [Link: https://developer.ibm.com/tutorials/cc-build-chatbot-ibm-cloud].)
> - *Botmake.io.* [Link: https://blog.botmake.io/how-to-build-an-effective-faq-chatbot]. The founder of this platform provides details regarding how to develop a chatbot using it. [Link: https://www.youtube.com/watch?v=hI-FJB87AUY&feature=youtu.be].
> - *Scratch.* [Link: https://scratch.mit.edu]. The developers of this tool provide a how-to-guide for creating a chatbot if you should need it [Link: https://en.scratch-wiki.info/wiki/Creating_a_Chat_Bot]. (An alternate that might prove simpler to use is *Scratch Jr.* [Link: https://www.scratchjr.org].)

Workbook Activity 10.4

Once you have selected a development tool, spend a minimum of 6 hours to create a simple chatbot that your students, or potential students can interact with in some fashion. It can be limited to 5 questions or fewer as in the *Sphinx Riddle Bot* example introduced earlier, or it can be more complex if you wish.

Think through what functionality your chatbot will provide to the user. This might be anything from a simple fun game style of interaction, a choose-your-own adventure story, a way for learners to find out information such as how to write an essay, and so on. You will also need to consider the chatbot persona, or its personality. For example, it might represent you, or an historical figure.

If following a decision tree model, contemplate the kind of questions or prompts that your target users might use with your chatbot. Write these out, along with the responses that the chatbot will provide. You will also need to develop appropriate responses to questions or user prompts that the chatbot is not designed to answer. Once this is complete, include this in the associated workbook. You can do this graphically or using text like that provided as an example for Sphinx. If you have used training data with your chatbot instead, then provide a list of the data that you supplied the model. In addition, respond to the following in the associated workbook.

10.4a What is the name of your chatbot?

10.4b What is the name of the development tool that you relied upon to create your chatbot?

10.4c What is the URL where your chatbot is located? (If it has one).

10.4d What does the decision tree/training data for your chatbot look like?

Workbook Activity 10.5

Consider the following, and answer these questions in the associated workbook.

10.5a How is the functionality of your chatbot useful for your learners or potential learners?

10.5b How would you apply this chatbot with your learners or potential learners? Provide a brief example use-case.

Summary

In this chapter you:

- Explored the emerging field of RALL (robot-assisted language learning).
- Gained a general overview of how robot-assisted language learning is being applied in the classroom.
- Established an appreciation for how chatbots can be utilized, particularly in education.
- Garnered an understanding of how chatbots work, and how they can be created with machine learning and decision-trees.
- Developed a working chatbot for use with your language learners.

Resources

Bika, N. (2021). *Get schooled by AI: Use cases of chatbots for education.* Acquire. https://acquire.io/blog/use-cases-of-chatbots-for-education

Botmake.io. (2021). *How to build an effective FAQ chatbot?* https://blog.botmake.io/how-to-build-an-effective-faq-chatbot

Chatbot Masters. (2020, January 06). *How to create a chatbot on Botmake.io?* Video. [YouTube]. https://www.youtube.com/watch?v=hI-FJB87AUY&feature=youtu.be

Chatcompose. (2021). *How to use chatbots for education and learning.* https://www.chatcompose.com/chatbot-learning.html

ChatbotPack. (2021). *Chatbots in Education.* https://www.chatbotpack.com/chatbots-in-education

DevTech Research Group, Tufts University., Lifelong Kindergarten Group, MIT Media Lab., & Playful Invention Company. (2021). *Scratch Jr.* https://www.scratchjr.org

Hobbs, H. (2021, June 06). *This AI chatbot named Oli is helping first-generation college students navigate the enrollment process.* Upworthy. https://www.upworthy.com/this-ai-chatbot-named-oli-guides-students-through-complicated-college-enrollment-process

IBM Developer. (2021). *Artificial Intelligence.* IBM. https://developer.ibm.com/technologies/artificial-intelligence

IBM Research. (2013, November 07). *Watson and the Jeopardy! Challenge.* Video. [YouTube]. https://www.youtube.com/watch?v=P18EdAKuC1U

IBM Watson Assistant. (2021*). Watson Assistant: Create a chatbot.* IBM. https://www.ibm.com/cloud/garage/dte/producttour/create-chatbot-plan-trip

i-Scream Media. (2020). *A digital educational content platform used by 90% of elementary school teachers – All-in-one coding robot.* 24-7 Pressrelease. https://www.24-7pressrelease.com/press-release/477613/pangyotechnovalley-koreas-first-digital-education-content-company-i-scream-media

Kim, E. (2021, January 13). *Chatbot Luda controversy leave questions over AI ethics.* Yonhap News Agency. https://en.yna.co.kr/view/AEN20210113004100320

Lardinois, F. (2016). *Duolingo's chatbots help you learn a new language.* TechCrunch. https://techcrunch.com/2016/10/06/duolingos-chatbots-help-you-learn-a-new-language

Kuki. (2021). *Kuki.* Chatbot. https://chat.kuki.ai

Maryam Ashoori. (2017, January 02). Make your robot respond to emotions. Video. [YouTube]. https://www.youtube.com/watch?v=KU8DNzZNdBY

NA. (2019, January 22). *QuizBot Video Figure.* Video. [YouTube]. https://www.youtube.com/watch?v=xL6_CTiD2DU&feature=emb_title

Ramos, D. (2018). *Artificial intelligence chatbots are changing the way you do business and may impact your bottom line.* Smartsheet. https://www.smartsheet.com/artificial-intelligence-chatbots

Siegel, J. (2021). *The ethical implications of the chatbot user experience.* User Experience Center, Bentley University. https://www.bentley.edu/centers/user-experience-center/ethical-implications-chatbot-user-experience

Schwartz, O. (2019, November 25). *In 2016, Microsoft's racist chatbot revealed the dangers of online conversations.* IEEE Spectrum. https://spectrum.ieee.org/tech-talk/artificial-intelligence/machine-learning/in-2016-microsofts-racist-chatbot-revealed-the-dangers-of-online-conversation

Scratch Foundation (2021). *Scratch.* https://scratch.mit.edu

Scratch Wiki. (2021). *Artificial Intelligence – Tutorial.* https://en.scratch-wiki.info/wiki/Artificial_Intelligence

SnatchBot. (2021). *Snatchbot.* https://snatchbot.me

Telegram (2021). *Sphinx Riddle Bot.* https://web.telegram.org/#/im?p=@SphinxRiddleBot

TJBot. (2021). *TJBot simulator.* https://my-tjbot.mybluemix.net

TrueTrue. (2018, May 15). TrueTrue | All-in-one coding robot. Video. [YouTube]. https://www.youtube.com/watch?v=hyj1mA9Yyco&feature=youtu.be

Welch, C. (2018). *Google just gave a stunning demo of Assistant making an actual phone call.* TheVerge. https://www.theverge.com/2018/5/8/17332070/google-assistant-makes-phone-call-demo-duplex-io-2018

Van den Berghe, R., Verhagen, J., Oudgenoed-Paz, O., Van der van, S., & Leseman, P. (2018). Social robots for language learning: A review. *Review of Educational Research, 89*(2). 259-295. https://journals.sagepub.com/doi/full/10.3102/0034654318821286

Varol, O., Ferrara, E., Davis, C., Menczer, F., & Flammini, A. (2017). Online human-bot interactions: Detection, estimation, and characterization. *Social and Information Networks, ICWSM'17.* https://arxiv.org/pdf/1703.03107

References

AbuShawar & Atwell (2015). ALICE chatbot: Trials and outputs. *Computacion y Sistemas, 19*(4), 625-632. https://10.13053/CyS-19-4-2326

Adamopoulou, E., & Moussiades, L. (2020). Chatbots: History, technology, and applications. *Machine Learning with Applications, 2.* https://doi.org/10.1016/j.mlwa.2020.100006

Bii, K., J. Too, & Mukwa, C. (2018) Teacher attitude towards use of chatbots in routine teaching. *Universal Journal of Educational Research, 6*(7). https://doi.org.10.13189/ujer.2018.060719

Fryer, L. (2006). Bots for language learning. *The Language Teacher, 30,* 8(33-34).

Fryer, L., & Nakao, K. (2009). Assessing chatbots for EFL learner use.

Fryer, L., Ainley, M. Thompson, A., Gibson, A., & Sherlock, Z. (2017). Stimulating and sustaining interest in a language course: An experimental comparison of chatbot and human task partners. *Computers in Human Behavior, 75,* 461-468, https://doi.org.10.1016/j.chb.2017.05.045

Pandey, A., & Gelin, R. (2017). Humanoid robots in education: A short review. *Humanoid robotics: A reference*, 1-16. https://link.springer.com/referenceworkentry/10.1007%2F978-94-007-7194-9_113-1

Randall, N. (2019). A survey of Robot-Assisted Language Learning (RALL). *ACM Transactions on Human-Robot Interaction, 9*(1), 1-36. https://dl.acm.org/doi/fullHtml/10.1145/3345506

Smutny, P., & Schreiberova, P. (2020). Chatbots for learning: A review of the educational chatbots for the Facebook Messenger. *Computers & Education, 151*. https://www.sciencedirect.com/science/article/pii/S0360131520300622

Turing, A. (1950). Computing machinery and intelligence. *Mind, 49*, 433-460.

Part Three:
AI in Practice

11. AI and the Design Thinking Process – Pedagogy Project

Overview

This chapter covers aspects of the design thinking process, and the expansion of this process to include equity-centered design. You will explore how these processes are able to assist in the development and the build of human-centered AI applications for education. Details relating to the development and design of a pedagogical project relying on these processes, and one for application in your (actual or potential) workplace is also presented.

Learning Outcomes

1. Earn the ability to identify the key components of the design thinking process.
2. Explore how design thinking can help build human-centered AI applications.
3. Work with the design thinking process to generate ideas for a pedagogy project.
4. Develop a pedagogy project for use in the workplace, and one that is based on the design thinking process for a given scenario.

The Design Thinking Process

The design thinking process begins with empathy, and moves through the phases of define, ideate, prototype, and then test (see Figure 11.1). It is through empathy that we are able to put ourselves in other people's shoes and connect with how they might be feeling about a problem, circumstance, or situation. Define is next and defining means to clarify a problem in order to understand what needs to be solved. It is a chance for the design thinker to define the challenge that they are taking on, basing this on what they have learned about the user(s) and context. This is followed by ideate, and ideation is essentially about idea generation. It represents a process of mentally 'going wide' in terms of concepts and outcomes. There are many brainstorming tools that can be used during this stage. Prototype is next, and this involves the refining of a product, and is intended to answer questions that will get you closer to a final solution. Prototypes are often quick and simple to make, but bring out useful feedback from users. Finally, test. During testing, designers receive feedback about the prototype(s), and have another opportunity to gain empathy for the people that they are designing a solution for. Testing focuses on what can be learned about the user and the problem, as well as the potential solution. Using a specific design methodology, such as the design thinking process, can help focus developers and designers when creating solutions that work better for users. You can learn more by spending a couple of minutes watching *What is design thinking?* [Video: https://www.youtube.com/watch?v=ldYzbV0NDp8&feature=youtu.be].

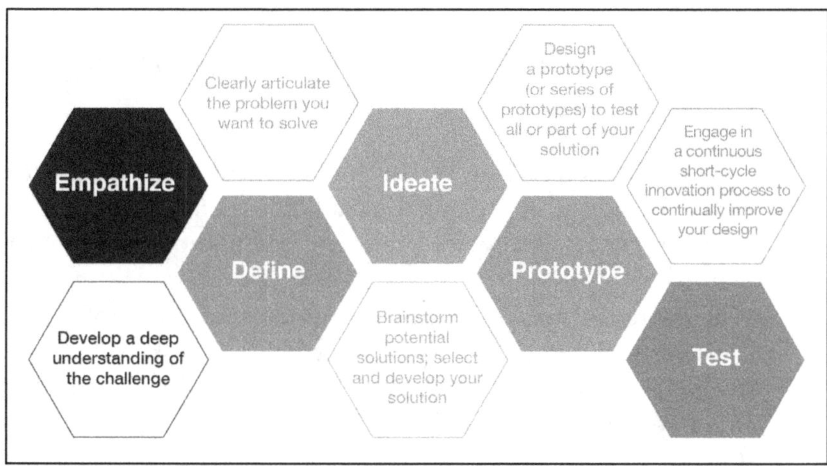

Figure 11.1 The design thinking process

Expanding on the Design Thinking Process: A Use-Case Example

As a process, design thinking is a human-centered design approach that is often applied to the development of AI technologies including that of robots. So, for now, imagine that you are on a development team for a robot, and before moving on you might wish to look over the article *design thinking in robotic automation* (https://dzone.com/articles/design-thinking-in-robotic-automation-1), and *Cozmo: Big brain, bigger personality* (https://www.digitaldreamlabs.com/pages/cozmo).

Before developing a solution, it is important to thoroughly understand both the problem and the user need(s). In the robotics industry, researchers collect this information by interviewing people, observing people in action, observing how the tools work, and documenting their observations. The empathy stage is an opportunity to get an authentic understanding of the challenges, experiences, and needs of clients before developing a product.

Empathize

In this hypothetical use-case example, a client, MeBots, has asked your team to create a robot that helps children who suffer from social isolation. Your team decides to explore the question:

> *What are some of the needs of children who are in weekly therapy for social isolation?*

Considering what you might do during the empathy, stage some strategies that you could apply might include those of:
- Developing a survey for children, parents, and teachers to complete.
- Talking to therapists to obtain case studies for user profiles.
- Watching children as they play with those robots currently available in the marketplace.
- Interviewing children and their parents.
- Observing children.
- Shadowing children.

Define

When data has been collected from the empathy stage, the information needs to be analyzed so the issues are clear and actionable. During the define stage of design thinking, the user of a potential product needs to be understood and the problem that the product will address explained. Questions such as the following are addressed:
- *What capabilities will the user need?*
- *In what type of environment will the product be used?*
- *What might get in the way of use?*
- *What is likely to hinder adoption?*

To this end your team needs to develop a user persona, with the following information helpful to include:

- The goal – this is the end goal that addresses: What do users want or need to accomplish using this product? Here, the end goal determines what the persona wants or needs to fulfill.
- A fictional name and photo – it is useful to personalize the product development and keep in mind that you are developing for a real person.
- Personal background – details such as age, gender, ethnicity, education level, persona group (e.g., teens), and family information (e.g., siblings, parents). The personal background should be based on user research so that it is authentic.
- A scenario – a 'day in the life' narrative of how a person would interact with the robot describes the typical interaction of the user with the product. It is important as it details how the user would interact with the product in a particular context to achieve the end goal. The scenario is usually written from the perspective of the persona and addresses the when, where, and how the product will be applied.

To better understand the empathy and define stages of the design thinking process, watch the *design thinking teacher training video* [Link: https://www.youtube.com/watch?v=qqM8lf3zfFo&list=PLAD1F871255 29A918&index=5].

Ideate

Ideation is the process where any and all ideas are welcomed, no matter how outrageous they may seem. After everyone has shared their ideas, without judgment, specific criteria is then used to evaluate those ideas and narrow the list. The most feasible ideas are chosen for further exploration. Storyboarding, or making a visual mockup of an idea, can also be useful during the ideation process.

Your team needs to consider the features of a robot that would help children who feel socially isolated. So, for this hypothetical project, your team might brainstorm ideas for features that a robot might need to help children, and then assess these from the perspective of those which realistically address the problem using robotic automation.

Prototype

During the prototype stage, a test product is built to meet the requirements and reflect the customer experience to determine if it is a viable solution. Robot designers consider functionality, mechanics, materials, and aesthetics when designing prototypes.

In our hypothetical scenario, your team determines that based on data, you could create a prototype with the following abilities, and one that:
- Teaches turn-taking skills.
- Requires children to take care of the robot.
- Helps to develop positive communication skills.
- Collects sensory data (e.g., body movements, and facial expressions).
- Complies with existing ethical, social, and legal norms.

Test

The test stage is the start of the iterative process, where continuous improvement is made. User testing involves observing which features get used the most; how someone uses the product; identifying if there are user patterns that get the users confused; and at what point users stop uutilizing the product.

So, your team in our hypothetical example, when testing the robot with socially isolated children would want to look for:
- How/if children talk to the robot.
- When children get frustrated.
- When children get excited.
- Children's facial expressions.
- How children physically interact with the robot.

Now watch *design thinking teacher training video part 2*, for further understanding of the ideate, prototype, and test stages of design thinking for education. [Link: https://www.youtube.com/watch?v=ziADZVyLTqo].

Workbook Activity 11.1

Review the below, and provide a response in the appropriate place of the associated workbook.

> **11.1** The design thinking process can be applied in your class. Consider the question: How can each stage of the design thinking method help you apply any particular AI content that you might be considering choosing for use with your learners? To do this, **a)** select an AI technology that you might consider using with your learners, and **b)** make short notes regarding it in response to each stage of the design thinking process.

Reconsidering Bias

At this juncture, we need to reconsider bias, and to help you understand this concept a little further. To do so, spend five minutes engaging with the website *data bias interactive* [Link: https://csfieldguide.org.nz/en/interactives/data-bias]. As you work with the website, consider the question:

> *How is data bias related to human bias?*

The question then is, as asked by Robin Hauser in her TED talk, *can we protect AI from our biases?* [Hauser https://youtu.be/eV_tx4ngVT0]. Hauser (2018) talks about bias being explicit and implicit and how, when this bias is written into our algorithms, it can wreak havoc throughout people's lives and society without being known. So, it is important that we look at design thinking as a way to combat that natural human bias.

In equity-centered design thinking the original design thinking model is extended by adding a noticing phase at the beginning, and a reflection phase to the end (see Figure 11.2). In revisiting bias, we engaged in an activity in relation to noticing bias, and how bias can affect what we see and perceive. The focus now will be on the remaining stages of the design thinking process, starting with empathy.

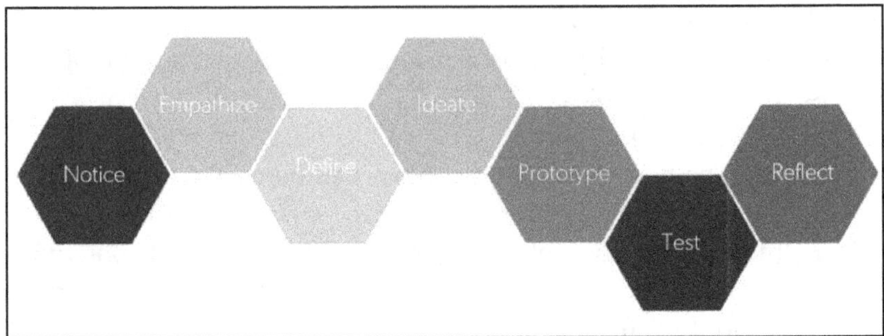

Figure 11.2 The equity-centered design thinking process

Empathy

Empathy in the design thinking process allows us to understand and share the same feelings that others feel. It helps us connect to them, and to help us understand how they might feel about their problem, circumstance, or situation. Working with an empathy map is one way to help you engage in empathizing during the design thinking process.

Empathy Maps

Empathy maps assist you in being able to put yourself in the shoes of the user. They are useful at the beginning of a project, or even midway if needing to refocus. (See Figure 11.3).

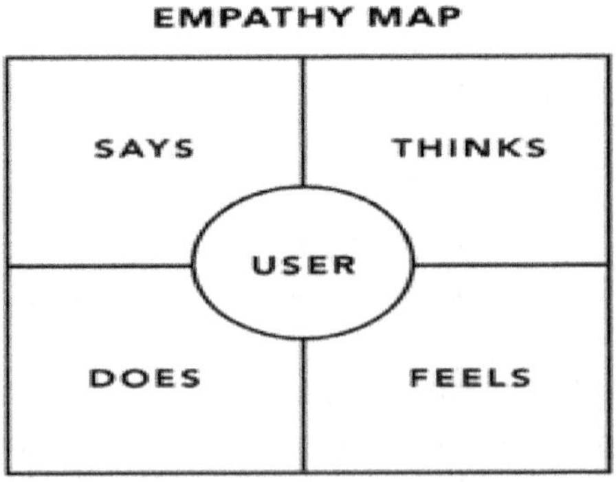

Figure 11.3 Empathy map

To start out using an empathy map:

1. Draw a square with four quadrants within it, and label them: 'says', 'does', 'thinks', and 'feels'.
2. Place your user in the center and give them a name, along with a description detailing what they do or who they are (the user persona).
3. Use sticky notes or points in each quadrant with one observation or note on each, annotate assumptions or unknowns, and add questions if any inquiry or validation is required.
4. Discuss observations and fill in any gaps collaboratively with others (i.e., cohorts, colleagues, potential users).

Empathy Map Example

The most important part of designing for somebody is to gain empathy for that person, and the empathy map can assist us in doing this. See Figure 11.4 for an empathy map example. This example illustrates how we might empathize with a user in thinking about a solution for them (e.g., how to work with an AI-enabled virtual assistant for use by a teacher/students during class).

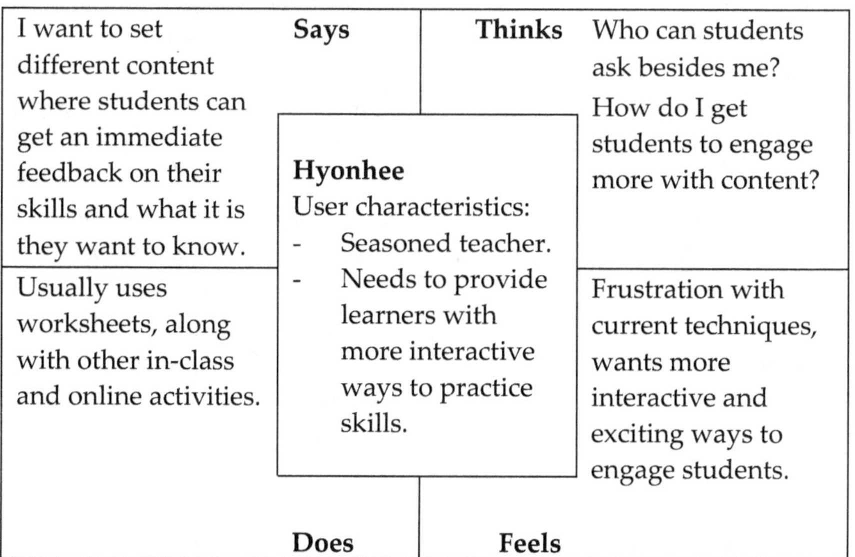

Figure 11.4 Empathy map example

Workbook Activity 11.2

Examine the following, and five minutes to respond in the appropriate section of the associated workbook.

> **11.2** Think of your own scenario and place your user background information in the middle of the empathy map. Be sure to add characteristics for your user in each 'says', 'thinks', 'does' and 'feels' section.

Define

In the define stage of equity-centered design thinking, we are trying to synthesize all of the learning and information gained in the notice and empathizing stages. We want to find a needs statement discovered from this process, and additional insights that might assist the target user(s). You can do this by writing the statement:

> *The user* needs a way to *do something that addresses their need* so that *they benefit directly*.

Focus on the points developed in the quadrants of the empathy map to get at the underlying problems, stay away from listing individual features but instead ask things like *What is the user really seeking?*, and *'What do they really want?'*. Cluster similar ideas together. A developed user statement for your users might look similar to:

> *The teacher needs a way to help students so that they can practice their listening and speaking skills in increasingly interactive and authentic ways.*

Workbook Activity 11.3

Take two minutes, and complete the appropriate section of the associated workbook in response to the following:

> **11.3** Develop a user statement regarding the AI solution that you are considering to apply with your learners, and have mentioned when completing *workbook activity 11.2*.

Ideate

In this stage of the design thinking process it is time for idea generation and not evaluation. It is here where you need to brainstorm solutions for your needs statement. It is not necessary for them to be realistic, just as many as you can think of. For the example user statement presented to you earlier, we might brainstorm ideas such as using a digital assistant to practice asking for authentic but set information (e.g., the time, the weather, asking for definitions of words, as well as synonyms, antonyms, and so on). The brainstorming box in regards to ideating about this example might look similar to that of *Figure 11.5*.

Brainstorming box example

Digital assistant use:
- *For time management*
- *Students to ask questions about vocabulary and spelling*
- *AI provides relevant and authentic information like weather and news*

Figure 11.5 Brainstorming box example

Workbook Activity 11.4

Examine the following, and take 2 minutes to respond in the appropriate section of the associated workbook.

> **11.4** Ideate about your user statement from *workbook activity 11.3* and brainstorm several ideas regarding to it.

Prototype

In the prototype phase of design thinking, we are making something that someone can engage and interact with, and one way to do this is to employ storyboarding. Imagine your scenario as a story with characters, a plot, conflict, and resolution. To do this, divide a page or piece of paper into six frames. In the example here, we have done this for our user, Hyonhee (see Figure 11.6). She wants to engage students more interactively and in more authentic ways, so we are prototyping a use-case where she introduces the Google Assistant to her class, and teaches them how it works with examples. Students then begin to interact with the device.

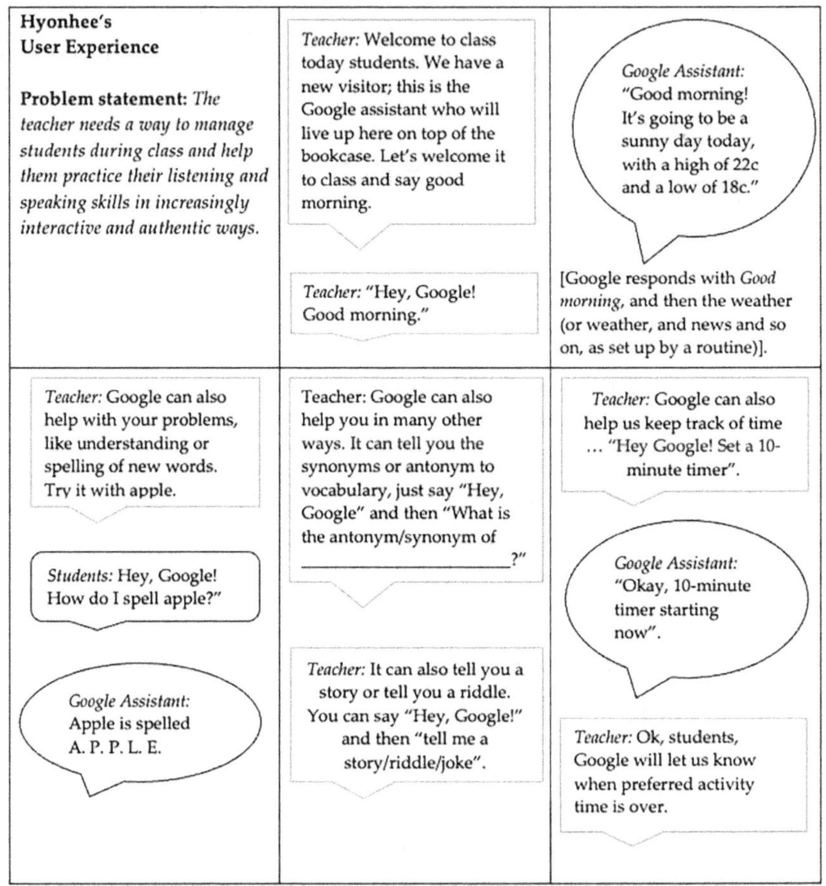

Figure 11.6 Prototype storyboarding example

Workbook Activity 11.5

Consider the following and take 5 minutes to complete the appropriate section of the associated workbook.

11.5 Develop a rough scenario sketch for your user, and base this on your user statement from *workbook activity 11.3*.

Test

In this phase of the design thinking process the prototype scenario can be tested in the real world. This is important as it allows the user to give you feedback, with any new insights then used to rework the model. You might like to reflect on the feedback with a feedback grid (see Figure 11.7).

Teacher directed interaction with the device.	**+ Things that worked**	**Things to Change ***	Location: place the Google Assistant high on a cupboard or on top of the bookcase, out of student reach. Awareness: Increase student invocation understanding.
What other things can we use: - Story Speaker action (create a choose-your-own adventure story tailored for the students).	**? Questions we still have**	**New Ideas to try !**	Provide students with worksheets to get them used to the phrases they can use.

Figure 11.7 Feedback grid example

A feedback grid is where you divide a piece of paper into quadrants, and in each quadrant focus on different aspects such as:
- Things that worked
- Things to change
- Questions we still have
- New ides to try

After completing a feedback grid, search for patterns and themes and ways to improve the user experience. You might like to then use the *'questions we still have'* quadrant to inform on assumptions and question the activity, use the *'new ideas to try'* quadrant to begin storyboarding solutions, or use the *'things to change'* quadrant as the basis for a to-do list of action items.

Workbook Activity 11.6

Consider the following and take 10 minutes to complete the appropriate section of the associated workbook.

> **11.6** How do you think your solution might work in the real world? Try to imagine its use in the real world, and then complete a feedback grid in response.

Reflect

In this final stage of the equity-centered design thinking process, the reflect phase adds time to consider those actions, emotions and insights that we noticed while walking through the design thinking cycle. Here, you need to be sure that you are reflecting from not only the perspective of the designer, but also that of the perspective of the user from within the scenario established.

Workbook Activity 11.7

Consider the following and take five minutes to complete the appropriate section of the associated workbook.

> **11.7** Respond to the following regarding the scenario that you developed for *workbook activity 11.5*.
> **a.** What did you like about your solution?
> **b.** What would you change about the design?

Pedagogy Project

We will use the design thinking process in completing a pedagogy project. This is a project that aims to assist either you personally, your students, or your colleagues. With this in mind, start by considering a person or the individuals who you would like to focus on as the 'user'.

Then, consider their problem and how you might solve it pedagogically with an AI-based solution. Potential scenarios for you to choose from are listed below.

Scenario 1 – Chatbot Implementation

Develop a chatbot for use with your students. The chatbot should help them develop a project, such as help them to write an essay or story, or engage them somehow to practice the skills they are learning with you (e.g., practicing vocabulary for a unit of study, or practice listening and speaking skills during a game-based situation).

Scenario 2 – Interactive Story Implementation

Develop an interactive story using Story Speaker with the Google Assistant. You can develop a short story (3-6 minutes), one that is level specific (e.g., lower intermediate), and one that is topic focused (e.g., travel unit focused). [Note, that this will require use of a VPN].

Scenario 3 – AI in the Classroom with Learners

Think of an AI technology (e.g., the use of a chatbot, digital assistant, Grammarly, the Duolingo smartphone application, and so on). Consider the means of using this technology with students in the learning process. Develop the means to use it with learners, and trial its use with them in the classroom/homework process.

Scenario 4 – Teacher Training Workshop

Think of an AI technology (e.g., the use of a chatbot, digital assistant, Grammarly, the Duolingo smartphone application, and so on). Then, develop a short training session/workshop for colleagues detailing how they can implement such a process with learners. (e.g., developing a workshop on how to use a digital assistant with learners of EFL to support in-class learning and skills practice.)

Scenario 5 – Alternate Uses of AI

Think of your own scenario using an AI technology with a specific user group of your choosing. You might like to take on board the one you have already started thinking through as we worked though this section, and have started to detail in the associated workbook for the text. Any use and application of AI is permissible for this scenario. As such, the stage of implementation is very broad.

Workbook Activity 11.8

Select a scenario for you pedagogy project, you might choose that which you have already worked through in the previous workbook activities for this chapter. After selecting a scenario, respond to the following in the associated workbook.

> **11.8** Complete the pedagogy project template based on a scenario of your choice.

Project Checklist

Ensure that your project meets the following criteria.

Project Details

Provide the appropriate information including the title, scenario chosen to pursue, your name and affiliation, the date(s) of implementation, the duration of the session(s), information about the learning and teaching context, as well as the materials, resources and equipment required.

Project Overview

Provide a summary with a brief description of the project. Include learning objectives that indicate the key knowledge and skills that users gain as a result of participation in the pedagogy project. List prerequisites, all the background knowledge and skills required of users and yourself prior to project implementation. Determine how your project will focus on AI, and describe how the user(s) is challenged to engage with AI tools or concepts that are authentic and based on real-word examples. Describe how you incorporate aspects of inquiry-based learning into the project by involving the user in the learning process (e.g., detail the approaches you use, such as small group discussion, guided learning, learning by doing and so on). Also consider how you will provide authentic learning that is connected to user interests and the teaching and learning context. Also, determine how the project engages participants, providing them with opportunities to make aspects of learning their own and in ways that they can see practical significance in what they are learning.

Design Thinking Process

The project promotes the use or learning of the design thinking methods and its process (empathize, define, ideate, prototype, test). Respond to each of these stages in the process, deciding the steps and aspects required for each.

Reflection, Revision, and Modification

Detail the how, what, and why of the learning being undertaken by participants, and take the opportunity to illustrate how it is that participants know this. (i.e., answer the questions Why are we learning this?, What are we learning this for?, and How are we learning this?) Then, describe what worked well, and what might require changing in future iterations of project delivery. After which you will be able to then describe any modifications that might be required. Note, if you have not delivered your project yet this can be a hypothetical. However, if you have delivered the project consider what worked well and what did not, and what in this regard might need keeping and what might need addressing in terms of any alteration to delivery.

Feedback and Assessment

Describe how you will give or receive feedback during the project in order to revise your ideas and to assist participants in deeper learning. Further, consider how learners are able to demonstrate their level of understanding to you, and how you assess learning throughout project delivery.

Worksheets and Activities

Include any handouts or worksheets provided to participants throughout the course of the project. Along with this, provide a listing and outline of the activities undertaken during the project. This might include instructions, and any items used to assist in the functionality of the activities for learners (e.g., photo of gameboards or screenshots of online-based activities).

Pedagogy Project Rubric

The following rubric might help you to focus on the various components and aims when seeking to develop a successful pedagogy project (see Table 11.1). Scores range from 1-5, across 6 Criteria, totaling to a score out of 30.

Criteria	1	3	5	/30
Project Details	No details included	Details could provide more clarity, but are completed accurately	Details provide clarity to context, and are completed accurately	/5
Project Overview	The Description of the project, learning objectives and audience prerequisites are not clear.	The Description of the project, learning objectives and audience prerequisites are somewhat clear.	The Description of the project, learning objectives and audience prerequisites are clear.	/5
	Audience members are not encouraged to explore AI, ask questions, and share ideas, and/or they are unable to make the learning and outcomes their own.	Audience members are somewhat encouraged to explore AI, ask questions, and share ideas in order to make learning and outcomes their own.	Audience members are encouraged to explore AI, ask questions, and share ideas in order to make learning and outcomes their own.	
	Various approaches such as small-group discussion, guided learning and learning by doing are not utilized during the project.	Various approaches such as small-group discussion, guided learning and learning by doing are somewhat utilized during the project.	Various approaches such as small-group discussion, guided learning and learning by doing are utilized during the project.	

Design Thinking Process	The project does not consider the design thinking process very well. Significant improvement is required to address this issue.	The project mostly considers the design thinking process, and displays pedagogical knowledge and experience but minimal improvement is required.	The project clearly takes advantage of the design thinking method, and displays pedagogical knowledge and experience.	/5
Reflection, Revision, and Modification	The project does not provide opportunities for participants to reflect on the why, what and how they are learning.	The project mostly provides opportunities for participants to reflect on the why, what and how they are learning.	The project provides opportunities for participants to reflect on the why, what and how they are learning.	/5
	The project does not include processes for the presenter/audience to give and receive feedback in order to revise their work and ideas.	The project mostly includes processes for the presenter/audience to give and receive feedback in order to revise their work and ideas.	The project includes processes for the presenter/audience to give and receive feedback in order to revise their work and ideas.	
	Modifications take into account what worked well and what did not and mostly addresses any shortcomings.	Modifications take into account what worked well and what did not and mostly addresses any shortcomings.	Modifications take into account what worked well and what did not and addresses shortcomings.	

				/5
Feedback and Assessment	Aspects of feedback are missing.	Feedback opportunities are mostly provided to the audience, with a means for them to provide feedback to the presenter mostly obvious.	Feedback opportunities are provided to the audience, with a means for them to provide feedback to the presenter obvious.	/5
	Assessment was neglected.	Learners are clearly able to demonstrate their levels of understanding and learning, and how assessment of this is carried out is mostly clear.	Learners are clearly able to demonstrate their levels of understanding and learning, and how assessment of this is carried out is clear.	
Worksheets and Activities	None were included.	Those that are included are mostly easy to follow, with instructions mostly provided as to how and when they are utilized.	Those that are included are clearly easy to follow, with clear instructions provided as to how and when they are utilized.	/5

Table 11.1 Pedagogy project rubric

Summary

In this chapter, you learned how to:

- Identify the key components of the design thinking process.
- Explored design thinking in order to see how it can assist in building human-centered AI applications.
- Worked with the design thinking process to generate ideas for a pedagogy project.
- Developed a pedagogy project for use in the workplace, and one that was based on the design thinking process for your selected scenario.

Resources

Bhaskar, B. (2017, July 07). *Design thinking in robotic automation.* DZone. https://dzone.com/articles/design-thinking-in-robotic-automation-1

CSFG. (2021). *Data bias.* Computer science field guide. https://csfieldguide.org.nz/en/interactives/data-bias

DDL. (2021). *Big brain, bigger personality.* Digital Dream Labs. https://www.digitaldreamlabs.com/pages/cozmo

Hauser, D. (2018, February 13). Can we protect AI from our biases? Video. [YouTube]. https://youtu.be/eV_tx4ngVT0

HFLIschools. (2012, July 04). Design thinking teacher training video Part 1 of 2. Video. [YouTube]. https://www.youtube.com/watch?v=qqM8lf3zfFo&list=PLAD1F87125529A918&index=6

HFLIschools. (2012, July 04). Design thinking teacher training video Part 2 of 2. Video. [YouTube]. https://www.youtube.com/watch?v=ziADZVyLTqo

IDEO U. (2018, December 06). What is design thinking? Video. [YouTube]. https://www.youtube.com/watch?v=ldYzbV0NDp8&feature=youtu.be

Notes

About the Book

Artificial Intelligence in Education: Fundamentals for Educators presents those issues in artificial intelligence (AI) that are of concern to teachers when coming to understand the various aspects involved with the field, and how they relate and can be applied to those in education. This includes developing a working knowledge of the key concepts behind AI, and an understanding of the characteristics and evolution of the field itself. The benefits, risks, biases, and ethics involved with AI design, development, and deployment are also considered, and this includes aspects of AI and human perception, how these differ, and what this means practically. The manner in which we can naturally come to interact with AI systems, along with an understanding of the differences and similarities between human-machine learning is also taken into account. After these fundamentals are established, the five big ideas in AI for education are introduced, and the more integral aspects of each, including their implications for society, are examined. This establishes a grounding for presenting what it now means to be teaching and learning in the era of the fourth industrial revolution; how digital assistants and voice user interfaces, along with chatbots and robots, can be applied in the teaching and learning context, particularly that of English language learning; and how the design thinking process can assist in the development of pedagogical projects in educational workplaces. The text also has a companion workbook in which all of the activities presented can be completed.

About the Author

David Kent is an Associate Professor in the Endicott College of International Studies at Woosong University in the Republic of Korea. He provides teacher education through the TESOL-MALL graduate program where he has served as Head of Department and coordinated an academic study skills program for doctoral students.

David is also a long-standing member of the academic community with a principal research focus that revolves around the digitalization of language learning. Serving as conference plenary and keynote, as well as invited speaker, he has won a number of teacher association and conference presentation awards.

To date, he has published a number of books, including *Teaching with Technology: Integrating Technology into the TESOL Classroom*, *Internet in Education: Integrating the Internet into the TESOL Classroom*, and a *TESOL Strategy Guide* series that focuses on the use of specific digital tools for teaching. He has also authored a number of multimedia applications.

Currently, he serves on the editorial board of several journals, and his research articles have been published at the Scopus and SSCI levels in such periodicals as *Teaching English with Technology* (IATEFL), *The Journal of Asia TEFL* (Asia TEFL), and *Language Learning and Technology* (NFLRC, University of Hawai'i at Mānoa/COERLL, University of Texas).